SAP® Exchange Infrastructure

 **PRESS**

SAP PRESS and the SAP NetWeaver Essentials are issued
by Bernhard Hochlehnert, SAP AG

SAP PRESS is a joint initiative of SAP and Galileo Press. The know-how offered by SAP specialists combined with the expertise of the publishing house
Galileo Press offers the reader expert books in the field. SAP PRESS features
first-hand information and expert advice, and provides useful skills for deci-
sion-making.

SAP PRESS offers a variety of books on technical and business related topics
for the SAP user. For further information, please also visit our Web site:
www.sap-press.com.

Steffen Karch, Loren Heilig
SAP NetWeaver
2005, approx. 350pp., ISBN 1-59229-041-8

Kessler, Tillert, Dobrikov
Java Programming with the SAP Web Application Server
2005, approx. 520 pp., DVD, ISBN 1-59229-020-5

Chris Whealy
Inside Web Dynpro for Java
A guide to the principles of programming in SAP's Web Dynpro
2005, 355 pp., ISBN 1-59229-038-8

Jo Weilbach, Mario Herger
SAP xApps and the Composite Application Framework
2005, approx. 270 pp., CD, ISBN 1-59229-048-5

Arnd Goebel, Dirk Ritthaler
SAP Enterprise Portal
The definite guide to administration and programming
2005, approx. 330 pp., CD, ISBN 1-59229-018-3

Jens Stumpe, Joachim Orb

SAP® Exchange Infrastructure

SAP PRESS

Contents

5 Mappings 93

6 Configuration 115

Introduction

In SAP NetWeaver '04, SAP has brought together various technologies in one product. It includes, among others, SAP Enterprise Portal (SAP EP), SAP Mobile Infrastructure (SAP MI), SAP Business Information Warehouse (SAP BW), SAP Business Process Management (SAP BPM), SAP Exchange Infrastructure (SAP XI), and SAP Web Application Server (SAP Web AS). SAP XI focuses on cross-system process integration—the exchange of messages between applications.

SAP XI is not an adapter, but a component of SAP NetWeaver with an open architecture that enables you to integrate a wide range of SAP and non-SAP systems within and outside your company's boundaries. Given the diversity of systems installed in today's companies and the increase in cross-company communication, the need for support in this area is greater than ever before.

SAP XI has considered these requirements in its upgrade from SAP XI 2.0 to SAP XI 3.0. Due to enhancements in Business-to-Business (B2B) application support and cross-component BPM in particular, the decision regarding which release the book should be based on was an obvious one. You should note that where it is not expressly mentioned, this book applies to SAP XI 3.0 with SP4 (Feature Pack). **Release**

Because this is the first book to be written on this topic, it is intended for all readers who need an introduction to guide them through their first steps with SAP XI. The first part describes the functions and most important concepts of SAP XI. **Target Group**

Chapters 1 and **2** are essential for understanding all subsequent chapters. **Chapters 3** through **5** concentrate on design and development with SAP XI, independently of a specific system landscape. **Chapter 6** summarizes everything discussed in the previous chapters: It describes how you configure the cross-system process for a specific system landscape, based on the developments made at the logical level. The order in which topics are addressed reflects the chronological order of the corresponding steps in an SAP XI integration project. Logically speaking, **Chapter 7**, which deals with SAP XI runtime, could also be read concurrently with all the other chapters. **Chapter 8** completes the first part of the book with its description of cross-component BPM, which marks the transition from stateless to stateful communication.

To illustrate how SAP XI is applied in a business context, the second part of the book examines two customer scenarios that have been realized with SAP XI. We selected typical scenarios and believe that scenarios that are similar to our examples can be applied at other companies. Naturally, we did not want the scenarios to be merely examples, but to also be technically demanding, each spotlighting a specific function of SAP XI. **Chapter 9** describes how cross-component BPM is used as part of an XI scenario at the Linde Group. **Chapter 10** shows how the B2B features of SAP XI help connect a Customer Relationship Management (CRM) system to an electronic marketplace over the Internet.

Acknowledgements This book could not have been written without the support of many people who, directly or indirectly, were involved in writing or checking the manuscript. First and foremost, we would like to thank Rachel Raw and Robert Sloan for translating the book into English so quickly and diligently. We are also indebted to the following colleagues from SAP XI development who found time to proofread sections from their specialist areas and resolve open questions: Jörg Ackermann, Frank Beunings, Andreas Dahl, Anton Deimel, Franz Forsthofer, Thea Hillenbrand, Frank Oliver Hoffmann, Christoph Hofmann, Jörg Kessler, Christoph Liebig, Michael Mühlberg, Stefan Rossmanith, Uwe Schlarb, Martin Tewes, Stefan Werner, and Manfred Zizlsperger. Finally, special thanks go to Florian Zimniak and the team at Galileo Press for their valuable support.

Jens Stumpe would like to thank the entire SAP XI Product Management Team for their involvement in the project, in particular Wolfgang Fassnacht for his organizational support; Alan Rickayzen for sharing his experience from previous book projects; Andrea Schmieden for her chapter on cross-system Business Process Management; Sindhu Gangadharan, Christine Gustav, Udo Paltzer, and Thomas Volmering for their useful contributions to the text; and everyone else who lightened Jens' workload during this time, enabling him to concentrate on the book. Last but not least, Jens would like to thank Jürgen Kreuziger, Margret Klein-Magar, and Sven Leukert for allowing him to work on the manuscript in conjunction with his other tasks at SAP.

Joachim Orb would also like to thank Matthias Allgaier, Thomas Grosser, Robert Reiz, Alan Y. Smith, and Xiaohui Wang for their support in both organizational and content issues. Thanks also go to Mr. Detlef Schulz from iWay Software for his critical review of Chapter 10, and to Dr. Klaus-Ulrich Meininger from the Linde Group for allowing us to include a scenario from his business area.

Joachim Orb would also like to thank Agnès Bouillé for her cooperation. Many evenings and weekends were sacrificed to produce this book.

The challenges of cross-system and cross-company processes arise from their multifaceted nature regarding the diversity of platforms, programming languages, involved applications, and communication parties. We hope that this book will give you the necessary guidance when using SAP XI to meet these challenges, and that it will contribute to the success of your integration projects.

Walldorf, February 2005
Jens Stumpe
Joachim Orb

1 Overview

Starting with SAP NetWeaver, this chapter describes the focus and components of SAP XI.

1.1 Introduction

SAP Exchange Infrastructure (SAP XI) is just one component of the SAP NetWeaver technology platform, which is summarized briefly in the next section. Section 1.2 introduces the world of process integration, but first, Section 1.1.2 clarifies at which level you integrate processes with SAP XI.

1.1.1 SAP NetWeaver

A company's competitiveness generally depends on whether it can manage quality and cost considerations to achieve a profit within a reasonable period of time. In the past, companies could achieve a competitive advantage simply by accelerating their existing processes. In recent years, however, another success factor has emerged: the ability to react to changes in the market and within a company. Such changes require you to adapt the existing processes in your company, and integrate your organizational units (including employees) into new organizational structures. The necessary changes have direct implications for the existing IT landscape of your company. Therefore, one of the major challenges facing the IT sector today is enabling companies to react quickly and flexibly to the constant changes and demands.

The Integration Challenge

The SAP NetWeaver product groups together various technological concepts and previous SAP platforms. The focus of SAP NetWeaver '04 is the integration of people, information, and processes in one solution. Figure 1.1 shows an overview of the capabilities of SAP NetWeaver. This book is an introduction to the area shown in white, but covers only the Business Process Management (BPM) aspects that are relevant to SAP XI (namely *cross-component* BPM). The components of SAP NetWeaver and the capabilities that they address are discussed below.

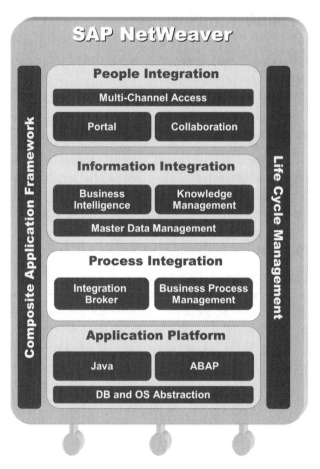

Figure 1.1 Capabilities of SAP NetWeaver '04

SAP Web Application Server (currently SAP Web AS Release 6.40) is the basis of all SAP applications and constitutes the application platform capability. The core of SAP Web AS is the "old" SAP Basis, which offers the recognized advantages of the ABAP development and runtime environment, which include reliability, scalability, and operating-system and database independence. SAP Web AS supplements these fundamental aspects with technologies such as the SAP J2EE Engine and the Internet Communication Manager (ICM), which handles Internet requests and distributes them to the individual components. Furthermore, SAP Web AS supports a wide range of technical standards such as HTTP(S), SMTP, WebDAV, SOAP, SSL, SSO, X.509, Unicode, HTML, XML, and WML.

The new SAP products Exchange Infrastructure and Business Process Management form the basis for optimized process management for process chains:

▶ **SAP Exchange Infrastructure (SAP XI)**
SAP XI acts as a data hub for SAP and non-SAP systems. Simply put, it is SAP's answer to the problems of enterprise application integration (EAI), which were previously tackled by using, and often combining, products of all types from different vendors.

▶ **SAP Business Process Management (SAP BPM)**
This capability encompasses all facets of BPM within SAP NetWeaver: modeling standardized workflows with SAP Business Workflow, modeling less structured or less frequently used *collaboration tasks* by using wizards in the Enterprise Portal, and stateful processing of messages in SAP XI with *cross-component Business Process Management*.

Before the dawn of the Internet and distributed systems, the problem for users was finding information about a particular topic. The challenge facing them now is filtering out what is relevant from the mountain of information available. The task of the IT sector is to find a solution to meet the requirements arising from this problem, which are often summarized under the term information management. SAP NetWeaver meets these requirements by means of the following components:

▶ **SAP Business Information Warehouse (SAP BW)**
SAP BW, an OLAP system, holds and retrieves data from SAP and non-SAP systems in order to enable differentiated information analysis by management (data warehousing). In addition to real-time data extraction and reporting options using MS Excel, SAP BW also offers Web-based reporting. SAP BW is the technical basis for the mySAP Business Intelligence solution.

▶ **Knowledge Management**
The Knowledge Management platform enables you to handle unstructured data. Its main functional areas are Content Management of the SAP Enterprise Portal and TREX (Text Retrieval and Classification Engine). The aim is to bring together information distributed across different servers (for example, file servers, Web servers, or in the SAP Knowledge Warehouse) in a central repository with tools for searching, classifying, and structuring the information. You can then use this information in SAP Enterprise Portal, for example.

▶ **SAP Master Data Management (SAP MDM)**
Consolidated master data management across system boundaries is becoming evermore important in the complex arena of information management. Many companies have heterogeneous distributed IT landscapes, not least because of the wide range of new SAP applications. All systems within these landscapes have to access the same master data, for example, business partners, address information, or warehouses. This has resulted in many complex distribution processes aimed at ensuring the consistency of this data. SAP's newest product, SAP Master Data Management, addresses this problem. SAP XI is the technological basis for SAP MDM.

People Integration Last but not least, we must not forget the employees of these companies, who, together with their colleagues, work with applications on a day-to-day basis. They, too, are constantly developing and changing areas, and need a particular selection of applications, or tailored access to these applications, depending on their function. SAP NetWeaver provides the technical solutions to meet these requirements via the following components:

▶ **SAP Enterprise Portal (SAP EP)**
SAP EP provides a company's employees with a central point of access to the applications of various back-end systems, tailored to an employee's user roles. They cannot only access applications, but also information from the intranet and Internet with Single Sign-On (SSO), using a uniform user interface of their Web browser. *SAP NetWeaver Collaboration* (see below) and Knowledge Management are integrated into the Enterprise Portal and give employees access to structured information and their personal network.

▶ **SAP NetWeaver Collaboration**
Good internal communication is an important success factor for a company. The challenge facing us here is that interdependent teams, and even employees within a team, often work in different buildings, towns, or even countries. SAP NetWeaver Collaboration has various tools to support the exchange of information: *collaboration rooms* (virtual rooms for exchanging documents), real-time collaboration with *instant messaging* and *application sharing*, and the *collaboration launch pad*, which displays all online employees. Moreover, you can integrate commonly used third-party tools (such as MS Exchange, WebEx) in SAP NetWeaver Collaboration.

▶ **SAP Mobile Infrastructure (SAP MI)**

Employees who spend a lot of time away from the office as part of their job need access to relevant information when they are on the move. A service technician, for example, needs access to information regarding the availability of spare parts. In the SAP NetWeaver framework, SAP Mobile Infrastructure is the technical basis for mobile applications of this type. In order to support as many mobile devices as possible, SAP MI has a platform-independent runtime for these applications. Synchronized access to data from one or more back-end systems supports, among other things, encryption, compression, synchronous and asynchronous data exchange, user-specific data replication, and conflict management. Also, SAP MI has a sophisticated development environment and a central administration and deployment tool.

These main components are supplemented by a *Composite Application Framework*, which provides a range of open interfaces (APIs), and *Lifecycle Management*, which extends the existing Transport Management System (TMS) to all SAP NetWeaver components.

1.1.2 Levels of Process Modeling

As mentioned in the previous section, the main factor for today's companies in gaining competitive advantage has less to do with their ability to accelerate their processes, and more to do with the flexibility necessary to adapt their processes to ever-changing requirements. What are these processes? There are many possible answers to this question, even within a single company.

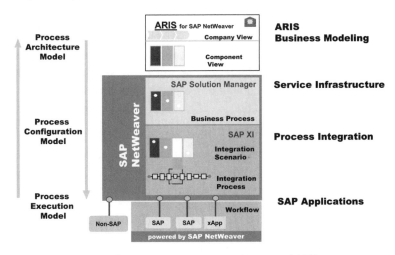

Figure 1.2 Overview of Process Types in SAP NetWeaver and ARIS

Process Types   To avoid misunderstandings, let us start by examining Figure 1.2, which shows an overview of process types within SAP systems, starting at the top with the more business-oriented level and progressing down to the execution of processes. At each level, you work with the model corresponding to that particular level of abstraction:

▶ *ARIS for SAP NetWeaver* supplements *SAP NetWeaver BPM* with process modeling at the business level. ARIS enables you to model the whole *process architecture* of a company, strictly from the business perspective, without referencing technical objects. You use this architecture model to describe the process strategy of your company.

▶ At the next level, you use one or more scenarios to describe the configuration of the *business process*, right down to the individual process steps. The process descriptions at this level go beyond the individual components of *mySAP Business Suite* and enable you to derive customizing activities, navigate to the component in SAP systems, and define relevant information for monitoring (for example, threshold values). For this purpose, *SAP Solution Manager* works with reference processes, which you configure during implementation by using customizing. You can synchronize process models between ARIS and SAP Solution Manager.

▶ At the next level of process modeling, you use SAP XI to describe cross-system process execution. This enables you to connect processes within applications in a flexible manner. You use *integration scenarios*[1] and *integration processes*,[2] which enable you to exchange messages not only within a company, but also between companies. You can import the corresponding models to the ARIS process architecture model.

Together, the joint solution of ARIS and SAP NetWeaver contains a universal and integrated description of the process architecture—from the business model to implementation of the process by SAP Solution Manager and integration of executable processes in SAP XI and the applications by SAP Business Workflow.

This book focuses on process integration using SAP XI. The terms integration process and integration scenario pertain to the development objects for describing a process. If we need to refer to the real process that our models describe, we differentiate it from the existing development

---

1 As of SAP XI 3.0 SP9, *business scenario* is renamed *integration scenario*. We use the new terminology in this book.

2 As of SAP XI 3.0 SP9, *business process* is renamed *integration process*. We use the new terminology in this book.

objects by using the term *collaborative* process. The next section covers the basic concepts of SAP XI.

1.2 Process Integration with SAP XI

If you visited the data processing department of any modern company of considerable size and looked at the hardware and software it uses, you would probably notice that the solutions employed are derived from more than just *one* software provider. Software solutions are becoming increasingly more interconnected, partly because cost considerations prevent companies from replacing entire software solutions, and partly because companies build their complete solution based on their own individual requirements. Furthermore, companies want to use software to automate cross-company business transactions.

Connected Systems

Companies have long been able to integrate a wide range of systems within a system landscape. A range of middleware technology is available for exchanging data between these systems. At first glance, the simplest solution would appear to be point-to-point connection of the various applications and systems. However, as the number of different systems increases, so does the complexity of the overall system landscape, and you would be well-advised by any computer engineer to "*never change a running system.*" Because the information regarding the integration of the applications is distributed across the various systems, it is extremely difficult to get an overview of the overall implementation. Therefore, making changes after the initial implementation is laborious, time-consuming, and expensive.

This is where SAP Exchange Infrastructure (SAP XI) comes into play—by making integration knowledge available at a central location. This means that you don't have to search through all the systems to find the relevant information; rather, you can access this information at a central location (*shared collaboration knowledge*). We'll look at this in more detail in Section 1.2.2. However, to give you a better idea of the cross-system scenarios supported by SAP XI, we'll assume that the required integration objects (mappings, interfaces, and so on) already exist, and examine the SAP XI runtime in the next section.

Shared Collaboration Knowledge

1.2.1 Communication Using the Integration Server

The central component of the XI runtime is the Integration Server, which receives and forwards messages of the application systems. The Integration Server uses a message format based on the *Extensible Markup Lan-*

XML

guage (XML), which has become the standardized exchange format on the Internet. Further standards and tools based on the XML standard exist that make working with XML even easier, such as XML Schema, XSLT, and XPath. XSLT (*Extensible Stylesheet Language for Transformations*), for example, enables you to define mappings required when two communication parties use different message structures.

Moreover, the XML standardized format makes it easier to connect to non-SAP systems. Once data from a non-SAP system has been converted to XML using an adapter, then it is a simple step to convert the data to other XML formats for other receivers. However, defining mapping pairs for all different systems is not recommended.[3] This is where the Integration Server comes into play: In SAP XI, all communication parties use it to exchange messages. Various *engines* work together on the Integration Server (see Figure 1.3):

Engines on the Integration Server

▶ **Integration Engine**
The Integration Engine receives messages using XI message protocol and performs central services such as routing and mapping for received messages. The XI message protocol is based on the W3C (Worldwide Web Consortium) note *SOAP Messages with Attachments*. As of SAP Web AS 6.40, SAP systems support this protocol directly using the *proxy runtime* and a *local Integration Engine*. Therefore, in this case, no adapters are required for communication with the Integration Engine on the Integration Server.

▶ **Adapter Engine**
You use adapters to connect other systems to the Integration Server. Apart from the IDoc adapter, all adapters run on the Adapter Engine, which provides central services for messaging, queuing, and security handling. Each adapter converts calls or messages from a sender into the XI message format for the Integration Engine. Conversely, the adapter receives messages from the Integration Engine and converts them for the receiver. You only need to convert the respective message protocol for communication with the Integration Server, and not for every single combination of application systems. In this way, you can use SAP XI to exchange messages with a wide range of different systems.

▶ **Business Process Engine**
Put simply, the adapters and the Integration Engine are limited to forwarding a message to the receiver or receivers and, if necessary, exe-

---

3   If there were n different systems, you would need n*(n-1)/2 different mappings.

cuting a mapping. Once a message has been sent successfully to the receiver, message processing is complete. The Business Process Engine now extends this Integration Server function to include *stateful* message processing: The engine processes a process model and, if necessary, waits for other messages before continuing with execution. We will address this fundamental enhancement in Chapter 8.

To process messages using the engines, the Integration Server accesses information from an *Integration Directory* and the *System Landscape Directory*. Before we look at these components in more detail in the next section, let's concentrate on the communication using adapters and the proxy runtime.

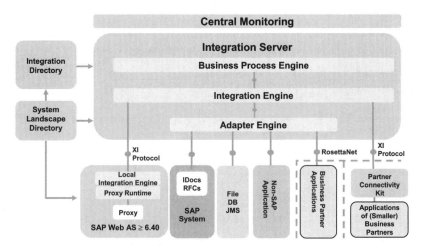

Figure 1.3 Communication Using the Integration Server

SAP ships SAP XI with adapters for internal company and cross-company communication. It would, however, be unfeasible for SAP to provide an adapter for every single type of third-party application. For this reason, SAP relies on partners to develop additional adapters for these applications. SAP then offers these adapters to customers via a reseller agreement, and is responsible for the first-level support for the adapters. The partners are responsible for second- and third-level support and use the same support system as SAP.[4] As of XI 2.0, SAP has been able to offer adapters in this way, to integrate applications from Siebel, PeopleSoft, and Oracle, for example.

Adapter Strategy

---

4 For more information about third-party adapters, see SAP Service Marketplace at *service.sap.com/xi • SAP XI in Detail • Connectivity*.

There are several installation options for the Adapter Engine. As shown in Figure 1.4, you can install the Adapter Engine either centrally on the Integration Server (recommended) or non-centrally. Both the (non-)central Adapter Engine and the Partner Connectivity Kit are based on the *Adapter Framework* with the core functions for adapter communication. This framework supports the *Java Connector Architecture (JCA)* standard and thus provides the foundation for the aforementioned development of new resource adapters. As we'll see in Section 6.5.1, you configure the adapters of the Adapter Engine centrally. The configured adapters then take on the inbound and outbound processing on the Integration Server for the Integration Engine, according to the respective protocol. The J2SE Adapter Engine is pre-SAP XI 3.0, and is of interest in only a few special cases.

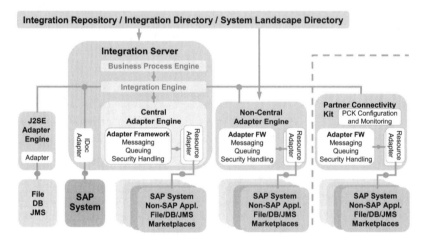

Figure 1.4 Adapter Architecture

What do you need to implement the message exchange using the Integration Server? To explore this question, we will look first at the implementation in the application systems. There are several common implementation features, even though implementation varies according to the system platform. The idea is similar to remote function calls (RFCs): Communication with another system is encapsulated using an interface, whose parameters are converted into a message. However, the significant difference here when compared to RFCs is that SAP XI always requires two interfaces for communication: one interface on the sender side, and one interface on the receiver side. At first glance, this may appear to be a disadvantage, but it is actually an advantage over RFCs because sender and receiver interfaces don't have to match exactly.

Figure 1.5 shows message exchange schematically from the perspective of the application. On the sender side, the application calls an *outbound interface* to transfer the data to the XI runtime (an adapter or the proxy runtime). The XI runtime uses the parameters of the interface to generate a request message, which can be processed by the Integration Server.[5] Before the message reaches the Integration Server, the message header merely contains specifications about the sender and does not yet have any receiver information. If you think back to our earlier goal, that is, to use sender-receiver assignments to access information at a central location rather than searching through all application systems, this immediately makes sense. The receiver of a message is determined on the Integration Server, which makes this decision on the basis of configuration data from the Integration Directory. On the outbound side of the Integration Server, an adapter or the proxy runtime must convert the request message into a call. It does this by calling an *inbound interface* at the receiver, which implements the inbound processing of the application.

Outbound and Inbound

With *synchronous* interfaces, the return parameters of the inbound interface determine the response message that the sender is waiting for before continuing the application. With *asynchronous* interfaces, the application does not expect a response. Here, the message exchange is complete after processing at the receiver. This *mode* must be the same for the outbound and inbound interface.[6]

Synchronous and Asynchronous

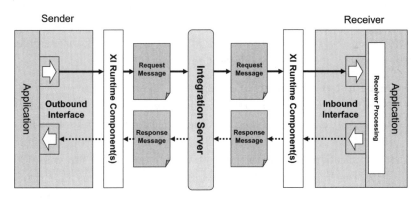

Figure 1.5 Communication Using Interfaces

In a real scenario, the outbound and inbound interface can be all manner of things, for example an RFC, an IDoc, or a proxy (we will examine the

Loose Coupling

---

5 Section 7.2.1 looks at the structure of such messages.
6 As of SAP XI 3.0 SP5, you can use a synchronous/asynchronous bridge within an integration process to forward the request message of a synchronous call.

differences in more detail below). The configuration for determining the receiver is based on the assumption that such interfaces exist. If this is not the case (for example, when exchanging messages using the file, JMS, or JDBC adapter), you simply work with an invented name for the non-existent outbound interface. What is important is that outbound and inbound interfaces separate (potential) senders and receivers. If the parameters of the interfaces for message exchange don't match, you map them to each other using a mapping. This *loose coupling* enables different senders and receivers to communicate with each other. In particular, it enables you to assign such interfaces to one another when one side of the communication cannot or must not be changed, for example, when using a proxy as the outbound interface, which calls an RFC in an SAP 4.6C system. In this case, the RFC has the role of an inbound interface.

Proxies and Adapters At the beginning of this section, we learned that you can either use proxies to exchange messages directly with the Integration Engine, or use an adapter, with the Adapter Engine as a mediator between the adapter and the Integration Engine. These two approaches have a fundamental difference, as shown in Figure 1.6. You develop interfaces that are to be connected to the Integration Server using an adapter in the application system. Proxies, on the other hand, are objects (classes, methods, and data types) generated from a language-independent description. The underlying goal is, again, to make all information relevant to integration available at a central location, and the interfaces for message exchange are undoubtedly part of this information. To achieve this goal, SAP XI works with a central *Integration Repository*, where you save interface descriptions, for example. For interfaces, there are two different development approaches:

▶ **Inside-out development**
When using adapters to connect systems, you develop the interfaces for message exchange as normal in the application system (or they may already exist there). You then import the interface descriptions from the application systems to the central Integration Repository. SAP XI allows this import for RFCs and IDocs. If you have the message structure in WSDL, DTD, or XSD format, you can import this structure to the Integration Repository as an external definition.

▶ **Outside-in development**
SAP introduced a new programming model with SAP XI, which you use to define language-independent *message interfaces* in the Integration Repository. You can then use proxy generation to create either ABAP or Java proxies in application systems.

Figure 1.6 shows both approaches in an example: An ABAP proxy calls a Java proxy, an IDoc, and an RFC. Proxy communication development starts with objects in the Integration Repository, and adapter communication development starts in the application system. You can access the interface description in the Integration Repository centrally in both cases. This separation of the description and the implementation enables you to use the interface description to develop mappings in parallel with the implementation in the application systems. In Chapter 4, we examine interface development in more detail.

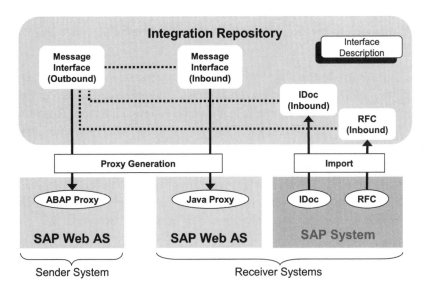

Figure 1.6 Proxy and Adapter Communication (Example)

Besides message interfaces, there are numerous other objects that are important for the implementation of a cross-system process, and which you develop centrally in the Integration Repository. Now that we have examined the runtime and some fundamental aspects, the next section takes us back to the beginning of development.

1.2.2 Design and Configuration

The Integration Server needs the technical address of a receiver to be able to forward messages. These addresses are dependent on the specific system landscape, but you can describe the collaborative process between the applications at the logical level without this information. Therefore, SAP XI divides the implementation of the collaborative process into the following phases:

▶ **Design time**

At design time, you describe the message exchange between applications (not between systems), based on the collaborative process to be implemented. You can then derive the required interfaces and mappings, for example, whether an integration process is required on the Integration Server to communicate between the applications.

▶ **Configuration time**

Put simply, at configuration time you assign systems to the applications and configure the message exchange. You not only reference existing objects of the design time, but also supplement this information according to the requirements of a scenario, for example, with security settings.

Implementation Phases

Figure 1.7 shows the different phases. The *Integration Builder* is the central tool of SAP XI, and you use it both at design time and when configuring the collaborative process in a specific system landscape. The Integration Builder creates *design objects* in the Integration Repository and *configuration objects* in the Integration Directory. At *runtime*, the Integration Builder accesses the configuration in the Integration Directory to process inbound messages. Moreover, the Integration Builder saves executable design objects directly on the Integration Server in order to be able to execute them at runtime (mapping programs, for example).

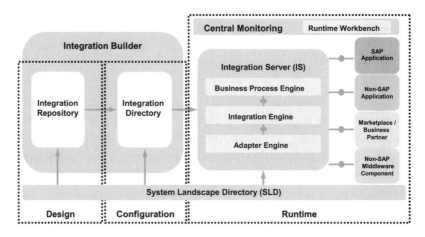

Figure 1.7 Implementation Phases

To illustrate the implementation of the collaborative process, let's compare it with the construction of a car. At design time, you use the Integration Builder to develop the design of the car. The design references the parts that you'll need to build the car at a later time. The design also leaves some individual options open for the customer. The color and the horsepower of the car, for example, are specified in the purchase order. At configuration time, the car is built according to a specific purchase order, and, if everything is done correctly, it will drive once finished.

Before we present an overview of design and configuration time, let's look at the advantages of this architecture:

Advantages

▶ The basic philosophy of SAP XI (unlike the construction of a car) is to make all information and objects required to integrate the applications available at a central location. No matter how many applications you want to integrate, you always use the Integration Builder to call the information from the Integration Repository or Integration Directory.

▶ At design and configuration time, you first define the collaborative process at the logical level, ignoring the technical details. Accordingly, at configuration time, you distinguish between logical and technical routing: Logical routing determines the logical receiver, whereas technical routing determines the technical address of the receiver. This separation means that you don't have to change your whole design and configuration if technical addresses change, for instance, in the event of a server change.

With regard to this last point, SAP XI uses the System Landscape Directory (SLD), which is where you save products, software components, and business systems for the logical level, and technical systems for the technical level. Among other things, you can use the SLD to determine which technical systems are installed in your system landscape, which of these are assigned to a business system for a cross-system scenario, and which products and software components are installed in this system. We'll discuss products and software components in Chapter 3, and technical and business systems in Chapter 6.

System Landscape Directory

This brings us to the end of the basics and overall concept of SAP XI. If you feel there are still pieces of information missing that prevent you from understanding the complete SAP XI picture, don't worry. The various areas of SAP XI are all interconnected, and it takes time to get a hold of this topic. In the next several chapters, you need only identify the individual components in their context to comprehend the material. Chapter 2 is an introduction to the SAP XI tools and presents a demo example to give you some practical experience.

However, let's first take a look at the different design and configuration objects. The Integration Builder is the tool for creating and managing objects, and these objects are stored in the Integration Repository and Integration Directory. To clarify whether a particular section relates to design or configuration time, we will often write as if we are working directly in the Integration Repository or in the Integration Directory. Don't let this confuse you: In both cases, you access the objects by using the Integration Builder.

Design Objects in the Integration Repository

Figure 1.8 shows an overview of the main design objects in the Integration Repository. Each design object is assigned to a software component version, which you must import from the SLD beforehand. The software component version clarifies which product and to which application the objects are assigned. This enables you to control which design objects are shipped with an application from the Integration Repository. Design objects are shipment objects, whereas the objects of the Integration Directory must be configured at the customer site.

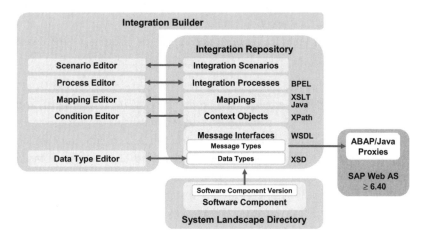

Figure 1.8 Design Objects and Editors in the Integration Builder

Graphical Editors The Integration Builder provides graphical object editors (listed on the left in Figure 1.8) to enable you to edit objects. The sequence of the design objects in the figure corresponds to a usage hierarchy; the Integration Builder supports both top-down and bottom-up development. Since the design objects are based on XML standards, there are export and import functions to enable you to use definitions in tools outside the Integration Builder as well, and vice versa. For example, instead of using graphical mapping in the Integration Builder, you can import XSLT or Java mapping programs to the Integration Repository and use them. As far as interface development goes, Figure 1.8 shows only the outside-in approach.

Configuration Objects in the Integration Directory

The configuration in the Integration Directory determines the message processing at runtime. Figure 1.9 shows the relationship: The routing rules (receiver determination and interface determination) determine the receiver, and whether mapping programs from the Integration Repository are to be executed. You use collaboration profiles to describe the technical options of the sender and receiver. Together with collaboration agreements between a sender and the Integration Server or between the Integration Server and a receiver, you can derive the inbound and outbound processing of the Integration Server and the logical routing. We will look at this in more detail in Chapter 6. You can specify just systems as the receiver, or an integration process executed by the Business Process Engine of the Integration Server. You use this integration process to relate messages to each other on the Integration Server.

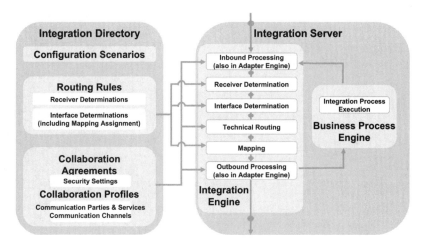

Figure 1.9 Configuration of Message Processing

For simplification, the figure shows only the essential services. Moreover, the figure represents only the logical process flow of message processing. The directory data, for example, is not actually read directly from the Integration Directory, but from a cache.

2   First Steps

This chapter provides you with an overview of how to access the tools in SAP XI. The Integration Builder is central to this topic. SAP also gives you demo examples, which guide you step by step through the technical concepts and tools.

2.1   Overview

The features of SAP XI can be divided into several task areas, each of which has corresponding user roles. Users require these roles to perform the tasks in their respective areas. Before we discuss the SAP XI tools in detail, we'll list the various task areas and refer you to the respective chapters in this book that cover these areas:

▶ **Administration**

An administrator sets up the various SAP XI tools and is responsible for system monitoring and user management. Because these tasks are closely linked to the installation of SAP XI, it is advisable for the administrator to be involved in the installation process.

▶ **Technical configuration**

The configuration of the SAP XI runtime components is referred to as *technical* configuration. It includes setting up the Integration Engine and the adapters. This configuration depends on the components used in the current system landscape. Configuration is performed by consultants or administrators, independently of the design and configuration of the collaborative process.

This book does not cover the installation or administration of the tools. Section 7.2 introduces the technical configuration of the Integration Engine. For more information, see the *Installation Guide* or *Configuration Guide* for SAP XI 3.0 on the SAP Service Marketplace at *service.sap.com/nw04installation*. The book focuses on the following task areas:

▶ **Design**

This area includes the design of collaborative processes by a development or consultant team. Chapter 3 first describes the organizational steps of this development and then addresses the modeling of the collaborative process using integration scenarios. This description provides the basis for an examination of the objects required to integrate

Task Areas

the applications: interfaces (Chapter 4), mappings (Chapter 5), and integration processes (Chapter 8). These objects, which you save in the Integration Repository at design time, are referred to collectively as *process integration content*, or XI content for short.

▶ **Configuration**
This area comprises the configuration of collaborative processes by a development or consultant team. You configure inbound and outbound processing, logical routing, technical routing, and mapping for a particular Business-to-Business (B2B) scenario or system landscape. This is discussed in Chapter 6. This task area also includes the maintenance of configuration data for the IDoc adapter.

▶ **Monitoring**
This area comprises the monitoring of collaborative processes at runtime. This includes monitoring of the message flow (with respect to throughput, for example), and analysis and further processing of messages that have not been processed (status tracking). The monitoring of processed IDocs and RFCs in the corresponding adapters also belongs to the monitoring task area. Monitoring is discussed in the runtime chapter (see Chapter 7, Section 7.4).

There is a seamless transition from the *technical* configuration (an administrative task) to the configuration of the collaborative process. For example, the IDoc adapter must access metadata that describes the structure of an IDoc. Which IDocs are to be processed depends on the collaborative process (configuration). In order to access the metadata of an IDoc, there must be an RFC connection to the system that will send or receive the IDocs (technical configuration). The latter task is likely to fall to an administrator, the former to a consultant.

User Roles   SAP XI consists of Java- and ABAP-based applications that run on SAP Web AS 6.40. Table 2.1 shows the authorizations that you need to access the functions of SAP XI. They are related to user roles and correspond approximately to the aforementioned task areas. These are composite roles and each references a single role for accessing the Java applications and a single role for accessing the corresponding ABAP transactions. Users must be assigned only the composite roles. This automatically gives them access to the ABAP and Java tools. Since user management is located on the ABAP side, users must log on to the ABAP side once to change their initial password. Other options for assigning authorizations to Integration Builder users are addressed at the end of Section 2.2.

Role	Task Area
SAP_XI_DISPLAY_USER	This role groups together the display authorizations for all SAP XI tools.
SAP_XI_DEVELOPER	Design
SAP_XI_CONFIGURATOR	Configuration
SAP_XI_CONTENT_ORGANIZER	Tasks related to the organization and structuring of the content of the Integration Repository, Integration Directory, and System Landscape Directory that are not usually performed by developers, for example, the maintenance of software components.
SAP_XI_MONITOR	Monitoring
SAP_XI_ADMINISTRATOR	Administration and technical configuration

Table 2.1 User Roles in SAP XI

Once a user has logged on to a client in an SAP system, a user menu that corresponds to the roles assigned to the user is displayed. To start the Java-based applications, you need a user at the client in which the Integration Engine is configured as the Integration Server (this is discussed in more detail in Section 7.2.1). You have to log on at least once to this client to change your initial password. Once you have done this, you can use the transaction **Start Integration Builder** (Transaction SXMB_IFR) to call the XI start page in the Web browser and log on to the Java applications by using the ABAP user.

Transactions and XI Start Page

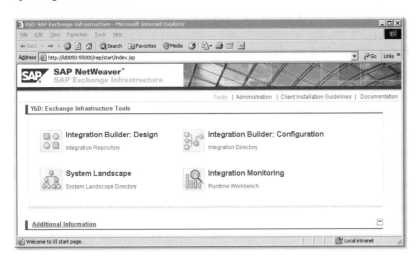

Figure 2.1 XI Start Page

Figure 2.1 shows the XI start page in the SAP system Y6D. From here, you can call the *Integration Builder* (for design or configuration), the *System Landscape Directory*, and the *Runtime Workbench* for monitoring. In Section 3.2 and Section 6.2, we look at the System Landscape Directory in more detail. The next section introduces the Integration Builder.

2.2   Introduction to the Integration Builder

The Integration Builder is the central tool for designing and configuring collaborative processes with SAP XI. Both Java applications use the same GUI framework and are started using Java Web Start (for information about installing Java Web Start, see the **Client Installation Guidelines** on the XI start page). The Integration Builder libraries are saved on the SAP Web AS after SAP XI has been installed. When you start the Integration Builder for the first time, Java Web Start transfers the required libraries to your PC by HTTP and starts the Java application. You can also change this HTTP connection (and all other internal HTTP connections of the Integration Builder) to the HTTPS protocol.

Logon and Personalization

The Integration Builder has its own logon dialog box. The user and password pertain to the client of the SAP system in which the Integration Engine is configured as the Integration Server. If Single Sign-On (SSO) is activated for the system, you only have to log on to the Integration Builder a first time. You can then call any subsequent sessions without having to reenter your user and password. You can change the logon language at any time by choosing **Tools · Personal Settings...** In addition to settings for navigation and searching, you can also select the original language for object documentation in the Integration Builder.

Navigation

Figure 2.2 shows the Integration Builder for design. The tab pages on the left side are for object navigation and for managing change lists. The respective *object editor* is displayed on tab pages on the right side (in this case the mapping editor). To compare several objects, choose **Detach Window** in the top right corner of the object editor (the pin icon). In addition to the navigation tree options, you can use the blue arrows in the main menu of the Integration Builder to navigate forward and backward in the navigation history, which remembers the sequence in which you have opened objects.

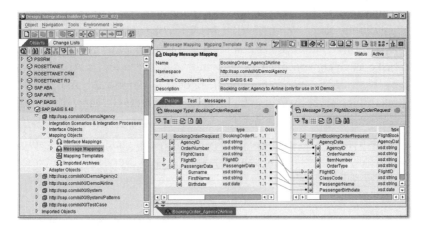

Figure 2.2 Integration Builder (Design)

Since the Integration Builder user interfaces for design and configuration are based on the same GUI framework, you operate the Integration Builder in the same way in both cases. There are differences, however, with regard to the object types and their organization. Before you can use the Integration Builder to create objects in the Integration Repository at design time, you need a software component version, which you import from the System Landscape Directory (see Section 3.2.2). Configuration objects, on the other hand, are not assigned to software component versions and can be grouped using *configuration scenarios* instead (see Section 6.1 and Section 6.2.2). The differences in the object types mean that they must be handled differently during copy or transport procedures. We'll discuss below how to edit objects in the Integration Builder and point out differences between design and configuration where applicable.

Editing and Managing Objects

To create a new object, choose **Object · New...** in the main menu, select the object type, and enter at least the required attributes. Required attributes are marked with a red asterisk (*) in the dialog box. If you use the context menu in the navigation tree to create objects, the Integration Builder deduces certain information from the position of the object in the tree and enters values in the corresponding fields (object type; in the Integration Repository **Software Component Version** and **Namespace**).

Once you have saved an object, the Integration Builder generates a new object version (status: **Being Processed**) and adds it to a user-specific *change list*. Change lists simplify object management:

Change Lists

▶ While an object is being edited in a change list, the changes are visible only to the user making the changes. The change list still has the status **Open**. This enables you to edit several objects in a change list and then make all changes visible to all Integration Builder users (status: **Active**) by releasing the change list. The change list is then **closed**. You can display older object versions by choosing **<Object> · History...** in the respective object editor menu.

▶ If the user doesn't yet have a change list, the Integration Builder automatically creates a new standard change list. Every user can create additional change lists. You can also reassign change lists of other users to yourself.

▶ In the Integration Directory, you release change lists to activate changes for runtime.

▶ In the Integration Repository, the change lists are grouped by software component versions. If objects belong to the same software component version, you can move them between different change lists by using drag and drop. Dependent objects are moved as well.

Object References and Copies

As is clear from the last point, software component versions are important for organization in the Integration Repository: They represent the smallest shippable unit. Limitations on object references and behavioral considerations when copying design objects stem from the requirement that objects that belong together must also be able to be shipped together. For example, the Integration Builder does not permit references between interface objects from different software components, because at least one interface must be shipped with all its dependent objects (message and data types) as a unit. Otherwise, a customer can end up with an interface definition, but cannot access the structure of the message. The Integration Builder differentiates object reference types in order to account for these shipping implications. Similarly to hyperlinks (in this case the object reference) in an HTML document (in this case the referencing object), the Integration Builder saves the references of an object to another object either relatively or absolutely to a software component version:

▶ **Relative object reference**
In this case, the reference in an object becomes invalid as soon as you copy the referencing object to another software component version. There is a good reason for this in interface objects, as mentioned above. Therefore, all object references between interface objects are relative. If you copy an interface object to another software component version, you can copy all dependent interface objects as well.

▶ **Absolute object reference**

In this case, the reference in an object is still valid, even when you copy it to another software component version.

In the Integration Builder, references are defined as absolute or relative. To check all relative object references after an object has been copied, choose **<Object> · Check** in the object editor menu. If objects are missing in the current software component version, these are listed in the processing log of the check function. Figure 2.3 shows an example: The message type myMT1 was copied to the software component version Ameise 1.0. The reference to the data type myDT1 has therefore become invalid. The processing log at the bottom of the editor screen shows the results of the check, that is, that the Integration Builder cannot find an active version of the data type myDT1 in the software component version Ameise 1.0.[1] When change lists are released, the processing log can contain a range of messages relating to different objects. You can navigate directly from the log to the object in the list. You can show or hide the processing log by using the pushbutton circled in Figure 2.3.

Object Check and Processing Log

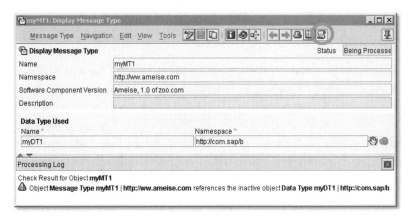

Figure 2.3 Results of an Object Check

Conversely, object references enable you to determine where an object is used. The Integration Builder provides a Where-used list in the object editor for this purpose. You use this Where-used list to identify either the direct user or the indirect (transitive) user. You can also search for objects:

Object Search and Where-Used List

▶ The search function in the toolbar of the navigation tree enables you to search for texts from the selected position in the navigation tree. You

---

1 The object check also considers the underlying software component version. This is discussed again in Section 3.2.

can use the wildcard * to mask any number of text characters and the wildcard ? to mask exactly one character. If the text is found, the Integration Builder expands the tree and selects the node. If the search is unsuccessful, it is performed again, starting at the top structure node.

▶ The search help (main menu **Object · Find...**) enables you to use **Search Requirements** to search for objects in the Integration Repository or Integration Directory. Examples of search requirements are header data (object type, software component version, namespace, name), changed on, changed by, and other object-dependent attributes. The latter enable you to select message interfaces by mode (synchronous or asynchronous), for example. In the extended search, you can logically link the search attributes.

So far, we have concentrated on the basic functions of the Integration Builder. To understand the concepts of SAP XI and the corresponding tools, it is helpful to use examples. SAP ships design objects and demo applications, which you can configure with the Integration Builder. The demo examples are presented in the next section, but first let's look at how authorizations are assigned in the Integration Builder, and the dependencies that exist between the Integration Builder and other SAP XI components.

Authorizations

Access to objects is determined by the roles assigned to the ABAP user. As shown in Table 2.1, there is one role for assigning display authorizations, one role for design, and one role for configuration. The role SAP_XI_ CONTENT_ORGANIZER exists for certain activities relating to the organization of process integration content in the Integration Repository (for example, the import of software component versions), because only selected users (and not all developers) can perform such activities. To add additional access rights for particular object sets, choose **Tools · User Roles** in the menu and create additional roles. The Integration Builder transfers activated roles to the *SAP User Management Engine*, which you use to assign the roles to user groups on the J2EE side. In the default setting, there are no restrictions on access to particular object sets in the Integration Builder. The user roles that you transfer to the SAP User Management Engine limit the existing authorizations to a selected group of people.

Dependencies and Caches

During configuration in the Integration Directory, you use the Integration Builder to reference the design objects in the Integration Repository. However, there are no references from the Integration Repository to the

Integration Directory. To accelerate access to objects, the following caches exist in the Integration Builder environment:

▶ **Runtime cache**

At runtime, the Integration Engine or the Adapter Engine must access configuration objects, mapping objects, and integration processes in the Integration Repository. The Integration Builder puts active object versions in the runtime cache. The cache is updated whenever you activate a change list in the Integration Directory or a change list in the Integration Repository that contains mapping objects or integration processes. To check whether the cache has been informed of changes, choose **Environment · Cache Notifications...** in the Integration Builder main menu. You can analyze the content of the runtime cache in the Integration Engine client by calling transaction SXI_CACHE.

▶ **SLD cache**

The Integration Builder accesses information about software components, business systems, and technical systems in the System Landscape Directory (SLD). This cache is updated every time the Integration Builder is restarted. Alternatively, you can declare the data in the cache invalid by choosing **Environment · Clear SLD Data Cache** in the main menu.

The next chapters describe the individual areas of SAP XI. The demo examples discussed in the next section help you to understand how to use SAP XI in practice.

2.3 Demo Examples

SAP ships demo examples as part of SAP XI 3.0. You use these examples to configure and execute basic communication scenarios. As is typical in a shipment of a cross-system SAP application, the process integration content in the Integration Repository and the example applications are part of the shipment, and you have to configure the scenarios yourself in the Integration Directory. The examples enable you to become familiar with SAP XI and perform tests. They are not intended for productive use. Detailed documentation is available on the configuration and execution of the individual scenarios.[2]

Because we will refer to the demo examples in the first part of the book, we will now provide you with an overview of them. To ensure that users

Application Scenario

---

2 For more information, see the online documentation at *help.sap.com* · *SAP NetWeaver '04* · *Process Integration* · *SAP Exchange Infrastructure* · *Overview* · *Demo Examples*.

can understand the demo examples without having detailed business knowledge, we based them all on the communication between a travel agency (as the vendor of flight tickets) and two airlines (that sell their tickets through the travel agency). The flight data model has been used successfully in many SAP technology courses, and since booking a flight is something that most people have personal experience with, SAP XI uses this experience as an example with which to demonstrate cross-system communication. Note, however, that not all aspects of this application scenario reflect how SAP XI is used in the real world. For example, the demo examples are based on the assumption that the travel agency books flights directly with the airlines. In reality, travel agencies use a central booking system for their flight bookings. The goal of the examples is not to mirror reality, but to demonstrate the central concepts of SAP XI.

Standard Configuration
The design of the demo examples does not stipulate a particular number of airlines. However, the documentation for configuring the demo examples is based on the assumption that exactly one travel agency exchanges messages with two airlines. Figure 2.4 shows the scenario for this *standard configuration*. The applications that communicate using SAP XI are usually part of different products, for instance SAP CRM and SAP APO. However, to keep the logistical effort involved in shipping the demo examples to a minimum, the demo example applications are implemented on SAP Web AS 6.40. This means that they are available on all systems based on SAP Web AS 6.40. Furthermore, in the standard configuration, the roles of travel agencies and airlines are performed by different clients of the same SAP Web AS. SAP does not provide any support for scenarios that differ from the standard configuration.

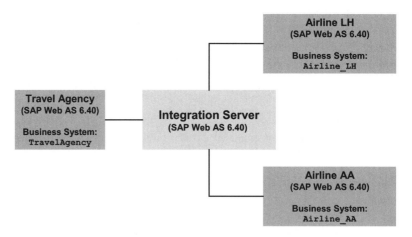

Figure 2.4 Technical Systems and Business Systems of the Examples

The documentation for the demo examples describes the general configuration steps for all the examples and the specific configuration steps for each example. The documentation also describes how to execute the examples.

Integration Scenario	Communication Types (→ Asynchronous; ↔ Synchronous)
Checking flight seat availability (CheckFlightSeatAvailability)	ABAP proxy ↔ ABAP proxy ABAP proxy ↔ RFC
Booking a single flight (SingleFlightBooking)	ABAP proxy → ABAP proxy ABAP proxy → IDoc
Booking connecting flights (MultipleFlightBooking)	ABAP proxy → ABAP proxy (using an integration process)
Distributing booking order data (DistributeBookingOrderInformation)	ABAP proxy → File system

Table 2.2 Demo Examples for the SAP XI 3.0 Feature Pack

The design objects required to integrate the travel agency application and the airline application are shipped with SAP XI 3.0. Table 2.2 gives an overview of the examples shipped with the Feature Pack (SP4). These objects are located in the Integration Repository in the software component version SAP BASIS 6.40. The aforementioned logical separation of the travel agency application and the airline application is reflected in the Integration Repository. All design objects that belong to the travel agency application are located in the namespace *http://sap.com/xi/XI/Demo/Agency*, and those that belong to the airline application are in the namespace *http://sap.com/xi/XI/Demo/Airline*. Design objects that don't belong to a particular application (such as integration scenarios, integration processes, and mapping objects) cannot always be assigned uniquely to one of the communication parties. The demo examples are based on the assumption that the airline application provides certain services, which form a complete integration scenario together with the travel agency application. Therefore, all such design objects are defined in the namespace of the travel agency. The available design objects form the basis for executing the demo examples for test purposes. Furthermore, you can use the design objects to examine how the content of the Integration Repository is structured, how various object types are used in the Integration Repository, and the dependencies between the design objects.

Design Objects of the Examples

This brings us to the end of the introductory chapters of this book. In the next chapters, we explore the individual areas of SAP XI in more detail.

3 Designing Collaborative Processes

To design a collaborative process, you need a range of objects that are all related to each other. This chapter looks at how SAP XI organizes these objects and how you use them to describe a collaborative process.

3.1 Introduction

As described in Chapter 1, SAP XI separates the design, configuration, and runtime phases to manage the complexity of collaborative processes. The term *collaborative process* means a cross-system process from the *real* business world, for example, the process for booking flights between travel agencies and airlines. The requirements of the process determine which design objects you need.

Definition

Before you can start the implementation, you make certain organizational steps or settings. These organizational steps are described in Section 3.2. The design of the collaborative process is closely linked to the planning and organization of the implementation and describes which components exchange messages with each other. You model the collaborative process in the Integration Builder using *integration scenarios*. These scenarios provide you with an overview of the message exchange and group the objects created at design time together semantically. This is discussed in more detail in Section 3.3.

3.2 Development Organization

In every type of software development project, you are faced with the challenge of grouping development objects and organizing them into appropriate units. For example, you may want to have a particularly high level of reusability, or minimize the communication between individual components. It is an important feature of SAP XI that all objects involved in message exchange are centrally available. Therefore, the first thing to establish about the organization of objects is that there are two general object types:

▶ **All design objects in the Integration Repository**
Because you use this content to describe and implement the collaborative process, these objects are collectively referred to as *process integration content* (or *XI content*).

▶ **Development objects in the application systems of applications that
use SAP XI to exchange messages**
Examples are Java and ABAP classes, client and server proxies generated by XI, ABAP programs, and other development objects that
implement the actual application logic (such as updates when a message is received).

Of course, these objects belong together semantically and must be
grouped together again for shipment of the cross-system application. The
next two sections describe how this is done: Section 3.2.1 discusses the
organization of products in the SAP System Landscape Directory, and
Section 3.2.2 shows how you use this information in SAP XI.

3.2.1 Describing Products in the Software Catalog

An application is a piece of software that is installed or can be installed in
a system. It can be updated and provides interfaces to enable other applications to access or transfer data. A cross-system application uses multiple systems and products. It helps both SAP and the customer to have an
overview of all systems and the components installed in these systems.
SAP stores this information centrally in the *SAP System Landscape Directory* (SLD):

▶ The SLD saves the information about the software that you *can* install
in a system in a *software catalog*. SAP differentiates between *products*
and *software components*. Software components can be shipped but
don't have to be executed. The executable product consists of software components. This is discussed in more detail later in this section.

▶ The SLD also contains information about the systems that make up the
system landscape in which the software is or can be installed. Because
the system landscape is defined at the customer site, system data is of
interest only at configuration and runtime. This is discussed in more
detail in Section 6.2.

In SAP XI, products and software components belong to design time, and system landscape data belongs to configuration time. Don't let the product name *System Landscape Directory* confuse you. The SLD is relevant for the whole of SAP; therefore, the differentiation usually made between *repository* and *directory* in XI does not apply.

System Landscape Directory and SAP XI

At the beginning of a software project, management defines the software components of a product. The SLD imports the relevant information to the software catalog. Initially, this catalog is just a list of *installable* software components. When a product is installed, the software components are assigned to a technical system in the SLD, and thus become *installed* software components. We should also mention that different versions of products and software components can exist. For example, the product CRM has *product versions* CRM 3.0 and CRM 3.1, which you can find in the software catalog.

Figure 3.1 shows an example of product version CRM 2.0A. It comprises three interdependent software component versions:

▶ SAP ABA 4.6A uses SAP BASIS 2.0A. Software component versions such as SAP BASIS 2.0A are referred to as *underlying* software component versions.

▶ SAP BBPCRM 2.0A uses SAP ABA 4.6A and SAP BASIS 2.0A.

This *use relationship* enables objects from underlying software component versions to be reused. Furthermore, a software component version can be used in different product versions. The actual functions for a product are developed in the application system. Developers work with packages[1] to divide the functions of a software component version into smaller units. In short, a customer never installs individual software component versions in a system; instead, an executable version of a product is installed. Developers, on the other hand, are more likely to work with software component versions, because they represent the smallest shippable unit. For example, SAP ships support packages on the software component version level, and not on the package level.

Use Relationship

---

1 Software logistics on SAP Web AS offers additional development units, which are not discussed in more detail here.

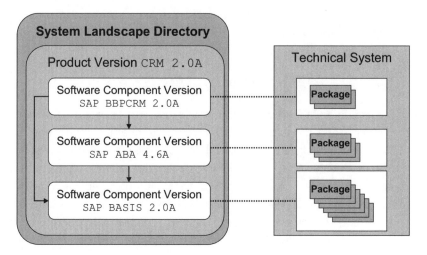

Figure 3.1 Software Component Versions and Packages

SAP provides information about the available SAP software in the software catalog in the SLD. Customers can add their own software components and products as third-party products. The SLD thus simplifies the administration of a customer's system landscape and provides a basis for describing the components that communicate using SAP XI. In Section 3.3, we'll see how to build on this description to model the communication between components and what to do if these components are outside your own system landscape.

3.2.2 Organization of Design Objects in the Integration Repository

You use the Integration Builder to edit all the design objects of your collaborative process. The responsibility for organizing this content lies with selected employees, called *content managers*. In order to perform the necessary steps, these content managers need special authorizations that go beyond normal developer authorization. Just as in development in the application systems, the design objects must be shippable, and therefore must be assigned to software component versions. The software component versions of interest are those that belong to the products for which you want to implement cross-system communication. The content manager imports these software component versions using the menu path **Tools · Transfer from System Landscape Directory · Import Software Component Version** in the main menu of the Integration Builder. After import, the software component versions are displayed in the navigation tree in alphabetical order. Displaying all the software component versions would unnecessarily complicate the overview.

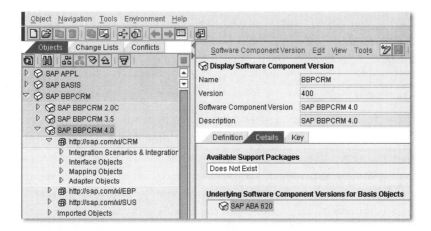

Figure 3.2 Software Components in the Integration Builder

Namespaces

Figure 3.2 shows the navigation tree of the Integration Builder in the central Integration Repository. The top level shows the software components, the next level shows the imported software component versions, and the level below that shows the namespaces. The content manager creates these namespaces after the import of the software component version to prevent naming conflicts between Integration Repository objects. Therefore, they are also referred to as *repository namespaces*. You use repository namespaces to identify design objects at different places in SAP XI: in the Integration Repository, in the Integration Directory, in application systems, and also in the message header. Since SAP XI uses the XML standard, there is also an entire range of other namespaces in addition to the repository namespaces:

▶ RFC and IDoc descriptions that have been imported to the Integration Repository each have a fixed, cross-software-component repository namespace.

▶ For messages and data type enhancements, you can assign an *XML namespace* as an alternative to the repository namespace. This is discussed in more detail in Section 4.4.1 and Section 4.4.2.

▶ In message monitoring, you'll find internal namespaces in the message, for example, for the message format.

Versioning

Unlike repository namespaces, software component versions aren't used to uniquely identify the object, and are relevant only for shipment and versioning at the software component level. Once the development of a software component version is complete, content managers import a new version of the software component to the Integration Builder. To transfer the design objects of the previous version, they can use the *release transfer.*[2] To do this, they must first create the same namespaces in the new software component version that were in the old version. Software components with different versions can therefore use the same namespace.

Object References   The division of the product into software components has repercussions. Objects that are dependent on one another should be in the same software component version. Otherwise, you cannot be certain that a shipment to the customer is complete. For this reason, the Integration Builder warns users if they try to create the same namespaces in different software component versions, because the objects of a namespace are usually closely related. The Integration Builder also limits the options for object references. For example, message interfaces in the Integration Repository point to message types, message types to data types. To ensure that all these interface objects are in the same shipment unit, an interface object can only reference interface objects of the same software component version, or an underlying software component version. Therefore, you cannot select any other software component versions in the input help in the Integration Builder. Such references are valid only within this context. However, you can copy objects to another software component version, but the object references become invalid. On the other hand, in cross-component communication, you can't avoid referencing objects in different software component versions. For example, in principle, a mapping is located between two components (see Section 5.1.2 for more information). In this case, the Integration Builder references the other objects *absolutely*, that is, the software component version is specified explicitly in the input help. These references remain valid when the objects are copied.

Since the concepts presented here also apply to other areas of software logistics, we'll discuss them in the next section. However, it isn't necessary to read Section 3.2.3 to understand Section 3.3, which looks at modeling collaborative processes using integration scenarios.

---

2   The release transfer function is in the main menu of the Integration Builder, under **Tools**.

3.2.3 Object Versioning and Transport

We have already seen that versioning occurs at the software component level. Versioning also exists at the object level (design objects in the Integration Repository and configuration objects in the Integration Directory) in the form of user-specific change lists. When an object is initially saved, a new object version is created, which is added to the change list. When users activate their list, this version of the object in the list is closed. All changes are then visible to all other users in the Integration Builder. One particular feature of this concept is that it enables the release of changes in the configuration collectively for the runtime environment in the Integration Directory.

Design objects are developed in a central Integration Repository. In Section 3.2.2, we learned that you can use the release transfer to transfer design objects in the Integration Repository to other software component versions. You can also exchange objects between *different* Integration Repositories, for the following reasons:

Transport and Shipment

▶ Design objects are necessary to configure the collaborative process at the customer site. Customers must import the process integration content to their Integration Repository.

▶ It is advisable to import the process integration content to an intermediate Integration Repository before the shipment for quality assurance reasons. This step enables import problems to be identified and corrected at an early stage. In very large development landscapes, you may want to use additional Integration Repositories for consolidation purposes.

Since the configuration of design objects is customer-specific, the Integration Directory does not contain shipped content. Therefore, there are no software component versions in the Integration Directory. Nevertheless, transports between different Integration Directories are still necessary to test the configuration before using it in a productive landscape. This is discussed in more detail in Section 6.7.

For the moment, however, let's take a closer look at design objects. They always have *one* original repository, that is, the Integration Repository from which the object originates. Within an Integration Repository, you differentiate between the original objects and the copies by using an attribute of the corresponding software component version. This originality principle means that transport landscapes for Integration Repositories are star-shaped. Figure 3.3 shows an example.

Original Objects

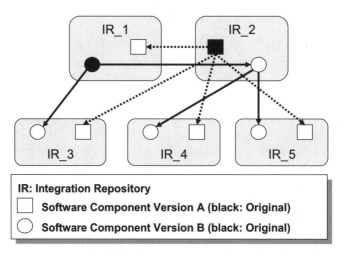

Figure 3.3 Transport Landscape

Mechanisms
for Ensuring
Consistency You must only make changes to an object in the Integration Repository from which the object originates. This ensures that during import to the target repository, the new versions of this object are created such that the object has the same version in both repositories. The object versions in the different repositories are always consistent. The following mechanisms ensure this:

▶ Content managers lock objects in the target repository against changes. They can, however, allow changes if they are necessary for an immediate correction. As long as development makes the same changes to the original, this does not cause a problem. If they don't, this results in a conflict, which the user can resolve during import in the Integration Builder.

▶ When older object versions are imported to a target repository, any existing newer object versions aren't overwritten. The imported older version is visible in the object history of the Integration Builder after import, but the new version remains the current valid version.

Transport Variants The latter mechanism ensures that multiple imports to an Integration Repository always have the same result, irrespective of their sequence. There are two variants for the transport itself:

▶ You export the design objects to an export directory as a file. You copy these export files to an import directory of the target repository and use the menu path **Tools · Import Design Objects** in the Integration Builder to import them.

► As of the SAP XI 3.0 Feature Pack, there is a transport connection from SAP XI to the *Change Management Service* (CMS) of the *SAP NetWeaver Java Development Infrastructure*. You use the same function in the Integration Builder as previously mentioned, but you don't need to copy the export files manually.

The next section looks at integration scenarios in the Integration Builder. Integration scenarios in the Integration Builder enable you to model the message exchange of the collaborative process, using the products that you learned about in Section 3.2.1.

3.3   Modeling the Collaborative Process

A collaborative process, whether existing or new, comprises a sequence of steps that must be performed to execute the process. Before you can implement the process, you must determine and document the required steps and their sequence. As we've already seen in Section 1.1.2, there are different process views in SAP, each with a different focus and level of detail in the steps. With regard to the level of abstraction, integration scenarios in SAP XI are primarily at the same level as *business processes* in SAP Solution Manager. However, they are used very differently:

► **Business processes in SAP Solution Manager**
In SAP Solution Manager, you work with *business scenarios*,[3] which you use to derive *business processes* that model the process flow across applications. Customers use the business processes to configure applications that are required in a scenario within the involved systems (for example, to customize these applications).

► **Integration scenarios in the Integration Builder of SAP XI**
These scenarios document the message exchange between application components (see Section 3.3.1 for more information).

Because we want to focus on SAP XI, we'll now look at modeling with integration scenarios in the Integration Builder. Using this approach, we'll focus on the following features:

► Documenting the message exchange between application components. You can reference involved design objects of the Integration Repository directly from integration scenarios, for example, point from a connection to a necessary interface mapping. Integration scenarios

---

3 SAP documents the business scenarios of its own solutions on SAP Service Marketplace in the portal for Integrated Business Content (*service.sap.com/ibc*).

therefore offer a central point of access. You can also derive and create all necessary design objects from an integration scenario or bundle existing design objects in an integration scenario.

▶ Providing a configuration template to use as a basis to generate and refine configuration content in the Integration Directory. This is discussed in more detail in Section 6.3.1.

Now, we'll examine how integration scenarios are used in the Integration Repository. Technically speaking, they aren't necessary to implement the collaborative process. However, it would be short-sighted not to use integration scenarios, because they provide an integrated overview of the design objects—thereby making them easier to maintain—and save time during configuration.

3.3.1 Mapping Application Components to Systems

As we saw in Section 3.2.1, a product is a piece of software that you can install and execute in a system. An installed product can also send and receive messages. To create a graphical model of these processes, integration scenarios use *application components*, which the integration scenario editor depicts by using colored lanes.

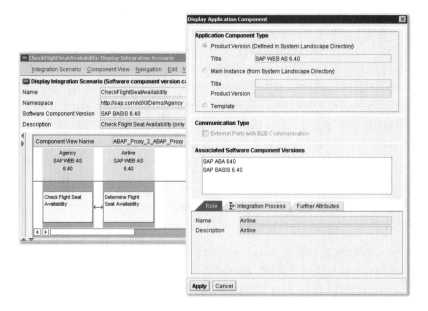

Figure 3.4 Application Components in the Integration Scenario Editor

Figure 3.4 shows a simple integration scenario that models a flight avail- **Application** **Component**
ability check. The left lane is an application component for the travel
agency (role `Agency`); the right lane is an application component for the
airline (role `Airline`). The same product version is assigned to both
application components (`SAP WebAS 6.40`). You would normally expect
there to be different product versions, such as SAP CRM and SAP APO.
However, the example shown in Figure 3.4 is part of the demo examples
that SAP ships with SAP XI. To ensure that the example is available in all
systems based on SAP Web AS 6.40, it is part of the same product version. The demo example is described in more detail in Section 2.3.

Application components of integration scenarios can reference product
versions from the SLD. You may ask yourself why you don't simply insert
product versions in the integration scenario. The reason is that this does
not cover the application cases where the product version is not known.
For example, only the product versions of a system landscape are saved in
the SLD. In cross-company communication, you can't access this information. In other cases, the product version may not be known at the time
of modeling. For these reasons, integration scenarios use application
components as the logical abstraction of all these cases. The common feature is that *applications* (and not systems) are integrated. Which systems
the applications are installed in is not relevant in modeling.

The dialog window on the right in Figure 3.4 shows the properties of the **Types of**
application component with the role `Airline`, with information about **Application**
the associated software component versions for the product version. The **Components**
upper part of the window displays the different types of application components:

▶ **Product version**
The application component references a product version in the SLD.
This does not have to be an SAP product. Partners and customers can
enter their own products and software components in the software
catalog of the SLD.

▶ **Software unit**
The application component references a software unit in the SLD. Software units are different variants of a product that are installed on different servers. In such cases, a reference to a product version is not sufficient, because there can be several software units for a product version, and these have different roles in the scenario. Since modeling
with software units is otherwise no different from modeling with product versions, we won't go into this particular case in any more detail.

▶ **Template**

The application component is not dependent on information from the SLD. You use templates if the implementation of the application component is not known (see above).

In addition to the type of the application component, you can also specify whether it is an external B2B communication party. Section 6.4 describes the configuration of such integration scenarios.

It's important to remember that application components are not systems, but units that provide an executable function. Determining in which systems (or how many) this function is to be installed isn't relevant for modeling. Let's take another look at the flight availability check example in Figure 3.5.

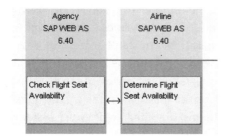

Figure 3.5 Integration Scenario CheckFlightSeatAvailablility

The integration scenario is the same, whether or not the status is to be queried at several airlines: There is one communication party with the role of a travel agency, and several communication parties with the role of an airline, all using the same product version. Therefore, you don't need additional application components for modeling. The final number of airlines to be checked is determined at configuration time. You can assign services of different systems to an application component in the Integration Directory. This abstraction simplifies the modeling of collaborative processes considerably. Figure 3.6 illustrates this principle for the flight availability check. At configuration time, the application component with the role `Airline` is assigned two business systems—`Airline_LH` and `Airline_AA`—for the airlines Lufthansa and American Airlines, respectively. Additional airlines are possible. In Section 3.3.2, we'll cover other examples of this type of abstraction and examine more closely how to describe the message exchange between the application components.

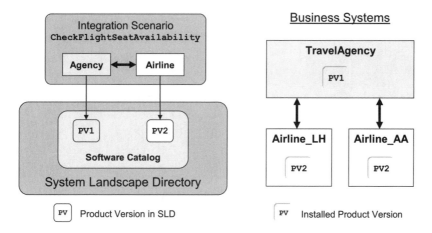

Figure 3.6 Modeling at the Application Component Level

The common feature of the application components that we have looked at so far is that you assign application systems to them at configuration time. Integration processes are an exception, as they are executed on the Business Process Engine on the Integration Server, that is, *during message processing* between different systems. In the integration scenario, you reference these processes from the **Integration Process** tab page of an application component. Which integration processes you can reference depends on the type of application component. We'll look at references in more detail in the next section.

Integration Processes in the Integration Scenario

So far, we have not yet mentioned what the *role* of an application component entails. It is a business description of the application component that aids the understanding of the integration scenario. A product can be used in different application components in different roles. The role consists of a technical name and a description, which is visible in the integration scenario editor in the header of the application component. Table 3.1 has examples of good role descriptions.

Roles

Type of Application Component in Integration Scenario	Role Description (Examples)
Business partner	Customer Vendor
Different application components of a business partner	Vendor—Customer Management Vendor—Production
There are application components of only one business partner in the integration scenario.	Customer management Production

Table 3.1 Role Descriptions of Application Components

Component Views

In the input field above all the application components, you can also assign a name for the corresponding *component view*. To start with, there is only one component view of the integration scenario, in which you model the message exchange for a particular combination of product versions. In some cases, the only difference between integration scenarios is that they support different combinations of product versions. If this is the case, you can use the component view to define different views of the same integration scenario. In this example, we don't recommend that you create a second integration scenario in the Integration Builder, because this would mean having two descriptions of scenarios that are essentially the same. Instead, you should proceed as follows:

1. Enter a role for each application component in the first component view. This role must be identical in all component views.

2. Enter a name for the first component view.

3. In the menu bar of the integration scenario editor, choose **Component View · Copy**.

4. To reference other product versions in a new component view, replace the respective application components with new components that use the same role name.

5. To the left of the graphical editor, the Integration Builder shows a screen area that displays a preview of all component views. To switch between component views, click the respective preview.

The component views are copies within an integration scenario. Technically speaking, they are independent of one another.

Now that we have examined application components in integration scenarios in detail, we'll explain how you can model the message exchange between application components.

3.3.2   Modeling the Message Exchange

In the previous section, we looked at application components as a modeling abstraction and examined how they are mapped to systems. We saw that application components reference product versions or templates. Moreover, a product version consists of software component versions. Every object that you ship with your product is part of such a software component version, even the integration scenario itself.

In this section, we'll study *actions* and how to use them to describe the message exchange. Actions are separate reusable objects in the Integration Repository that are assigned to a software component version. At first glance, you might think that this appears to be somewhat complicated. Therefore, we'll return to the start of modeling and ask ourselves where we create which objects, where we can use them, and why. Then, we'll look at the modeling of the message exchange in detail.

Actions

Initial Modeling Considerations

We'll start with the integration scenario itself. Since the integration scenario describes the message exchange between application components, it is at a higher level than the components and encompasses all of them. There are two ways to define which software component version the integration scenario should belong to:

▶ You define a "leading" application component of the collaborative process, which is responsible for higher-level design objects. These objects can also be mapping objects, which are located between the application components (see Section 5.1.2). In this case, you create the integration scenario in a software component version for the product version of the application component.

▶ You define a separate software component version for the integration scenario, which is not assigned to a product of the application component. However, the result of this is that the integration scenario is not automatically shipped with one of the products that exchange messages with each other.

The first option is recommended because the integration scenario, in this case, is shipped along with a product.

Once you've decided which option to use, you need to consider how many integration scenarios you need to describe the different subprocesses of the collaborative process. The subprocess should be an appropriate and self-contained unit of manageable scope. Sometimes it's possible disconnect subprocesses at the start or end. (The use of component views for differentiating between different product versions was covered in the previous section.) You must also consider which parts of the process to configure together. You should group these parts into an integration scenario and transfer them collectively to the Integration Directory (see Section 6.3.1).

Let's look again at the application components. Section 3.3.1 described the mapping of application components to systems in detail. The important factor in modeling is that an application component offers a range of functions and can later be installed in multiple systems. If the following prerequisites are met, you can use an application component to model several communication parties of a collaborative process that is to be modeled in the integration scenario. The communication parties must:

▶ Have the same business role

▶ Offer the same functions

▶ Use the same product version

Once you have identified the necessary application components, you must clarify one more technical detail, namely, whether the application component relates to a product version or whether you're using a template:

▶ Ideally, a product version is known and entered in the SLD that provides the functions of the application component. In this case, you reference the product version from the application component.

▶ If the product version is not (yet) known, use a template. In this case, you may be dealing with non-SAP products that aren't entered in the SLD. Therefore, the principal use of templates is to model cross-company processes.

You may ask yourself why it isn't simpler to always use a template. Aren't templates sufficient enough to produce a graphical description of the integration scenarios? Why not simply enter the missing information (the product version) in the templates by hand? Indeed, this is how you proceed with products outside your own system landscape. However, using this method within your system landscape would mean forfeiting numerous advantages:

▶ Since templates are separate from the SLD, all attributes of the template simply serve as documentation. Consistency checks aren't possible.

▶ A reference to a product version in the SLD bridges the gap to configuration in the Integration Directory: The Integration Builder can call the product versions installed in systems in the SLD. This enables you to identify the services of a system. In this way, application components of the product version type simplify the subsequent development and are more than mere documentation.

Therefore, you should use application components of the product version type for all products in the SLD that are part of a collaborative process.

To describe the message exchange between application components, you use *actions*. We have already met actions in the flight availability check in Figure 3.5 (*Check Flight Seat Availability* is an action), although they were not identified as such. Before we look at the modeling of actions in more detail, let's examine the different types of actions that exist and where you can use them. These restrictions are necessary to ensure that actions are shipped together with the integration scenario in which they are used:

Internal and External Actions

▶ Actions relating to a function of a product version should be shipped using a software component version of that product version (or, alternatively, using an underlying software component version). These actions can be used only within the corresponding product version, and are therefore referred to as *internal actions*.

▶ In templates, the product version is not known, so you cannot assign an action to it. Such actions are defined outside a product version, and are therefore referred to as *external actions*. To guarantee that the actions are shipped together with the integration scenario, you can use only external actions in integration scenarios of the same or an underlying software component version.

Besides referencing actions, you can also reference integration processes from application components. The Integration Builder allows references in a similar way. Table 3.2 provides a summary of the software component versions for which you must create actions and integration processes in order to be able to use them in application components. In principle, either the product version of the application component or the software component version of the integration scenario determines which objects you can use. To simplify the table, we use two terms:

▶ **Product-version-based**
The object to be inserted is determined by the product version of the application component. Therefore, you create the object in a software component version (or underlying software component version) of the product version.

▶ **Integration-scenario-based**
The object to be inserted is determined by the software component version of the integration scenario. Therefore, you create the object in the same software component version, or an underlying software component version of the integration scenario.

To summarize, the following can be said of actions: External actions can be used in all application components of the corresponding integration scenario, whereas internal actions can be used in only the respective product version.

Object to be inserted	Application Component Type	
	Product Version	Template
Internal action	Product-version-based	(not applicable)
External action	Integration-scenario-based	Integration-scenario-based
Integration process	Product-version-based	Integration-scenario-based

Table 3.2 Possible Uses by Application Component Type

Modeling with Actions and Connections

How do you model the actual message exchange of a collaborative process in the integration scenario? Integration scenarios focus exactly on this point: the modeling of the message exchange, and nothing else. Therefore, the only steps that you model as an action in the integration scenario are those required to exchange messages with other application components. Local processes within an application component are irrelevant, and you should insert them only as actions if they are required for the understanding of the integration scenario.

The communication between actions of different application components is indicated by an arrow and is referred to as a *connection*.

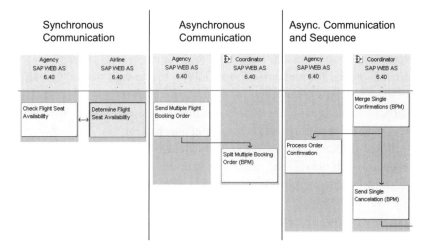

Synchronous Communication		Asynchronous Communication		Async. Communication and Sequence	
Agency SAP WEB AS 6.40	Airline SAP WEB AS 6.40	Agency SAP WEB AS 6.40	Coordinator SAP WEB AS 6.40	Agency SAP WEB AS 6.40	Coordinator SAP WEB AS 6.40

Figure 3.7 Examples of Connection Types

Figure 3.7 shows an example of each connection type:

Connection Types

▶ A double-headed arrow (↔) represents *synchronous communication*. To graphically represent that the execution of the process can only be continued after receiver processing, the two relevant actions are shown at the same level.

▶ In *asynchronous communication,* the sender and receiver are separated by a time difference, and only a request message is sent. Therefore, the actions are not shown at the same level.

▶ A *sequence* is not a type of communication, but a sequence of actions within an application component that is important for the understanding of the integration scenario. In the example shown above, there are two follow-up actions, and thus branching takes place. Since you don't define routing until configuration time, you can't assign conditions to this or to other connection types.

Of course, at the start of modeling, no actions have been inserted. You insert application components and actions in the integration scenario editor by using the context menu. All you must remember is that the connection type is determined automatically from the position of the actions. For example, if two actions are at the same level, you can insert only synchronous connections by using the context menu. Therefore, you must arrange your actions according to the connection type you want to use, and comply with the rules described above. To select the actions that you want to connect, hold down the SHIFT key and then click both actions, one after the other. Alternatively, select them by using the mouse to drag a box around the actions (rubberband function).

Modeling at the Type Level

Figure 3.8 shows the attributes of the `DetermineFlightSeatAvail-ability` action from Figure 3.7. In addition to the type of use, you also specify the relevant outbound and inbound interfaces for the step that you are modeling with the action. Multiple outbound or inbound interfaces may be necessary to execute the action successfully. The semantics of an integration scenario don't stipulate which interfaces should be called in which order. This means that in an action, you can specify alternative interfaces, which refer to different versions of a product. You can then work with the same action in different component views of an integration scenario. It is essential that the specifications you make identify which interfaces are involved in each communication. This simplifies the later configuration in the Integration Directory.

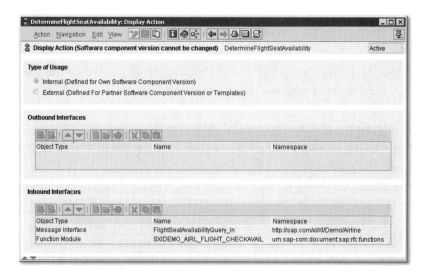

Figure 3.8 References to Interfaces in Actions

Level of Detail of Connections

The level of detail in connections is kept just as simple. A connection between two actions describes the communication between these actions using selected interfaces of these actions. It is irrelevant how often messages are exchanged until a particular function of the application component is successfully executed. In the flight availability check in the example, two actions and one connection will suffice to model a successful availability check for a flight. The model does not specify whether the query must be made several times at the receiver end.

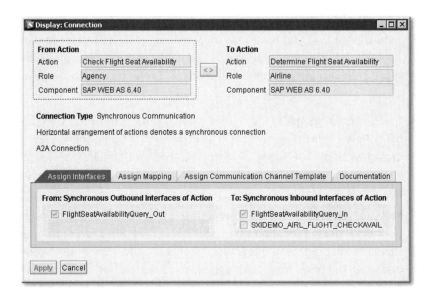

Figure 3.9 Connection for Synchronous Communication

The `DetermineFlightSeatAvailability` action is implemented on the receiver side using a server proxy. For older systems, there is an alternative implementation using RFC. In a connection, you assign an outbound interface to each inbound interface. In the synchronous connection in Figure 3.9, two message interfaces are selected for communication. If a mapping is necessary, specify it on the **Assign Mapping** tab page. The Integration Builder can evaluate this information automatically at configuration time. The information that you specify also documents the integration scenario and enables you to navigate directly to the respective interfaces and mappings. You can reference existing objects (bottom-up development), or create these objects from the integration scenario (top-down development).

In individual cases, it may be necessary to define multiple connections between two actions, for example, if a connection has different mappings, depending on customer requirements. If this is the case, you simply create additional connections between the actions. The integration scenario editor displays alternative connections in the same way as a single connection, and you can display or edit them using the context menu. If alternative connections exist, you must first select the connection you want to use in the corresponding dialog box. There can be only one valid connection at configuration time and at runtime.

Alternative Connections

Advanced Functions

The knowledge that you have now amassed regarding software logistics and modeling integration scenarios will enable you to work intuitively with the graphical integration scenario editor. Therefore, all that remains is to point out the following useful commands:

▶ You can print integration scenarios by using the menu path **Component View · Print** or export them as a graphic via **Component View · Export as JPEG**. The latter, in particular, saves you time if you want to insert the component view of an integration scenario into Word documentation.

BPEL File ▶ You can use the same editor menu to export integration scenarios as Business Process Execution Language (BPEL) files. BPEL is a cross-tool standard that enables integration scenarios and processes to be imported to other tools and edited, for example, in *ARIS for SAP NetWeaver*.

In closing, we should point out that integration scenarios in the Integration Repository contribute significantly toward a better understanding of the whole collaborative process and the need to reduce configuration effort. The effort that you expend at the start will save you time later on. In this way, SAP also simplifies the configuration of RosettaNet standards, as we will see in Section 6.6.

4 Interfaces, Messages, and Proxy Generation

Interfaces are at the heart of message exchange with SAP XI. This chapter looks at the different programming models from the point of view of interface development, and how you communicate with parties that are not interface-based.

4.1 Introduction

In all types of communication, you are faced with the question of how the sender is to transfer the data and how the receiver is to *collect* it. Software developers are used to using function calls to transfer data within a program, and it's hardly noteworthy to use this established form of data exchange to transfer data between systems; *Remote Function Calls* (RFCs) follow this principle, for example. Therefore, it isn't surprising that in SAP XI, every message is assigned to an interface to simplify the sending and receiving of messages, as well as the configuration steps that you're required to make.

The most straightforward scenario is if all the systems you want to connect use the same interface technology. However, in reality, this is rarely the case. At the same time, the demand for cross-company applications (for example, Business-to-Business (B2B) applications and marketplaces) is increasing. The challenge is therefore to bring together the various approaches, while at the same time not lose sight of the current requirements for cross-company communication. SAP XI supports the following programming models:

Inclusion of Different Interface Technologies

▶ You can create interface descriptions directly in the Integration Builder and generate executable proxies in application systems that are based on SAP Web AS 6.40.[1] Systems such as these can exchange messages directly with the Integration Server.

▶ You can use established SAP interfaces from SAP systems (RFCs, BAPIs, IDocs) or other interfaces from third-party systems. In this case, the interfaces exchange messages with the Integration Server by using adapters. Later we'll see that it is also possible to use these adapters to connect third-party systems that don't use interfaces to exchange messages.

---

1 This applies to SAP XI 3.0 only. The relationship between SAP XI 2.0 proxies and SAP XI 3.0 proxies is explained in greater detail later.

This chapter will look at both models with regard to the development of interfaces and their use in the design process. You should be familiar with the terms *outbound interface*, *inbound interface*, *synchronous*, and *asynchronous* before continuing (see Section 1.2.1).

4.2 Developing Using the Proxy Model

You can significantly improve the maintainability of cross-system applications if you can access all relevant objects centrally. Interfaces play an important role here, because the signature of an interface determines the structure of the message. If you don't know the structure of a message, you cannot, in turn, define a mapping or model an integration process.

Outside-In   When you develop using the proxy model, you use the Integration Builder to create *message interfaces* in WSDL (*Web Services Description Language*) directly in the Integration Repository. A message interface is actually a *description* that cannot be executed. In fact, you don't need to be able to execute it during the remainder of the design process, because just knowing the structure of the message will suffice. You use this description to generate proxies in ABAP/Java in your application system. Since you develop the interfaces outside the application system, this approach is known as *outside-in*.

Why Proxies?   At first glance, it may seem odd that SAP has created yet another kind of interface technology. Here are a few reasons why proxies were used:

▶ The interface technology is not really new, because the target languages already exist (ABAP Objects, Java).

▶ Using WSDL enables you to develop interfaces according to recognized standards. This is particularly important for minimizing the amount of effort required to coordinate cross-company scenarios.

▶ You can use a message interface in both ABAP and Java scenarios. The range of target languages could be increased, although none are planned at present.

4.2.1 Interface Development in the Integration Builder

Referenced   Before you can start exchanging messages by using proxies, you must cre-
Objects   ate the relevant message interfaces in the Integration Builder. Message interfaces can reference the following objects:

▶ *Message types*, which you create in the Integration Builder

▶ *IDoc* or *RFC* messages, which you import to the Integration Repository via the Integration Builder

▶ *External messages* from imported WSDL, XSD, or DTD documents

We'll begin by concentrating on the first case in which you create the interface description directly by using the Integration Builder. This primarily concerns new developments in which no interfaces in SAP or third-party systems need to be accessed. Other scenarios are addressed in Section 4.3.

Structure of Message Interfaces

Message interfaces from the Integration Repository are based on WSDL. For this reason, their structure is similar to that of a WSDL document. You don't need to be a WSDL expert to develop message interfaces in the Integration Builder, however, it's useful to know the basics. Figure 4.1 shows which objects you use to construct message interfaces in the Integration Builder, and to which WSDL elements these objects correspond.

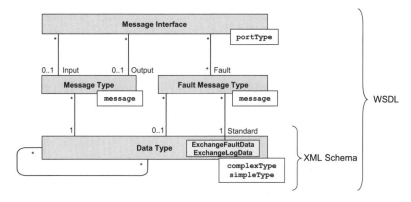

Figure 4.1 Message Interfaces and WSDL

You use the various object types as follows:

Object Types

▶ **Message Interfaces**
This is the *outer shell* for all messages. The attributes of a message interface determine the mode (synchronous or asynchronous) and the type of communication (outbound or inbound, from the perspective of the application system). *Abstract* message interfaces don't have a direction and aren't implemented in an application system. You use them in the RNIF adapter and to define the process signature of an integration process.

► **Message Types**

Message types describe the structure of the message by referencing a data type. A message type does not specify a particular direction and can be used for describing both inbound and outbound messages. This depends on whether the message type in the message interface is used as an output or input message type.

► **Fault Message Types**

Fault message types enable developers to send information about errors in the receiver application program to the sender or to monitoring by using a fault message. In most standard cases, the structure specified by the `ExchangeFaultData` and `ExchangeLogData` data types is sufficient. You can also reference other data types, if required.

Fault messages aren't available for asynchronous outbound message interfaces or asynchronous abstract message interfaces. In the case of these message interfaces, you can query the status by using *acknowledgment messages* in the application program or in the integration process.

► **Data Types**

The message type predefines the structure of a message. However, the message type determines only the name of the message instance. Although this *intermediate layer* seems superfluous at first, it corresponds to the WSDL standard and enables the message instance to be identified via an element. You use data types to describe which elements and attributes may be used to construct the message. Data types can reference other data types, but recursive definitions aren't permitted.

WSDL Export The range of WSDL commands has been restricted to simply cover the scenarios that are most important for message exchange. The cardinalities shown in Figure 4.1 and the range of XML Schema commands used in data types are therefore just a subset of WSDL. For those readers interested in using Web services, note that the Integration Repository does not contain any information about the technical receiver of a message. While it is possible to use the Integration Builder to export message interfaces as WSDL,[2] the exported WSDL document does not contain any receiver information for an executable Web service. You don't use the export function to publish Web services, but you do need it to use interface objects created in the Integration Repository externally (for example,

---

2 By choosing **Tools • Export WSDL** in the editor menu. There is also an export function for (fault) message types and data types.

to archive them or to use a message type for an XSLT mapping that you have developed using external tools). However, we'll see later that the world of SAP XI message interfaces and the world of Web services complement each other (see Section 7.3.2).

When developing message interfaces, the largest amount of time is spent developing data types. For this reason, we'll look at data types in more detail in the next section. Information about reusing message types and data types can be found in Section 4.4.

Importing Data Types As a Template

Within WSDL, data types are described using XML Schema. A data type in the Integration Builder is therefore also an XML Schema Definition (XSD) that you can create and edit by using an XSD editor. You have two options:

▶ You can create a new data type and use the XSD editor to describe its structure from scratch, or

▶ You can use an existing XSD in the Integration Builder as an editable template

The second option would obviously save you the most time. However, you must ensure that the XSD editor supports the range of commands in the XSD file that you want to import.[3]

References Between Data Types

If you want to define multiple data types in an XSD, the XSD editor can import only one of the globally defined data types. The XSD editor does not import any other data types that the XSD data type, which is to be imported, can reference. Once imported, the references become invalid. You can, however, import the data types into the Integration Repository one after the other. After the import, the Integration Builder automatically completes any references that were previously invalid.

To import a data type, proceed as follows:

1. To import a data type from an XSD file to the Integration Repository, first check whether the XSD file contains multiple global data type definitions. You can import only one definition with each import.

2. Using the Integration Builder, create a data type that has the same name as the data type that you want to import from the XSD file. If the

---

3 For an overview of supported XML Schema commands, see SAP Service Marketplace at *service.sap.com/xi* • *Media Library* • *Documentation* • *SAP XI 3.0 (SP1)— Supported XML Schema and WSDL (EN)*.

XSD file has a `targetNamespace`, it must be identical to the repository namespace in which you want to create the data type.

3. In the XSD editor, choose **Tools · Import XSD**, and then select an XSD file from the subsequent dialog box.

   If the file contains more than one global data type definition, the processing log shows that the remaining data type definitions have been ignored.

4. Any references to other data types that the imported data type contains—if there are any—are shown in a corresponding message. You import these data types by following the procedure described in the last two steps.

You can now change and enhance the data types you have imported by using the XSD editor. The original file remains unchanged.

Editing Data Types Using the XSD Editor

You use XML Schema to define the elements and attributes that can be used in an XML document.[4] In other words, an XML Schema Definition (XSD) describes a kind of grammar for the message payload. You don't need to know the exact XSD syntax when using the XSD editor: Once you've created and saved a data type with the XSD editor, it automatically becomes valid (the Integration Builder checks the objects before saving).

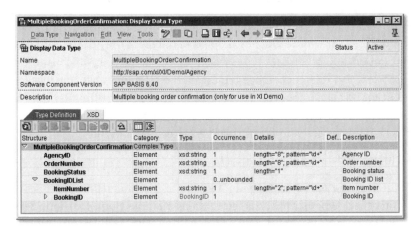

Figure 4.2 XSD Editor

---

4 The term *XML instance* is more generally used when the way that the XML document is saved is not important (as a file, in the main memory, and so on).

Figure 4.2 is a screenshot of a data type. A line in the XSD editor corresponds to the definition of either an element or an attribute. The root element (the first line in the editor) specifies the category of data type:

Root Element

▶ **Simple Type**
Simple data types correspond to the `<simpleType>` tag in XML Schema. They are scalar data types for which you restrict the value range, for example, by using a string pattern or by specifying a maximum permitted value in the **Details** column. The data in this column corresponds to the *facets* in XML Schema.

▶ **Complex Type**
Complex types correspond to the `<complexType>` tag in XML Schema. You use complex types to define structures by adding sub-elements to the root element or to other existing elements.

You assign a data type to an element or an attribute in the **Type** column. This can either be a scalar data type that is built-in using XML Schema (for example, `xsd:string`) or a data type that is already in the Integration Repository. References such as these enable you to construct complex data types from other data types, and to reuse data types.

Occurrence

There are no tables in XML Schema. Instead, you specify how often the individual elements may occur in the XML instance in the **Occurrence** column. In Figure 4.2, the `BookingIDList` element has the occurrence value `0..unbounded`, which means that it can occur any number of times.

Once you have described the structure of your message by using a data type, you can use the definition for further processing in the Integration Builder. Now we'll look at how message interfaces are converted to executable interfaces in the application systems.

4.2.2 Proxy Generation

Proxies are classes and interfaces that developers use to implement the exchange of messages. Figure 4.3 shows an example in which two message interfaces are used as the basis for generating proxies for communication via the Integration Server: A *client proxy* for the outbound message interface, and a *server proxy* for the inbound message interface. You can of course also use message interfaces to generate server proxies for Java and client proxies for ABAP.

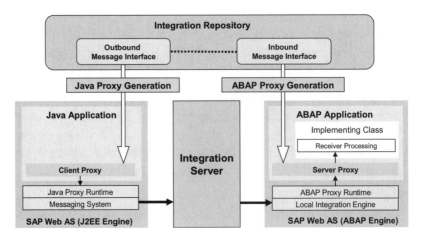

Figure 4.3 Example of Proxy-to-Proxy Communication

Regeneration When you generate proxies, the executable parts (classes and interfaces) are created in the application system. Proxy generation also saves the name of the original message interface as metadata, because the data in the Integration Repository must be consistent with the data in the application system. If any changes need to be made to an interface, simply regenerate the proxies after the changes have been made to make them visible in the application system as well. The relationship between the Integration Repository and the various application systems begs the question of what happens if you need to migrate SAP XI or perform a system upgrade. Note the following:

▶ Proxy generation is already available in application systems based on SAP Web AS 6.20 with the SAP XI 2.0 Add-On. This has the following result when you upgrade the application system or SAP XI:

  ▶ When you upgrade an application system from SAP Web AS 6.20 to SAP Web AS 6.40, you must regenerate any proxies created in SAP XI 2.0 (Java and ABAP) in the application system before you can use them in SAP XI 3.0.

  ▶ You *don't* need to regenerate the proxies when you migrate the SAP XI 2.0 Integration Repository to the SAP XI 3.0 Integration Repository.

▶ In application systems with the SAP XI 2.0 Add-On (SP4), you can use ABAP proxy generation to create ABAP proxies for message interfaces in the SAP XI 3.0 Integration Repository. Note, however, that you can implement only the message interfaces, message types, and data types in the same way that you implemented them in SAP XI 2.0.[5]

For the purpose of simplification, the following section on proxy generation covers only application systems based on SAP Web AS 6.40 and SAP XI 3.0. Figure 4.3 also shows the runtime components that are involved in sending the message. This aspect is covered in more detail in Chapter 7.

ABAP Proxy Generation

To generate ABAP proxies, you must log on to the application system in which you want to use proxies for exchanging messages. You can access ABAP proxy generation as follows:

▶ If your user is assigned the relevant SAP XI role, you can call ABAP proxy generation from the role menu. This entry calls the transaction SPROXY. Similar to the Integration Builder, this transaction provides you with an overview of the software component versions that exist in this application system.

▶ ABAP proxy generation is integrated in the Object Navigator (Transaction SE80). You access proxy objects from the navigation tree in the Object Navigator.

You can use both transactions for generating proxies. In transaction SPROXY, the software component versions in the Integration Repository are the starting point for creating or locating proxies. In the Object Navigator, you create a new proxy or locate an existing one by starting with the packages in the ABAP Repository. This way of working is more straightforward, because application developers can concentrate on the objects in their packages better.

Proxies are part of the Web Service Library in the ABAP Repository. In Figure 4.4, proxy generation displays the properties of the II_SXIDAG_ MULT_BOOKORD_CONFIRM server proxy in the Object Navigator:

▶ The data in the **Identification** frame provides the reference to the original object in the Integration Repository. In this example, it is an asynchronous inbound message interface.

▶ The **Proxy Interface** frame displays the name of the generated ABAP Objects interface for the inbound message interface. Proxy generation creates an ABAP Objects class as a client proxy for outbound message interfaces.

5   For more details, see the SAP XI 3.0 online documentation.

▶ To provide a service in the application system, the application developer implements the generated proxy interface. If there is no separate class name of an existing class with an appropriate signature in the **Implementing Class** frame prior to generation, ABAP proxy generation creates a proxy class for server proxies in addition to the proxy interface.

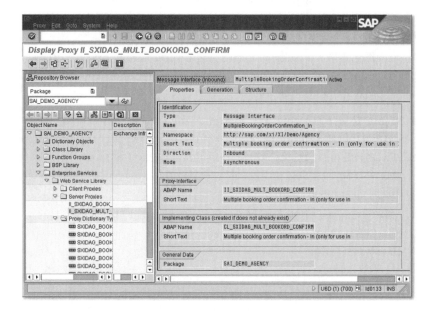

Figure 4.4 ABAP Proxy Generation in the Object Navigator

ABAP Proxy
Generation in the
Object Navigator

To generate a proxy in the Object Navigator, proceed as follows:

1. Call the Object Navigator (Transaction SE80) in the system in which you want to generate a server proxy or a client proxy. Select a package and then choose **Create · Enterprise Service/Web Service · Proxy Object** in the context menu.

2. In the subsequent dialog box, choose **XI Repository** as the source of the WSDL document. If you specify this source, you can use the proxies you generate both for communication via SAP XI, and for communication via the Web service runtime.[6]

---

6 As already mentioned above, the range of commands in the WSDL from the Integration Repository has been restricted. For this reason, you cannot specify any other source (*URL/HTTP destination*, *local file*, or *UDDI*, for example) for the generation of proxies that you want to use in proxy communication with the Integration Server.

3. The hierarchy of software component versions in the Integration Repository is displayed in the subsequent dialog box. Select an interface object for which no proxy has been generated, and confirm by choosing **Apply**.

4. In the subsequent dialog box, enter the name of the package in which the proxy objects are to be created. You can also specify a prefix for the names of all objects to be created to avoid naming conflicts with any existing objects in the system.

Note the following important information:

▶ To enable the ABAP proxies and the ABAP proxy runtime to be accessed from the application program, there must be a use access to the `SAI_PROXY_PUBLIC_PIF` package interface. Note that if there is a parent package, you must also create a use access to the parent package interface `SAI_TOOLS_PIF`.

▶ The creation of dictionary objects and classes/interfaces during proxy generation can result in a large number of objects that require translation. Because it isn't necessary to translate proxy objects since they aren't on the user interface, you must ensure that they're separated at the package level. Create a separate package for the proxy objects and set it as not relevant for translation.

To create the proxies, ABAP proxy generation uses HTTP to read the WSDL description of the message interface and then converts it into proxy objects. However, this does not happen immediately, because there may be objects in the application system that have the same name. Furthermore, technical names in XML can be as long as required, while in ABAP they are restricted to a certain number of characters. Technical names are also not case-sensitive in ABAP. To make the names easier to read, ABAP proxy generation inserts underscores, shortens any names that are too long, and adds a counter in the event of naming conflicts. Since this doesn't always result in appropriate names, a dialog box is displayed in the last two examples, indicating that you can check and modify names on the **Naming Problems** tab page.

Converting Names in ABAP

You can also change the other ABAP names to fit your requirements by calling the context menu on the **Structure** tab page. No objects will be created in the ABAP Repository until you activate the proxy. Only the proxy object metadata is saved when you save but do not activate the proxy. The name mappings to the object in the Integration Repository, which are also required at runtime, are saved in the metadata. Messages sent using proxies don't contain any ABAP names, just the original names of the WSDL definition. For this reason, transport requests for ABAP transports include both the generated proxy objects and the corresponding metadata.

Converting from WSDL to ABAP

Finally, we want to take a brief look at converting WSDL to ABAP proxy objects.

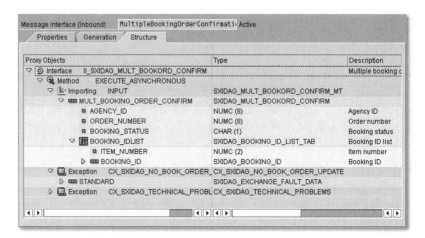

Figure 4.5 Structure of a Generated ABAP Server Proxy

Figure 4.5 shows the structure of the `II_SXIDAG_MULT_BOOKORD_CON-FIRM` server proxy. The input message type was converted to an importing parameter `INPUT`, which references a structure that is determined by the data type `MultipleBookingOrderConfirmation` (compare with Figure 4.2). To go into detail about conversions would exceed the scope of this book. Instead, note the following:

Converting Data Types in ABAP

▶ Proxy generation converts elements in the XSD that can occur an unlimited number of times (`0..unbounded`) into a table type and a structure for the line type. Although it's common practice in ABAP, in XSD do not define isolated data types for tables, because unnecessary types will be created.

▶ XML Schema defines an exact value range for built-in data types; this value range does not always match the value range in ABAP. ABAP proxy generation lists any data types that cannot be mapped exactly on the **Type Mappings** tab page.

Java Proxy Generation

Java proxy generation is part of the Integration Builder (Design). You can call Java proxy generation from either the context menu for a message interface in the navigation tree, or from the main menu under **Tools**. You can generate Java proxies for J2EE applications on the SAP Web AS. Proxy generation creates J2EE beans and proxy classes for this purpose. The generated beans comply with the EJB 2.0 standard.

As in XML, in Java technical names are not case-sensitive; in addition, they aren't restricted in length, which also holds true in ABAP. To avoid as many naming conflicts as possible, the corresponding WSDL tags are appended to the names as a suffix (see Figure 4.1). This conversion is based on the JAX RPC specification:[7]

Converting Names in Java

▶ Namespaces are mapped to packages.

▶ Classes for interfaces have the suffix _PortType.

▶ Classes for data types have the suffix _Type.

If naming conflicts do nevertheless occur (for example, because a data type has the same name as a Java keyword), Java proxy generation resolves the conflict by simply changing the name (by adding an underscore or appending a counter).

Due to these prerequisites, the developer does not need to make any changes to the technical names. Therefore, to generate a proxy, all you need do is select the message interfaces that you want to convert, and specify the archive in which the classes to be generated are to be saved. If you want to regenerate a proxy, specify the existing archive in Java proxy generation. The message interfaces it contains are displayed and can be included when you regenerate.

Using Java Archives

The generated Java package is part of the J2EE application and must be compiled together with it. To gain a better overview of what has been generated, it is recommended that you use the Java standard tool java-doc to create HTML documentation for the generated classes. Just as we did for the ABAP proxies, here, too, we will only briefly cover the most important conversions during generation:

▶ A Java interface is generated for inbound message interfaces; the application developer uses this Java interface to provide a service. If Java-Interface is the name of the generated Java interface, then the

---

7 http://java.sun.com/xml/downloads/jaxrpc.html.

implementing class must be `JavaInterfaceImpl`, and it must be in the same package as the generated Java interface.

Converting Data
Types in Java

▶ A class is generated for each complex data type that contains `set`/`get` methods for accessing the respective fields.

▶ Classes are not required for simple data types. For example, if you use a simple data type like `xsd:string`, Java proxy generation does not generate a separate global class for the data type; instead, it uses the corresponding Java data type `java.lang.String`.

▶ You can access elements that occur an unlimited number of times by using either list methods or an array.

▶ To access fields that have an enumeration specified as their value range, Java proxy generation generates a Java class for type-safe access to the enumeration's value set by creating constants for each value and restricting access to only methods.

Once the proxies have been generated, developers can then implement the message exchange for an application in the application system. For more details about programming with client and server proxies, see Section 7.3.

4.3   Supporting Adapter-Based Communication

So far, we have looked at development using only the proxy model. As a prerequisite for this, the application system must be based on either SAP Web AS 6.20 or SAP Web AS 6.40 (see Section 4.2.2). To connect SAP legacy systems or non-SAP systems to the Integration Server, you use adapters. In principle, an adapter works similarly to the proxy runtime: It converts XML and HTTP-based messages from the Integration Server to the specific protocols and formats of the application, and vice versa. The programming model is quite different, however. When using the proxy model, development occurs in the Integration Repository; when using adapters, development either takes place, or has already taken place, in the application system.

Communication
Parties Without
Interfaces

The first question you should ask is what information must be available in the Integration Repository for further development to take place. At configuration time, you require an interface name and a corresponding namespace to configure how messages should be exchanged. This also applies to those adapters for which the interfaces are not important, for example, the file adapter or the JDBC adapter.[8] In such cases, you must define a corresponding interface name and namespace when configuring the adapter. You cannot, of course, import interfaces that aren't available. Therefore, you can enter interface names manually in the Integration Builder, because this enables you to also connect application systems to the Integration Server from which you cannot import interfaces or descriptions of the message structure. You need these user-defined interface names, for example, for interface mappings, which are required later for executing mapping programs. (We'll look at interface mappings in more detail in Section 5.1.2.)

Ideally, however, you can import the interfaces' signature or required message structure descriptions to the Integration Repository. Since the information you are accessing is already available in the application system, this is known as the *inside-out approach*. The following section explains which Integration Builder mechanisms are available to you specifically for this purpose. Just like the message interfaces or message types discussed in Section 4.2, this information is then available centrally so you can use it during the remainder of the design process.

Inside-Out

4.3.1   Importing Interfaces and Message Schemas

You can import SAP interfaces and various message schemas using the Integration Builder. Both cases are discussed below.

Importing SAP Interfaces

Until the introduction of SAP XI, the established SAP interfaces used for exchanging messages between systems were BAPIs, RFCs, and IDocs. One way of including these interfaces in the SAP XI design process would be for the Integration Repository to contain one interface description for all existing BAPIs, RFCs, and IDocs. Indeed, in the early days of SAP XI, efforts were made to make all these interfaces available to customers in XML format. The result of these efforts is the *Interface Repository* (*http://ifr.sap.com*). However, applications use only a few of these interfaces for SAP XI scenarios. Therefore, you can import interfaces using the Integration Builder import mechanism. This enables each application to import to the Integration Repository those interfaces that they actually require in a scenario.

---

8 However, this only applies to inbound processing in the Integration Server. This is addressed in more detail in Section 6.5.

You can use the Integration Builder to import interface descriptions of BAPIs, RFCs, and IDocs from SAP Release 4.0 and higher to the Integration Repository.[9] You enter an SAP system from which the interface descriptions are imported for each software component version in the Integration Repository. To do so, open the relevant software component version by double-clicking on it in the Integration Builder navigation tree.

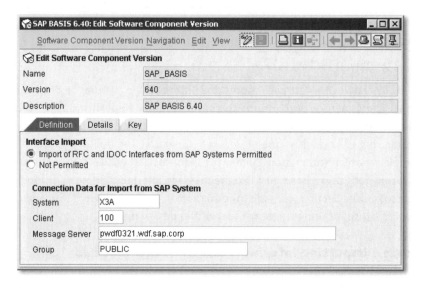

Figure 4.6 Attributes for Importing Interfaces from SAP Systems

Determining the Connection Data for the Import

Figure 4.6 shows an example in which the connection data for importing from an SAP system is specified. To determine this information for the SAP system, proceed as follows:

1. Call the logon dialog for SAP systems (SAP Logon) and choose **Groups**.

2. In the **System ID** field, enter the system ID of the SAP system from which you want to import the interfaces. The **Message Server** field then displays the address of the message server.

3. Choose **Create List**. All the available groups with which you can log on to the system are displayed, for example, PUBLIC.

Once you begin the import, the **Imported Objects** node is added as a subnode to the software component version node in the Integration Builder navigation tree. To import the interfaces, call the context menu

---

9 This is because the relevant function modules with which you can call this information don't exist in older systems. However, the RFC and IDoc adapters support SAP Release 3.1I and higher.

for this node. You can also temporarily overwrite the connection data given in the software component version. Once the import is complete, you can reference the imported interfaces from other objects in the Integration Repository. This is covered in more detail in Section 4.3.2.

Importing External Definitions

There are many different standard schemas that can be used to describe the message structure at runtime, for example, WSDL, XSD, or DTDs (*Document Type Definitions*). If the description of a message structure is already in one of these formats, you can reuse it in the Integration Repository by importing it as an external definition instead of having to enter it manually in the data type editor.

As we saw in Section 4.2.1, message interfaces in the Integration Builder are based on WSDL. Furthermore, other Integration Builder editors expect this WSDL description, or rather, the XSD description that it contains. For this reason, the Integration Builder converts all external definitions to WSDL during the import. However, you can define which parts of the external definition are to be interpreted as message schema beforehand. For example, when you import an XSD document, you can decide whether all global elements or just those that are not referenced are to be included in the definition of a message. The result of the conversion is a WSDL document that contains the identified message definitions. If external definitions reference each other, simply import them one after the other and enter the source for each definition. An example of a source is a URL that other documents use to reference this definition.

Converting to WSDL

As we have already seen, the Integration Builder specifies restrictions for WSDL descriptions. Therefore, even if the import has been successful, this does not ensure that you can use the imported external definitions everywhere in the Integration Builder. It would be too restrictive to prevent an external definition from being imported merely because it is not supported by the mapping editor, for example, because you may not even want to use the definition for a mapping. Table 4.1 shows the possible applications of external definitions.

Unfortunately, there is currently no check available during the import to determine in which areas you can use a specific external definition. For an overview of supported tags, see the Media Library on SAP Service Marketplace at *service.sap.com/xi* (*Documentation SAP XI 3.0 (SP1)—Supported XML Schema and WSDL (EN)*).

(Part of) External Definition	Use
Entire Definition	Archiving in Integration Repository
Message	An external message in the graphical mapping editor, XSLT, or Java mappings
	An external message in message interfaces
Complex Type	In mapping templates to map data types to one another

Table 4.1 Applications of External Definitions

4.3.2 Developing with Imported Interface Objects

In Section 4.2, we saw which steps you need to make in the Integration Builder (Design) to develop objects using the proxy model approach. In this case, we assumed that both communication parties exchange messages with the Integration Server by using proxies. But how does it work when adapters are used to exchange messages? In the following examples, we assume that one of the parties (either the sender or receiver) uses an adapter to communicate. Note the following different cases:

Proxy Model Support
▶ The application system at the other communication party supports development using the proxy model approach.

Create a message interface that references the imported message schema for this party. This can be an RFC message, an IDoc message, or an external message. The imported messages are then used in the same way as message types. You do not need to define a mapping, because the message interface references the same message schema that the adapter uses.

Proxy generation can process both RFC and IDoc messages. External messages can also contain language constructs that are not supported by proxy generation; this can result in proxy generation being aborted.

No Proxy Model Support
▶ The application system at the other communication party does not support development using the proxy model approach.

If RFCs or IDocs are involved, use them on the same level as message interfaces in the Integration Builder. In the case of third- party systems, enter the interface names and namespaces manually, and reference imported messages. The adapters do use the message protocol of the Integration Builder, but the payload schema is adapter-specific. Therefore, technically speaking, a mapping is required if both communication parties are using different adapters.

The adapter configuration is described in section 6.5. You can use the imported message schemas during the rest of the design phase, for example, in the mapping editor (see Section 5.3.1). The Integration Builder also has a series of other export and import options to enable you to develop using external tools. Note once again that you do not have to import message schemas to the Integration Repository to exchange messages with the Integration Server by means of adapters. However, if you do import the message schemas to the Integration Repository, you have the advantage of being able to access them centrally and use them for further design purposes in the Integration Builder.

4.4 Enhanced Concepts

So far we have only covered the fundamental concepts behind development using the proxy model approach and adapter-based communication. This last section looks at the concepts for some general topics. Sections 4.4.1 and 4.4.2 only concern development using the proxy model, while Section 4.4.3 covers both development models.

4.4.1 Using Message Types Across Components

Message instances generally need to be assigned to a namespace. Enter this namespace for (fault) message types in the Integration Builder in the **XML Namespace** field (see Figure 4.7). In the default setting, the Integration Builder uses the repository namespace[10] in which the (fault) message type was created.

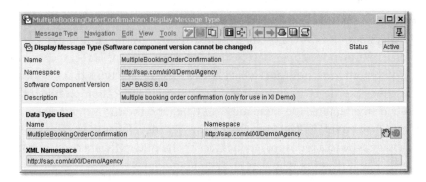

Figure 4.7 Message Type with Default XML Namespace

---

10 These are the namespaces that the Integration Builder (Design) displays in the navigation tree. See also Section 2.2.

In the following instance, it is advisable to use a different XML namespace to the repository namespace: Two applications communicating with each other by using XI are normally located in different software component versions that are not necessarily shipped to customers together. To ensure that the customer does not receive incomplete message interface definitions, the Integration Builder only permits references from message interfaces to (fault) message types in the same software component version or a sub-software component version. However, both applications want to regularly use the same message types for communication. Since it is not possible to use a reference, the only solution is for one of the applications to copy a message type from the other application to its repository namespace (see also Section 2.2). If the copy, in turn, had the new repository namespace as its XML namespace, this would be the only difference from the original. Even though the message structure is otherwise identical, a mapping would be required, because the message instance belonging to the message types has a different namespace.

The XML namespace therefore enables two applications to agree on a namespace for a message. The XML namespace is applied by proxy generation and used by proxy runtime in the message instance: An XML namespace for a message type or a fault message type qualifies the element tag for the message. In certain cases, you may not need to or want to use an XML namespace for the message instance. In this case, leave the **XML Namespace** field empty.

The following example refers to an SAP development project. However, it could quite easily also be a new customer or partner development project: A message is to be used to send a customer sales order from an APO system to a CRM system. Within a CRM software component version, the CRM developer has created the message type SalesOrder in the Integration Repository, which references a data type that in turn describes the structure of the message. The APO application on the outbound side requires the same message type (and the corresponding data types that are referenced from there). The APO developer then copies the message type to a repository namespace in the APO software component version, and uses the following copy-function options:

▶ **With All Dependent Objects**: The message type and all data types that describe the structure of the message are copied to the APO software component version.

► **Save Original As Reference**[11]: A reference to the original object is saved in the copy. This is useful if the original object is changed in CRM and the change must also be made to the copy in APO. You can display the original object from the object properties of the copy.

The APO developer agrees with the CRM developer to use the CRM namespace for the `SalesOrder` message type. The developer then enters the namespace *http://sap.com/CRM* in the **XML Namespace** field of the copy. This XML namespace is set automatically by the Integration Builder in the original message type, because it corresponds to the repository namespace for `SalesOrder` in the CRM application. Listing 4.1 shows how proxy runtime sets the XML namespace in the message instance.

```
<ns1:SalesOrder xmlns:ns1="http://sap.com/CRM">
   <OrderHeader>
   . . .
   </OrderHeader>
   <OrderItems>
. . .
   </OrderItems>
</SalesOrder>
```

Listing 4.1 XML Namespaces in Message Instance SalesOrder

Since CRM and APO have specified the same XML namespace, the message instances are identical. If the APO developer had not changed the namespace in the copy, the namespaces would have been different, and a mapping would have been required.

4.4.2 Enhancing Partners' and Customers' Data Types

SAP applications enable customers to enhance application programs without the need for modifications[12] to satisfy customer-specific demands that go beyond what is provided in the standard shipment. The applications can use Business Add-Ins (BAdIs) for this purpose, for example.

If the SAP application uses proxies to exchange messages, such enhancements must be seen as cross-system enhancements: The customer may want to not only access data that is available locally in the system, but

Cross-System
Modifications

---

11 This feature is only used internally at SAP and is not released for customers.
12 "Without the need for modifications" here means that customers' enhancements are not lost when the SAP application is upgraded.

also exchange data between the applications in the communication scenario. Since proxy objects cannot be modified in the application system, this kind of enhancement applies to the data type definition in the Integration Repository. In the following section, we want to investigate how customers or partners can enhance data types in the Integration Builder without the need for modifications. The proxy runtime does not provide a generic solution for enhancements in the application program. The application developers must decide which methods they want to use for customer enhancements.

To explain how customers and partners can use data type enhancements, we need to look at some different aspects. We will use the APO and CRM example from Section 4.4.1 for this purpose.

Using Top-Node Software Component Versions

CRM and APO ship the message type `SalesOrder` as part of their application by using the software component versions `SAP_APO 2.0` and `SAP_CRM 2.0`. Figure 4.8 shows which interface objects `SalesOrder` references, in other words, where this message type is used, for software component version `SAP_APO 2.0`.

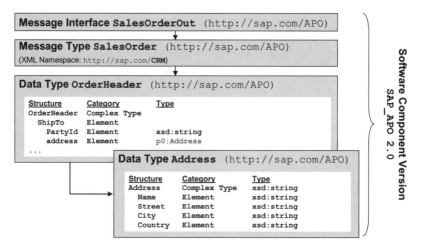

Figure 4.8 Interface Objects from SAP_APO 2.0

If a customer wants to enhance the data type `Address`, they cannot do so directly in software component version `SAP_APO 2.0`. Such an enhancement would be a modification, which would mean that if SAP were to change the data type again, for example in a support package, the customer enhancement would be lost.

The first step when making a data type enhancement is to create a customer-specific software component version in the System Landscape Directory, for example, CUST_APO 2.0. To be able to use objects of SAP software
component version SAP_APO 2.0, declare it as a sub-software component
version of CUST_APO 2.0: This means that CUST_APO 2.0 is based on SAP_
APO 2.0. Once you have imported CUST_APO 2.0 to the Integration
Builder (Design), all objects of SAP_APO 2.0 are available in the navigation
tree under **Basis Objects** of CUST_APO 2.0. You can now create your own
objects in CUST_APO 2.0 and reference objects from SAP_APO 2.0.

To enhance the data type Address in software component version CUST_
APO 2.0, create a data type enhancement there that references the data
type from SAP_APO 2.0, for example, AddressE. You can add elements,
structures, and attributes at the uppermost hierarchy level in the data
type enhancement. The relationship to interface objects that previously
referenced Address remains unchanged. If you display objects starting
from the Basis Objects branch of the software component version CUST_
APO 2.0, it appears that these objects also exist in CUST_APO 2.0. You
then reference AddressE automatically (see Figure 4.9). It helps if you
imagine that all other objects "shine through" to the software component
version that is based on SAP APO. For example, if you opened message
type SalesOrder in branch **Basis Objects** of CUST_APO 2.0, the header
data would show software component version CUST_APO 2.0 as owner
and the structure of the message type would include the data type extension of AddressE (although the original message type still points to data
type Address). However, you can retrieve the original software component version SAP_APO 2.0 via menu **Message Type · History**.

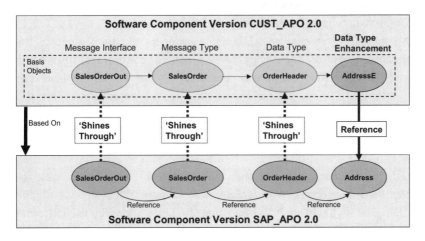

Figure 4.9 Objects in SAP_APO 2.0 and CUST_APO 2.0

If you enhance the data type Address in CUST_APO 2.0, you must do the same for the CRM data type Address so that the additional data that is transferred can also be processed at the receiver. Therefore, you must also create a customer-specific software component version CUST_CRM 2.0 for software component version SAP_CRM 2.0, and perform the same steps as for CUST_APO 2.0.

Proxy Generation and Data Type Enhancements

Once you have released the data type enhancements, you can regenerate the proxies in your application systems:

ABAP
- ▶ In the case of ABAP proxies, select the data type enhancement AddressE in the customer-specific software component version CUST_ CRM 2.0 or CUST_APO 2.0. ABAP proxy generation maps data type enhancements to APPEND structures in the ABAP Dictionary.

Java
- ▶ In the case of Java proxies, select the messsage interface of the customer-specific software component version CUST_CRM 2.0, which references the data type enhancement. The message interface is located under **Basis Objects**. The elements and attributes of the enhancement are recognized by proxy generation, but they aren't handled in a special way. You cannot determine which classes or attributes originate from the data type enhancement from the generated objects. There are no separate Java objects for enhancements.

XML Namespaces for Data Type Enhancements

Avoiding Naming Conflicts
In Section 4.4.1 we saw that CRM and APO had to be in agreement on a common XML namespace for the shared message type. The same applies for the data type enhancements in CUST_APO 2.0 and CUST_CRM 2.0. In the message instance, an XML namespace is used to distinguish the enhancements from the original SAP elements and attributes. Thus, if SAP uses the same field name as a customer in an enhancement in a later release, you can avoid a naming conflict. Data type enhancements also have an XML namespace that must be identical at the sender and receiver; otherwise, the XML namespaces would have to be mapped to each other via a mapping.

Let's assume that the customer decides to use the XML namespace *http://customer.com/CRM/AddrExtension* in both CUST_APO 2.0 and CUST_CRM 2.0. Listing 4.2 shows that the fields added by the customer have an additional qualifier added to the *http://customer.com/CRM/*

AddrExtension namespace. The fields that have been added to the `Address` data type in Figure 4.8 are shown in bold.

```
<ns1:SalesOrder
xmlns:ns1="http://sap.com/CRM"
xmlns:ns2="http://customer.com/CRM/AddrExtension">
   <OrderHeader>
     <ShipTo>
        <PartyId>1234</PartyId>
        <Address ns2:Airport="SFAirport" >
           <Name>Johnson</Name>
           <Street>Lombard Street 10</Street>
           <City>SanFrancisco</City>
           <Country>US</Country>
           <ns2:State>California</ns2:State>
        </Address>
     </ShipTo>
   </OrderHeader>
   <OrderItems> ... </OrderItems>
</ns1:SalesOrder>
```

Listing 4.2 Enhanced Data Type Address

4.4.3   Accessing Message Fields by Using Context Objects

To process messages on the Integration Server, you must be able to access the content of a message. For example, the Integration Server reads fields from the message header in order to use this information, and it reads fields from the configuration in the Integration Directory to forward the message to the correct receiver. Furthermore, applications can define conditions for logical routing or an integration process, which reference fields in the payload.

Since the payload is an XML document, you can access the different parts of it by using XPath. XPath is a syntax that enables you to identify parts of an XML document in the same way that you access the directory structure of a file system. Have a look at the following message instance:

Context Objects Instead of XPath

```
<InvoiceOut>
   <customerData>
     <address>
        <name> ... </name>
           <postalCode> ...</postalCode>
```

```
. . .
    </address>

    . . .
  </customerData>
</InvoiceOut>
```

To access the content of the `<postalCode>` field, you would use the following expression in XPath:

`/InvoiceOut/customerData/address/postalCode`

If you require this expression in multiple conditions, you have to type it out each time or copy it. Instead, you can assign a context object to the `<postalCode>` field. Give this context object the name `postalCode`, for example. Now, when you require the value of the `<postalCode>` field for a condition, you only need to use the `postalCode` context object, which makes your conditions easier to read:

▶ Comparison using XPath
`/InvoiceOut/customerData/address/postalCode > "69120"`
▶ Comparison using a context object
`postalCode > "69120"`

Reference Types for Context Objects In the Integration Builder, you create context objects as interface objects; they only consist of a name and a reference type. The type determines what kind of comparisons are in the conditions in which you want to use the context object (lexicological, numerical, date comparison, time comparison). In order to use this reference type in conditions, you must have already assigned it to a field. As you can see in Figure 4.10, you must select the **Context Objects** tab page in the message interfaces editor for this purpose.[13]

There are also *technical context objects*, which you can use to access assigned fields of the message header. Therefore, you don't need an assignment for these context objects.

---

13 You can also assign context objects for RFCs and IDocs.

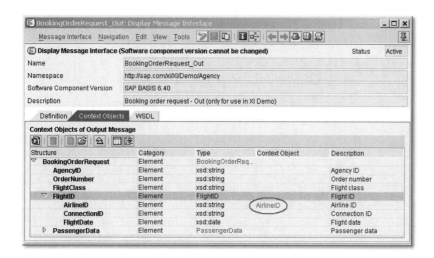

Figure 4.10 Assigning a Context Object

5   Mappings

In the previous chapter, we saw how to describe the structure of messages and assign them to an interface. This chapter looks at how message structures and value representations differ at the sender and receiver sides and explains how they can be mapped to one another.

5.1   Overview

Data exchange within a single system is relatively unproblematic. Even in a complicated development project where developers may be working in different components using different programming languages, they are nevertheless working in a relatively homogenous environment. In a heterogeneous system landscape, the components that exchange data with each other are distributed across different systems. When implementing a cross-system process, development takes place in more than one system, and you must consider the following additional factors:

▶ The involved systems can originate from different vendors with different technologies.

▶ Even if all systems are from one vendor, the systems that need to communicate with one another may be different release versions, and you might not be able to change the interface signatures of the older systems.

▶ Even if the semantics of objects in components from different systems are identical, this does not mean that they are identified using the same values. For example, the passenger class of a flight can be coded as a number or a string.

Mapping XML Documents

The emergence of XML raised hopes of a uniform XML-based data exchange format, which would improve the implementation of cross-system processes. Unfortunately, there are now countless such data exchange formats. However, using the XML standard enables you to map different XML languages to one another relatively easily. Figure 5.1 shows a mapping in which the whole structure of the source document and the value of the ⟨hh:class⟩ element are mapped to a target document. This chapter explores the options for structure and value mappings in SAP XI.

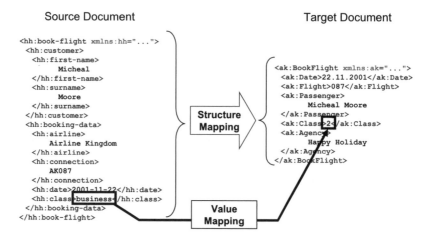

Figure 5.1 Structure and Value Mapping

5.1.1 Mapping Programs in SAP XI

To execute a mapping, you need a *mapping program*. Generally, the mapping program must be available on the Integration Server at runtime. Table 5.1 shows which mapping programs are supported by SAP XI and where they are executed.

Mapping Program	Runtime
Message mapping	J2EE Engine of the SAP Web AS on which the Integration Server is running
Java program	
XSLT program	
ABAP program	ABAP Engine of the SAP Web AS on which the Integration Server is running
XSLT program	

Table 5.1 Runtime Environment for Mapping Programs

Note the following:

▶ Mapping programs that are executed at runtime on the J2EE Engine of SAP Web AS must exist in the Integration Repository. You create message mappings directly in the Integration Repository, and you can import Java and XSLT programs to the Integration Repository. For message mappings, developers use a graphical editor in the Integration Builder to create a mapping. The Integration Builder uses this graphical description to generate an executable Java program.

▶ There is no delivery mechanism for mapping programs that are executed at runtime on the ABAP Engine of SAP Web AS. Customers can develop mapping programs on the same SAP Web AS on which the Integration Server is running via the ABAP Workbench. For this reason, the option for this mapping program type is deactivated in the Integration Builder default settings.

Due to the restrictions on mapping programs on the ABAP Engine, we will concentrate solely on the mapping programs that are executed on the J2EE Engine. Figure 5.2 shows the (sub)objects in the Integration Repository for which you can develop these mapping programs. You can structure them hierarchically in the same way as messages:

Mappings for Data Types and Messages

▶ You can create mapping programs for data types or complex types from RFCs, IDocs, or external definitions. You can use the same hierarchical structure of these types for mapping programs as well.

▶ To map a source message to a target message, you need a mapping program that maps the message schemas to each other. You can use mapping programs for data type mappings in this mapping program.

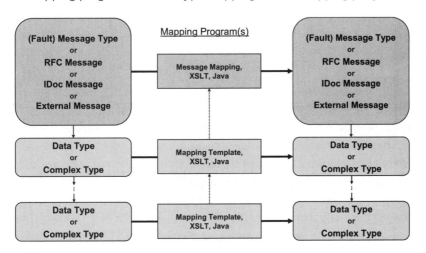

Figure 5.2 Hierarchy of Mapping Programs

There are different concepts for using one mapping program in another, depending on the mapping program type. You can use either a reference (to call a lower-level mapping program, in the same way as a subroutine) or a copy. In some cases, the various mapping program types (message mapping, XSLT, or Java program) can use each other.

Hierarchy Concept

Value Mappings

If a sender and receiver identify the same object in different ways, the corresponding values must be converted during message transfer. At first glance, the solution seems simple: Identify all source values using conditions in the mapping program, and transfer them to target values. However, this solution is not practical if there are countless values. Furthermore, this solution hides the mapping in the program. A preferable alternative is to save the values to be mapped in a value-mapping table and read them during the mapping.

Value-Mapping Table

SAP XI uses a value-mapping table for all mapping programs. At design time, developers can specify the fields in the message schema for which a value mapping is to be executed, either in a Java program or within a message mapping. However, the actual values are often not known until configuration time, because they're dependent on customer-specific data. Therefore, you save the values for the value-mapping table in the Integration Directory rather than the Integration Repository (see Section 6.3.3).

Value-Mapping Context

The entries in the value-mapping table must be assigned to a value-mapping context. The values that you enter using the Integration Builder interface automatically belong to the context *http://sap.com/xi/XI/System*. You use the context to separate value mappings from different areas.

Mappings in Integration Processes

Chapter 8 looks at how to process multiple messages in a process model in integration processes. Messages that are transferred from the Integration Engine on the Integration Server to an integration process are processed according to this model. Among other things, the model can stipulate that a certain number of messages must arrive and be processed before the integration process sends a result message to a receiver. This way of processing multiple messages enables you to bundle purchase order items from several messages into one message for a collective purchase order, for example. For integration process application cases such as these, the one-to-one mapping of messages would not suffice.

Multi-Mappings

To map multiple messages to each other, the mapping runtime has a special feature: If a mapping has multiple source messages, the mapping runtime puts all involved source messages into one structure. The structure is always the same: The `<Messages>` root element has `<MessageN>` elements as subelements for each source message with a different message schema. For example, if an integration process expects two messages from a proxy, and these messages both use the `<Order>` message type in the Integration Repository, then an instance of the dynamic source structure would look like this (without namespaces):

```
<Messages>
   <Message1>
      <Order>
         ...
      </Order>
   </Message1>
   <Message1>
      <Order>
         ...
      </Order>
   </Message1>
<Messages>
```

The second occurrence of the `<Message1>` tag refers to the same message type. If the message types are different, the dynamic structure contains a corresponding number of additional tags with a higher counter.

As soon as more than one message is involved in the mapping, on either the source or target side, the mapping runtime uses this dynamic structure for the source and the target messages. In this way, mappings of multiple message instances are reduced to a mapping of one XML instance. Developers can develop these *multi-mappings* in the Integration Builder, or by using external tools:

▶ The mapping editor for graphical message mappings in the Integration Builder allows you to specify multiple source or target messages. In the mapping editor, you define the message mapping with the message schema for the structure described above in the normal way.

▶ For multi-mappings in XSLT or Java, you can export the message schema from an *interface mapping* (see Section 5.2; interface mappings are explained in the next section). If your message schema does not exist in the Integration Repository, you can construct the schema for the dynamic structure yourself, as described above.

So far, our explanation of mapping programs has focused entirely on the messages that are to be mapped to each other. In the next section, we examine the implications for the higher-level interfaces when a mapping is required for message exchange.

5.1.2 Preconfiguration and Testing of Mapping Programs

In Chapter 4, we saw that you specify interfaces for message exchange in SAP XI. You specify these interfaces explicitly in the Integration Directory during the configuration of an *interface determination* (see Section 6.3.2). In the simplest case, you assign an inbound interface to an outbound interface. Once the Integration Server has read the outbound interface of an inbound message from the message header, it can use the interface determination to identify the inbound interface to which the message is to be forwarded. Depending on the type of the two interfaces, you use the interface determination to configure the exchange of not just one message, but of several. For example, you use synchronous message interfaces to exchange a message for a request first, and then a message for the response. Therefore, each interface pair may require several mapping programs.

Interface Mappings

In principle, users could reference the respective mapping programs for the request, response, and fault message from the interface determination. However, to do this, the consultants involved in the configuration process would have to know which mapping programs to use for which interface pairs. Moreover, it is more efficient to execute several mapping programs one after the other. To put it briefly, this enables you to map multiple message formats to a central message format. This reduces the number of mapping programs, since the communication parties involved need only one mapping to the central message format instead of numerous mappings for each communication party. This is a configuration task for the developer designing the entire mapping. For this reason, and to minimize the later configuration effort, developers create *interface mappings* in the Integration Repository, which act as an *outer shell* for mapping programs:

▶ Before making the actual configuration settings in the Integration Directory, you define which mapping programs are to be executed for an interface pair during the processing of the request, response, or fault message. With the exception of multi-mappings, you can specify several mapping programs to be executed one after the other for each direction.

▶ You can also create multiple interface mappings for an interface pair, for example, if there are different customer requirements for mappings between an interface pair.

▶ Interface mappings have an integrated test environment for mapping programs of the Integration Repository. We'll look at this in more detail in the next section.

▶ You can export the message schema for external XSLT and Java programs. You can also export the message structure for multi-mappings in the same way. Because these mappings are intended just for integration processes, this is only possible for asynchronous abstract message interfaces.

If the messages that are exchanged between an interface pair don't require a mapping, you also don't need an interface mapping. In all other cases, interface mappings are mandatory.

Figure 5.3 shows an example of an interface mapping. It references a source and a target interface, and mapping programs for the request, response, and fault message. Interface mappings can reference mapping programs from the same or an underlying software component version. There are no restrictions on references from interface mappings to interfaces. In this example, the mapping objects are assigned to the same software component version S1 as the source interface. This is, however, not necessary from a technical point of view. From a logical perspective, mappings are located between two application components. Therefore, the issue of which application component, and thus which software component version, a mapping should belong to is purely organizational. The communication parties involved could just have easily agreed to save the mapping objects in software component version S2. An argument against having a separate software component version for mapping objects is that mappings are part of the application to be shipped.

Mapping Programs and Software Component Versions

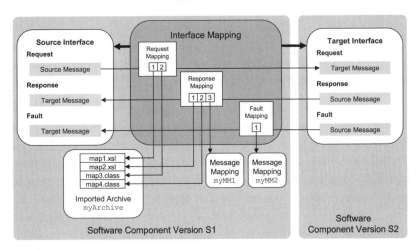

Figure 5.3 Example of an Interface Mapping

Since you have already configured the mapping program, all you need to do at configuration time is specify the respective interface mapping for an interface pair. The configuration in the Integration Directory enables the Integration Builder to recognize which mapping programs must be executed on the Integration Server at runtime. To ensure that these programs are available at runtime, the Integration Builder automatically copies all mapping programs to a system directory on the Integration Server.

Mapping Test Environment in the Integration Builder

We will now look at how to test mapping programs in the Integration Builder at design time. In order to do this, the mapping programs must be available in the Integration Repository. You can test message mappings—or Java or XSLT programs that have been imported into the Integration Repository—in the Integration Builder.

Test Instances

The test environment is integrated into the editor for interface mappings. To test an interface mapping, simply select the corresponding tab page. Figure 5.4 shows an example of a test instance, which is shown on the left side. In the default setting, the test environment generates an XML instance for the source message and displays it in a tabular tree representation:

▶ The first column displays the hierarchical structure of the XML instance. To edit this hierarchy, use the options in the context menu.

▶ The second column is where you enter the values for the respective fields.

The test environment functions also enable you to load other XML instances into the test environment and select other views for display or editing purposes, for example, a text editor.

Trace Level

Figure 5.4 shows an interface mapping for asynchronous communication. In synchronous communication, you test the mapping programs for the request, response, and fault directions separately. In this case, the test environment has an additional list box so that you can switch between directions. You can also set a **Trace Level** for testing of all mapping programs in a particular direction. The trace level relates to the messages that you write to the mapping trace within mapping programs. The mapping runtime has methods that enable you to differentiate between status information, warnings, and debugging information. The **Debug** trace level also displays messages of the mapping runtime itself. The Integration Builder displays the trace outputs and information about the test execution status in the lower area of the test environment. The result of the transformation is displayed on the right.

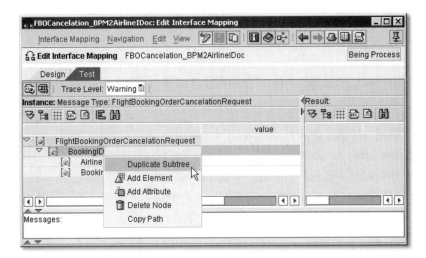

Figure 5.4 Test Environment in Interface Mapping

Of course, you can test individual Java and XSLT programs outside the Integration Builder by exporting the required message schemas from the interface mapping. Message mappings have the same test environment as the one integrated into the editor for interface mappings. In the mapping editor, you can also manage the test instances that are shipped with the message mapping.

We will now look at the different mapping program types in more detail. Section 5.2 deals with mapping programs in Java and XSLT. In Section 5.3, you'll learn that you can call Java programs as subroutines in graphical message mappings.

5.2 Java and XSLT Mappings

We will start by looking at two established mapping program types: You can develop mapping programs in Java or as XSLT programs. Because there is a whole range of development environments for these program types, the Integration Builder does not have its own tools to support this assortment. However, this does *not* mean that you cannot use Java and XSLT programs. To develop Java or XSLT programs for mappings in SAP XI, you proceed as follows:

1. Export the schemas for which you need a mapping from the Integration Repository.

   For example, you can use the export function under **Tools** in the editor menu to export message types. However, the simplest method is to first create an interface mapping for the relevant interfaces. Once you've imported the interfaces in the interface mapping editor, you export the XSD schema of the respective request or response message as a Zip file. The Zip file can contain several schema files that reference each other, in a multi-mapping, for example. In this case, the schema with the global element that is the root element of the message has the name `MainSchema`.

2. Use the exported schemas to develop your mapping program with a third-party tool. It may be that you are using a schema that cannot be imported to the Integration Repository.

3. Save your mapping programs in one or more archives. These can be Zip or JAR files.

4. For each external Zip or JAR file, create a mapping object of type imported archive in the Integration Builder. Objects of this type enable the external archives to be imported to the Integration Repository.

5. After the import, use the mapping programs in interface mappings by accessing the archive. You can make minor changes to XSLT mappings in a simple editor in the Integration Builder. You can change Java programs only externally, and you must reimport them.

The development of Java and XSLT programs is explained in depth in the technical literature. Therefore, Section 5.2.1 and Section 5.2.2 cover only those features that pertain to the development of mapping programs for SAP XI.

5.2.1 Java Mappings

There are various technologies for parsing and transforming XML in Java. For example, the *Document Object Model* (DOM) allows access to the entire XML tree via methods. Although this approach is straightforward and easy to understand, it is not suitable for large XML documents, because loading such large documents is too memory-intensive. The best approach to use depends on the application.

Working with
Streams

For this reason, SAP XI does not provide an all-purpose API with fixed access methods. Instead, the mapping runtime transfers XML documents to Java programs as a *stream*, and similarly expects the result to be a stream. Developers have the freedom to choose which transformation method is best-suited to meet their needs. For example, you can use *Java API for XML Processing* (JAXP), which supports DOM, as well as *Simple API for XML* (SAX).

Now, we'll use the API to access the stream. Listing 5.1 shows an example of how to use the API of the mapping runtime:

```java
import java.io.InputStream;
import java.io.OutputStream;
import java.util.Map;
import java.util.HashMap;
import com.sap.aii.mapping.api.MappingTrace;
import com.sap.aii.mapping.api.StreamTransformation;
import
com.sap.aii.mapping.api.StreamTransformationConstants;
public class JavaMapping
implements StreamTransformation {
  private Map          param = null;
  private MappingTrace  trace = null;
  public void setParameter (Map param) {
    this.param = param;
    if (param == null) {
      this.param = new HashMap();
    }
  }
  public void execute(
  InputStream in, OutputStream out) {
    try {
    trace = (MappingTrace)param.get(
    StreamTransformationConstants.MAPPING_TRACE);
    trace.addInfo('...');
    // ...
    String receiverName = (String)param.get(
    StreamTransformationConstants.RECEIVER_NAME);
    // Parse input stream
    // and create output stream
      }
    }
}
```

Listing 5.1 Framework of a Java Mapping Program

To implement a Java mapping, a developer must implement the Java interface `StreamTransformation` with the following methods:

▶ `setParameter()`
The Integration Engine calls this method to transfer runtime constants to the mapping program before it is executed. The implementation of this method is always the same. Simply use the method in Listing 5.1. The method makes the constants within the implementing class accessible using a `Map`, which has the name `param` in this example.

▶ `execute()`
The Integration Engine calls this method at runtime to execute a mapping. This method receives an input stream for the source document, and an output stream for the target document as parameters. You can parse the substructures to be converted from the input stream, and output the converted target document in the output stream.

As the listing shows, you can access runtime constants of the interface `StreamTransformationConstants` within the `execute()` method. All but one of these constants are string constants, which you use, for example, to exchange sender and receiver information in the Java program. The constant `MAPPING_TRACE`, on the other hand, provides an object for trace outputs at runtime. Such trace outputs are visible in tests and in monitoring.

The mapping runtime provides an API for executing value mappings. The values are saved in a Java database table. For more information about the API, see the online documentation.

To conclude, here are a few important notes about programming mapping programs for SAP XI in Java:

▶ Java mapping programs must always be stateless. Do not write data to a database table during a Java mapping, for instance. The Integration Server cannot track such side effects. Therefore, if an attempt is made to resend a message that has not been received by the receiver, the data may inadvertently be written to the database twice in a Java mapping.

▶ When using static variables in Java mappings, note the following points:

  ▶ Mappings can be executed in parallel. Therefore, several instances of a mapping may access a static field for read or write purposes at the same time.

▶ If mapping programs are executed more than once, the content of a static field may be lost, for example, because the Java class in question is reloaded. Moreover, during cluster operation of the mapping runtime, the classes of the mapping programs are loaded separately to each node of the cluster, so that each node has its own static fields.

Therefore, static fields can be used only for constants and as a buffer, taking into account, of course, the aforementioned points.

5.2.2 XSLT Mappings

The XSLT (*eXtensible Stylesheet Language Transformations*) standard belongs to the XSL language family. It was developed by the W3C (*World Wide Web Consortium*) for XML, to transform one XML structure into another. XSLT includes XPath, a syntax for selecting substructures in an XML document. In XSLT, you define mappings by using templates to define bindings for the selected substructures. A W3Schools tutorial (*http://www.w3schools.com*) is available for free and provides a good introduction to XSLT.

We won't elaborate further on the extensive options provided by XSLT. Rather, we'll examine just a few aspects. As is typical with Java programs, you can access mapping runtime constants in XSLT programs as well. For example, the `$ReceiverName` constant provides the name of the receiver interface at runtime. To use the constant in an XSLT program, you must declare it using the `param` statement:

Runtime Constants in XSLT Programs

```
<xsl:param name="ReceiverName">
```

You can call Java methods within an XSLT program. Since the XSLT standard does not define this enhancement mechanism, the precise procedure depends largely on the XSLT processor used. The XI online documentation includes an example of a Java enhancement, which is supported by the features of the SAP J2EE Engine. You'll also find a list of the runtime constants for XSLT programs.

Java Enhancements

5.3 Developing Mappings in the Integration Builder

The Integration Builder has an integrated mapping editor that you can use to describe mappings graphically. Since these mappings are between messages, this description is referred to simply as a *message mapping*. The Integration Builder uses the message mappings to generate Java programs, which are compiled for runtime and packed in JAR files. The user does not need to concern herself or himself with this; she/he works with just the message mapping in the Integration Builder at design time and at configuration time. Section 5.3.1 provides us with an introduction to the basic concepts of the mapping editor.

The challenge for all graphical mapping tools is to reconcile the need for clarity with the wide range of functions that can be integrated graphically. In Section 5.3.2, we'll investigate which standard functions exist in the mapping editor for describing mappings without developing program code. If the requirements are complex, the graphical description can become more complicated than the equivalent program code. If this is the case, you can enhance the pool of standard functions by adding your own user-defined functions in Java. Section 5.3.3 explains how to create and reuse mappings for data types.

5.3.1   Introduction to the Mapping Editor

In all mappings, source fields of a source structure are assigned to target fields of a target structure. A field can be an element or an attribute of the respective XML document. This can be displayed in a graphical mapping tool by using lines to connect the corresponding fields of the source and target structure. If the XML document is large and many fields have to be mapped to each other, this representation can become very complicated. In addition to field mappings, calculations and format conversions are also required, which means that there are even more graphical elements for the mapping tool to represent.

Target-Field Mappings in the Data-Flow Editor
The mapping editor in the Integration Builder divides mappings into sub-mappings. In Figure 5.5, the mapping editor shows a submapping in the lower area. It refers to the target field PassengerName, whose value is obtained by linking the FirstName and Surname source fields. Since the representation in the lower area describes a data flow from the source to the target fields, this part of the mapping editor is called the *data-flow editor*. It always shows a mapping to a target field. Therefore, the whole message mapping in the mapping editor consists of *target-field mappings*.

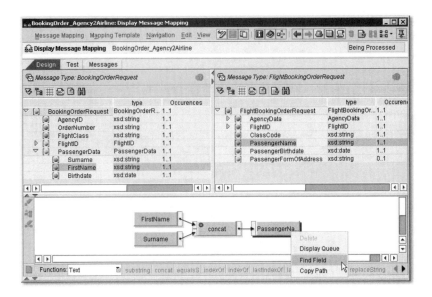

Figure 5.5 Mapping Editor

The *structure overview* in the middle area is closely linked to the data-flow editor:

▶ To create a target-field mapping, double-click a target field or drag it to the data-flow editor using drag and drop. If a target-field mapping already exists, use the same actions to navigate between the different target-field mappings that you want to display in the data-flow editor.

▶ To transfer source structure fields to the data-flow editor for a currently displayed target-field mapping, double-click the source field or drag it to the data-flow editor using drag and drop.

Similarly, you can drag fields from the source structure to target structure fields (and the other way round) to assign them to one another.

Separating the structure overview and the target-field mappings in the data-flow editor may seem unusual at first, but it reduces the complexity of the display. The mapping editor also offers several functions for easier orientation. These include a where-used list for source fields, quick infos for target fields showing existing target-field mappings, and a general field search in functions of the data-flow editor and the structure overview. By using the **Text Preview** (▤) function in the editor toolbar, you can also display an overview of all target-field mappings in place of the data-flow editor. In the example in Figure 5.6, the header area and the structure overview are hidden as well. Besides the text preview, there is also a graphical overview function, which you can use to display the dependencies between source and target fields directly in the structure overview.

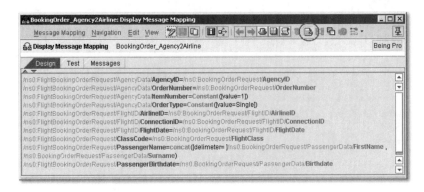

Figure 5.6 Text Preview

Loading Messages into the Structure Overview We will now look at the procedure for designing a message mapping in the mapping editor. Once you have created a message mapping, you first load a source structure and a target structure into the structure overview. You can load a schema from the Integration Repository ((fault) message types, IDocs, the request, response, or fault part of an RFC, and message schemas from external definitions) or an XSD or XML document from a local file. The latter enables you to define message mappings for message schemas or message instances that cannot be imported to the Integration Repository.

The mapping editor displays the loaded message schema in a simplified XML representation in the structure overview, in a tabular tree view. Table 5.2 provides an overview of the node symbols.

Node Symbol	Meaning
	Attribute
	Element
	Element with `maxOccurs = unbounded`
	Deactivated element
	Recursive element

Table 5.2 Node Symbols in the Structure Overview

If a field can appear more than once in the target structure, the tree view displays only one node in the mapping editor, just as there is only one tag for the field definition in the XSD. In this representation, it is not graphically possible to assign the value of a source field to a particular position in the target field. In such cases, you can use the **Duplicate Subtree** function in the context menu of the target structure to display multiple positions and specify them as the target. Section 5.3.2 looks at additional functions for accessing positions and structures of XML instances. The context menu contains several other functions, for example, for deactivating or activating fields, or using mapping templates. These functions are covered in Section 5.3.3.

Positions and Restrictions of Target Fields

When designing and analyzing mappings, it helps to imagine that the fields and values of the target structure must first be generated. The target structure in the mapping editor specifies which conditions must be fulfilled for the generated structure to be valid. The mapping editor displays these conditions in the columns of the tabular tree view, and uses colors to differentiate them:

▶ White fields have not yet been assigned and, according to the target structure specifications, must not necessarily be generated.

▶ Red fields must be included in the target instance, according to the target structure specifications. At runtime, a rule for the generation of these fields is required.

▶ Yellow fields have already been assigned to some extent, but the target-field mapping in the data-flow editor is not yet complete.

▶ Green fields represent a complete target-field mapping.

Only when there are no more yellow or red fields in the target structure is the message mapping *complete* from a technical point of view. In the Integration Builder, you can test and release only complete message mappings.

If you want to develop a multi-mapping for an integration process, the procedure is the same as described above. The only extra step is to specify all source and target messages and their occurrence on the **Messages** tab page. The mapping editor then displays the structure of the multi-mapping in the structure overview, as described in Section 5.1.1.

Multi-Mappings

Work Method of Message Mappings

When a message mapping is complete, this simply means that it can be compiled, as when a Java program has the correct syntax. To enable you to understand runtime exceptions and undesired mapping results, let's take a brief look at the behavior of message mappings at runtime:

Queues 1. Message mappings import source XML instances into queues. Using queues improves performance and enables very large messages to be processed.

2. Queues are processed by the functions of the target-field mapping. The functions themselves have result queues that can be assigned further functions.

3. Finally, the result queues are read for the target fields and compared against their occurrence attributes. For example, if an upper limit has been specified for the occurrence of a target field, then any further result values of the result queue are ignored. The source XML instance probably had too many values. If it has too few values, this triggers an exception.

If you have already loaded a test instance on the **Test** tab page, you can track each step of a target-field mapping on the **Design** tab page by calling the **Display Queue** function for the objects in the data-flow editor. The target field queue is the result queue that compares the message mapping against the target structure restrictions at runtime. Figure 5.7 shows an example.

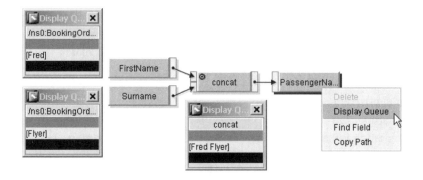

Figure 5.7 Queues in the Data-Flow Editor

5.3.2 Mapping Functions in Message Mappings

Before we look at the different types of mapping functions, we'll examine the hierarchical arrangement of XML structures. In the XML tree, the field of an XML instance is always in a *context* of the higher-level field. For example, in the XML instance below, the `<person>` element is in the `<street>` context, and the `<city>` element is in the `<root>` context.

```
<root>
   <city>
      <street>
         <person> Fix </person>
      </street>
      <street>
         <person> Foxy </person>
      </street>
   </city>
</root>
```

The closing tag of the higher-level element marks the end of the context (the context is also referred to as *closed*). For example, `Fix` is in the first `street` context and `Foxy` is on the second `street` context (the two obviously live in different streets). Let's assume that you want to map this XML structure to a list of all inhabitants of the town, that is:

```
<AllCitizens>
   <citizen> Fix </citizen>
   <citizen> Foxy </citizen>
</AllCitizens>
```

In this mapping, you must delete all contexts between `<person>` and `<root>` in the source structure. In other words, assigning all `<person>` elements to the `<root>` context simplifies the mapping. You would then have to assign only the `<person>` source field to the `<citizen>` target field. In the **Context** context menu of the data-flow editor, you can set the context of each field of the source structure individually. In our example, you set the context of the `<person>` source field to `<root>`. The data-flow editor displays the names of the fields where the standard context has been changed in *italics*.

Generally, you require a range of additional mapping functions in a mapping. You access these functions in the mapping editor, in the lower area of the data-flow editor. Figure 5.8 shows the standard functions of the **Boolean** function category. Standard functions for text mappings, arithmetical calculations, (runtime) constants, conversions (for example, for accessing the value-mapping table), date conversions, statistical functions for all fields of a context, and functions for specific structure mappings are also available.

Standard Functions

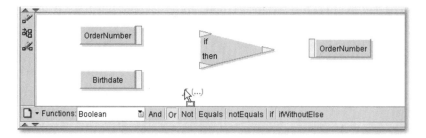

Figure 5.8 Standard Functions of the Boolean Function Category

Technically speaking, values of elements and attributes of the source message are a string. Therefore, all standard functions expect string-type arguments and return a string-type value. Nevertheless, the transferred value can have a different semantic data type, namely, the one that you specified when you defined the schema for the payload for the field. Standard functions exhibit the following standard behavior:

▶ Depending on the standard function, data type conversions are used to ensure that the values are transferred in a format suitable for the function (using a *cast*). If the value cannot be interpreted, the mapping runtime triggers a Java exception.

▶ If-clauses evaluate conditions that deliver Boolean values. Standard functions that return Boolean values return the string `true` or `false`. Standard functions that expect Boolean values interpret the values "1" and "true" (not case-sensitive) as `true`, and all other values as `false`.

User-Defined Functions

If the standard functions for a target-field mapping are not sufficient, or the complexity of the mapping means that the graphical display is unclear, you can create a user-defined function. You can use this function to create Java source code. The Integration Builder includes the function as a Java method in the Java program that is generated for the message mapping. You can use the following user-defined functions:

▶ **Simple functions**
These functions process individual input values of assigned fields for each function call. Therefore, simple functions expect strings as input values and return a string.

► **Advanced Functions**

These functions process multiple input values of a field for each function call. Before you call the function, you can either import all the field values of a context or the whole queue for the field in an array.

Clearly, you may want to use Java methods from imported archives in user-defined functions. You can access the following objects in user-defined functions:

► Java programs from imported archives that are in the same software component version as the message mapping or an underlying software component version

► Mapping runtime objects for trace output and for transferring values between user-defined functions

► Standard packages of the Java Development Kit and the J2EE environment

The comments on the implementation of mappings in Java at the end of Section 5.2.1 also apply to user-defined functions.

5.3.3 Developing Data Type Mappings in the Integration Builder

Thus far, we have explored how to develop mappings for messages in the Integration Builder. To enable you to reuse parts of message mappings, the Integration Builder supports *mapping templates*, which you edit using the same mapping editor as you would for message mappings. There are two ways to create a mapping template:

► You can use a message mapping or mapping template by selecting an element in the source and target structure that references a data type in the Integration Repository. Using the context menu of the target structure or using the editor menu, you can save the mapping for the two selected data types as a mapping template.

Creating Templates

► You can create a data type template—directly in the Integration Builder—and load a data type into both the source and the target structure.

You can use saved mapping templates in other message mappings or other mapping templates as a *template*. This means that the Integration Builder copies mapping templates into other mappings; it does not reference them. You can then adapt the target-field mapping of the copied template to meet your requirements. The original mapping template is not modified by these changes. In the mapping editor, you can display the mapping templates that have been copied to the editor. Alternatively, you can develop mapping templates in the same way as message mappings, as described in the previous section.

6 Configuration

The design of the collaborative process is independent of the technical details resulting from the system landscape of the customer. This chapter describes how to configure this information centrally to control message processing at runtime.

6.1 Introduction

At design time, we look at collaborative processes at the logical level. In this view, messages are exchanged between application components and not between systems. In this chapter, we make the link between this abstraction and the settings that are required at runtime to actually implement message exchange. These settings concern the following areas:

▶ Information about the actual system landscape and the products installed there. This is discussed at the beginning of Section 6.2.

▶ Information regarding the services provided within a system landscape and which technical communication channel other systems in the system landscape use to access a service. This is discussed at the end of Section 6.2, once the basics have been covered at the beginning of the section.

▶ Information about how the services are linked to one another by messages (logical routing) and whether a mapping is necessary. This is described in relation to internal company communication in Section 6.3.

▶ Information about services that you want to make available to business partners outside your own system landscape. This is described in Section 6.4, which builds on the concepts introduced in Section 6.3.

With the exception of the area listed in the first bullet, you configure all the necessary information centrally in the Integration Directory. You have the following options:

▶ If there is an integration scenario for your collaborative process in the Integration Repository (see Section 3.3), we recommend that you use this scenario for configuration. This is discussed in more detail in Section 6.3.1.

▶ If there is no integration scenario, a configuration wizard is available to guide you through the individual configuration steps.

▶ Alternatively, you can make the configuration settings manually. Unlike the first option—where the Integration Builder automatically recognizes from the integration scenario which configuration objects can be reused and which objects must be generated—manual configuration is very time-consuming.

Processes and Scenarios

To avoid confusion, we want to reiterate that the term *collaborative process* means a process that exists in the real world and a process that you want to implement using your software technology. An *integration scenario* is a design object in the Integration Repository that you use to model the collaborative process. *Integration processes* are also design objects that enable you to consider dependencies between messages in cross-system message exchange.

During the configuration of a collaborative process, you can choose whether or not you want to work with an integration scenario from the Integration Repository. On the one hand, making the integration scenario an integral part of the Integration Repository would be too restrictive. On the other hand, the lack of an integration scenario means that there is nothing to hold together the configuration objects of a scenario. By way of a compromise, the Integration Builder works with *configuration scenarios.*[1] These scenarios are simply a container for all the configuration objects that are required to configure a collaborative process. Figure 6.1 shows the configuration scenario MyCheckFlightSeatAvailability in the Integration Builder. The **Configuration Scenario Objects** tab page shows all the objects that are assigned to a configuration scenario. In this case, the objects were generated or suitable existing objects were automatically assigned using the CheckFlightSeatAvailability integration scenario. However, you don't have to use an integration scenario from the Integration Repository and can assign any configuration objects of your choice to a configuration scenario.

No matter which configuration option you choose, it is critical that you understand the various configuration objects. We'll take a step-by-step look at how these objects are used below.

---

1 As of SAP XI 3.0 SP9, **scenario** is renamed **configuration scenario**. We use the new terminology in this book.

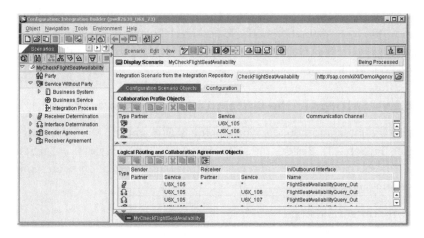

Figure 6.1 Configuration Scenario MyCheckFlightSeatAvailability

Configuration in the Integration Directory is designed to support as many configuration scenarios as possible. Depending on the protocol, the configuration scenarios can have very different technical requirements. However, the procedure for configuring the configuration objects is valid for many configuration scenarios. Sections 6.2, 6.3, and 6.4 explain this procedure and highlight any exceptions. Sections 6.5 and 6.6 address the special features of the various adapters. Finally, Section 6.7 focuses on the transport of configuration objects.

The Integration Builder also enables you to publish a service as a Web service at configuration time. Since we'll meet Web services again in a different context later in the book, we'll review this topic in its entirety in Section 7.3.2.

6.2   Describing Systems and Services

To configure a collaborative process within your system landscape, you must first describe the system landscape in the System Landscape Directory (SLD). This is discussed in more detail in Section 6.2.1. Basically, you have two options when it comes to dealing with the sequence of the configuration steps in the Integration Directory: You can work from the collaborative process (logical level) to the technical systems (technical level), or vice versa. The advantage of the latter option is that a system generally offers services for a wide range of collaborative processes and plays a role in different configuration scenarios. The technical options provided by the systems for message exchange are more constant and you only need to enter them once for all configuration scenarios in a *collaboration pro-*

file. For this reason, it is advisable to focus on this profile first, and then move on to configuration at the logical level. Therefore, we'll look at the settings in the SLD first and then examine the configuration of the collaboration profile in Section 6.2.2.

6.2.1 Settings in the System Landscape Directory

Like the Integration Builder, you call the SLD from the SAP XI start page (see Section 2.1). Besides the software catalog, which we met in Section 3.2.1, you can also enter and call the following information about your system landscape:

▶ Technical Landscape
In this area, you can access information about the technical systems in your system landscape. Examples of technical systems are an SAP Web AS (ABAP) or an SAP Web AS (Java).

▶ Business Landscape
In this area, you can access information about the business systems of your system landscape. This area is specific to SAP XI and enables you to identify those systems in your system landscape that use SAP XI to exchange messages.

Technical Systems   The information about the technical systems of your system landscape is not just of interest to SAP XI users. It can also be used by SAP support employees and customers to get an overview of the installed systems:

▶ Technical SAP systems
The SLD categorizes the technical SAP systems by the Basis or SAP Web AS release that they run on. The following systems register themselves automatically in the SLD when they're installed: SAP Basis 4.0B, and all SAP Web AS ABAP systems and SAP Web AS Java systems as of Release 6.40. They also transfer data about their installed products. You must register all other technical SAP systems in the SLD manually by using a wizard, and then assign them products from the software catalog.

▶ Third-party systems
You also register third-party systems in the SLD manually by using a wizard. You can assign these systems third-party products from the software catalog.

The technical attributes of a system are stored in the SLD. Examples of attributes for technical SAP systems are: system name, system clients, message server, and installed products. Furthermore, you can use the

Exchange Infrastructure option to display all technical SAP systems on which SAP XI runtime components are installed, for example, the Integration Server. These components register themselves automatically in the SLD as soon as they're launched.

If a technical system is part of a cross-system process, you must also assign it to a business system. (In SAP systems, every client represents a business system.) During configuration, you then work with the name of the business system and not with the name of the technical system. First, this ensures that only those systems relevant to the process are displayed during configuration. Secondly, you can make changes to the technical system landscape without affecting an existing configuration.

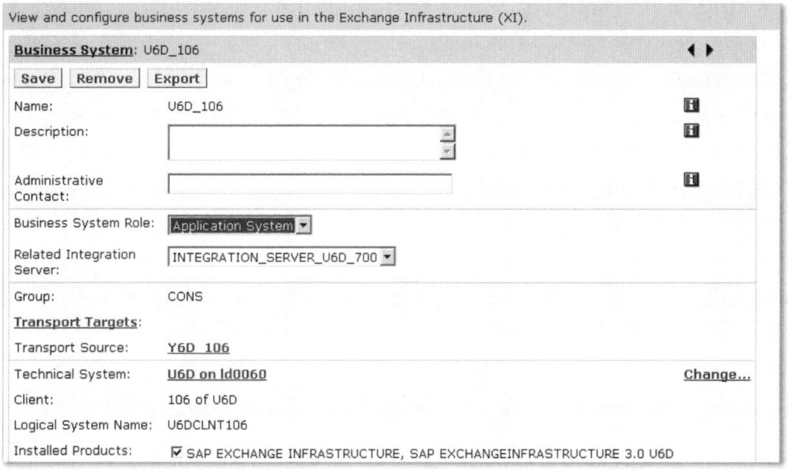

Figure 6.2 Attributes of a Business System in the SLD

Business systems are used exclusively for cross-system applications with SAP XI. Therefore, the attributes of a business system in the SLD relate directly to the particular application case. Figure 6.2 shows a screenshot of a business system in the SLD. As well as the header data (**Name**, **Description**, **Administrative Contact**), you must also define the role of the business system.

▶ If it is an application system, you must assign it an Integration Server, with which the business system will exchange messages. Since you usually test the message exchange before using the process in a productive environment, there can be multiple Integration Servers within a system landscape.

► Alternatively, you assign the business system the role of an Integration Server.

Just like the other data in the SLD, this information is merely descriptive. Therefore, defining a business system as an Integration Server in the SLD does not relieve you of the task of making the corresponding configuration settings for the respective clients in the technical system (see Section 7.2.1). Other SAP XI runtime components may also call data in the SLD. As will be discussed again later in Section 6.7, the **Group** and **Transport Targets** attributes are required for the transport of configuration objects between different Integration Directories.

Evaluating the SLD Data We will now focus on the uses of the data in the SLD for configuration in the Integration Directory. At the bottom of the screenshot in Figure 6.2, you can see the first of the installed products (SAP EXCHANGE INFRA-STRUCTURE). The products listed here and the derived software component versions are used by the assigned technical system (in this case, the client 106 of SAP system U6D). Since business systems are used in the Integration Directory to configure internal company communication, the Integration Directory accesses information about business systems and associated technical systems from the SLD to derive further details. For example, the Integration Builder can use the software component versions of a system to determine all the interfaces for a business system that have been saved in the Integration Repository for message exchange. Figure 6. illustrates this query. The Integration Builder also uses this mechanism for checks and input help.

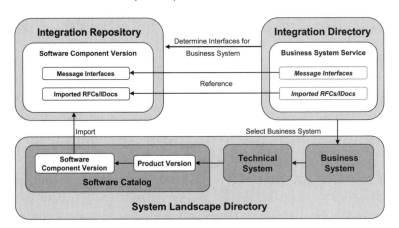

Figure 6.3 Referencing Content of the Integration Repository

The use of the software catalog in the Integration Repository, discussed in Section 3.2.1, completes the loop. The *business system service* shown in Figure 6.3 leads us to our next topic: the Integration Directory. The next section explains the configuration procedure in the Integration Directory.

6.2.2 First Steps in the Integration Directory

The Integration Builder provides a whole range of objects for configuring a collaborative process. Before we delve into how to use these configuration objects in detail, let us first get a general overview. Because there are dependencies between the various objects, it is advisable to adhere to the following sequence during configuration:

1. The configuration objects *communication party*, *service*, and *communication channel* reference each other and together form a *collaboration profile*. To exchange internal company messages, it is generally sufficient to use collaboration profiles, where the services and communication channels are specified. Therefore, for now, we'll leave the discussion of communication parties, and return to it in Section 6.4.

2. At this stage, the collaboration profile is still independent of a specific configuration scenario. You use the configuration objects *sender agreement* and *receiver agreement* to define the communication options that you want or have to use. These agreements are collectively referred to as a *collaboration agreement*.

3. Finally, you use *receiver determinations* and *interface determinations* to configure the logical routing, which defines where a message should be forwarded and whether a mapping is necessary beforehand.

The description of the collaboration profile is the basis for the following configuration steps. You can use the profile in different configuration scenarios. Therefore, let's take a closer look at this area before moving on to the configuration of internal company processes in Section 6.3.

Figure 6.4 shows the object hierarchy of communication parties, services, and communication channels. As we already mentioned, we'll look at communication parties in more detail later on. At this point, you need only know that a company uses a communication party to enter the services provided by a business partner in the Integration Directory. Therefore, you don't actually need a communication party as a configuration object for internal company processes. (The exception to this is a configuration scenario with IDocs. We'll look at this in more detail in Section 6.5.2.)

Collaboration Profile

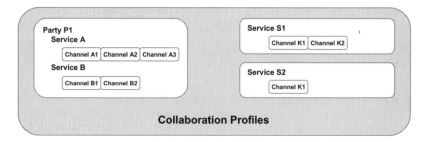

Figure 6.4 Object Hierarchy in Communication Profiles

Service

The *Service* object was introduced with SAP XI 3.0 as an additional level for business systems to enable other sender and receiver types to be modeled and addressed. There are three types of services:

▶ **Business system service**
This service refers directly to a business system from the SLD. To create business system services, you call the context menu for the **Service Without Party** or **Business System** node in the Integration Builder navigation tree and choose **Assign Business System**...

▶ **Integration process service**
This service refers to integration processes from the Integration Repository. Configuration with integration processes is discussed in more detail in Chapter 8.

▶ **Business service**
This service enables business partners to address receivers of your system landscape without you having to publish the receivers. We will look at this in more detail in Section 6.4.

A service offers a range of interfaces for communication using SAP XI. These interfaces are displayed on the Sender and Receiver tab pages. In the previous section, Figure 6.3 showed that the Integration Builder automatically determines these interfaces for business system services from the Integration Repository. Consequently, they're displayed in the input help (that is, the help that users can call up to enter a value in an entry field) in subsequent configuration steps. If the interfaces of a business system are not in the Integration Repository because they have not been created or imported, you must enter them manually in the subsequent configuration steps.

Communication Channel

When creating a business system service, the Integration Builder automatically creates communication channels for the service, which you must then adapt to your configuration scenario:

► For an SAP system, separate receiver channels are generated for RFC, IDoc, HTTP, and proxy communication (**Adapter Type XI**).

► For a non-SAP system, an HTTP receiver channel is generated.

Communication channels define the inbound and outbound processing in the Integration Server. To start with, the channels of a business system service simply reflect the options in the business system for receiving and sending messages. You define the channel to be used for a selected communication for the sender or receiver by using the collaboration agreement.

You may be asking yourself which system a *receiver* channel refers to: the Integration Server or the application system? This is a good question, and Figure 6.5 provides the answer. The communication channel for the sender configures the sender adapter, which converts the sender message for more processing in the Integration Server. Therefore, the channel for the sender determines the inbound processing in the Integration Server. Outbound processing works in a similar way. All configuration object names in the Integration Directory are based on the symmetry displayed in Figure 6.5. A configuration object for the receiver always refers to the receiver application system or the receiver business partner, and *not* the Integration Server sending the message.

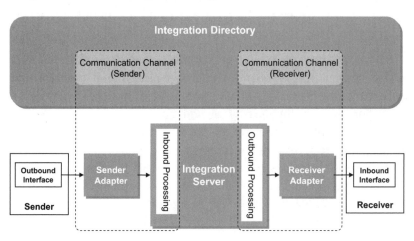

Figure 6.5 Sender and Receiver in Configuration

The representation of the adapters in Figure 6.5 reflects the logical point of view. It does not show where the runtime components of the adapters are actually installed. The proxy runtime, in particular, is installed in the application system. Nevertheless, you configure the proxy runtime in the

Sender and Receiver Configuration

same way as the other adapters, that is, by using a communication channel and choosing **Adapter Type XI**. We will look at adapter configuration in more detail in Section 6.5. You should now understand the symmetry of the configuration objects with respect to the sender and receiver. In configuration, however, you don't always require both sides. Since the Integration Server must define a receiver for the message, the configuration objects for the receiver side are mandatory. On the sender side, however, whether you have to configure anything depends on the adapter type and the configuration scenario. For example, the proxy runtime in the sender application system uses information from the SLD to determine the address of the Integration Server. Therefore, in this case you make configuration settings in the Integration Directory on the sender side only if security settings are required for message transfer.

Let's take another look at the object hierarchy of the collaboration profile from Figure 6.4. In the Integration Repository, we saw that namespaces ensure that object names are unique. Objects in the Integration Directory don't have any namespaces. Instead, the name of the higher-level object type serves as the namespace in collaboration profiles. It is normal for two communication channels of different services to have the same name, since the adapter type of the channel is often the same. For example, the names of the communication channels generated for business system services are always the same. The configuration of the channels, on the other hand, is specific to the business system.

Communication
Channel
Templates

For those adapter types where no communication channels can be generated, it would prove laborious to always have to edit the frequently used attributes manually. Certain attributes are often known at design time. For example, the *RosettaNet* industry standard stipulates security settings (encryption, signature) for the respective *Partner Interface Processes* (PIPs). To accelerate the configuration of such scenarios, the Integration Builder provides communication channel templates, which you create in the Integration Repository and reuse in the Integration Directory. Section 6.6 explains how SAP XI supports industry standards. You can use communication channel templates for all adapter types.

6.3 Configuring Internal Company Processes

So far, we have looked at the basic settings that form the foundation for a whole range of configuration scenarios. This section focuses on internal company scenarios. In Section 6.3.1, we use a demo example[2] to explain the configuration, using the corresponding integration scenario. In this case, the Integration Builder supports the automatic generation of configuration objects using information from the integration scenario. We will use this example to explain the general concepts in the following sections.

6.3.1 Configuration Using Integration Scenarios

We were introduced to the integration scenario `CheckFlightSeat-Availability` in Section 3.3. This scenario models a flight availability check in which a travel agency exchanges messages with one or more airlines. In the demo example, there are two airlines. For the purpose of simplification, let's say that these airlines are two different clients of the same SAP system:

▶ Client 105 is the travel agency on the sender side.

▶ Clients 106 and 107 are the airlines Lufthansa and American Airlines, respectively, on the receiver side.

The following steps are based on the assumption that the description of the technical systems and the business systems is already contained in the SLD. When writing this book, we worked with SAP system U6X and created the business systems U6X_105, U6X_106, and U6X_107. We also created the corresponding business system services, as described in Section 6.2.2, and generated and adapted the required communication channels.

Now we'll explain how to configure this scenario in the Integration Builder. To do this, first choose **Tools · Transfer Integration Scenario from Integration Repository...** in the main menu to access the integration scenario from the Integration Repository. This creates a configuration scenario that references our integration scenario. After the transfer, the **Integration Scenario Configurator** dialog box appears, which displays the first **component view** of the integration scenario (see Figure 6.6).

---

2   The demo example is described in Section 2.3.

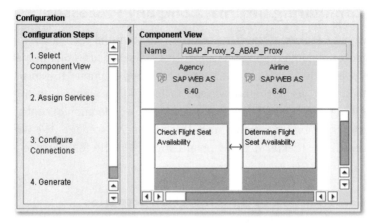

Figure 6.6 Configuration Steps for Integration Scenarios

To make the configuration settings, perform the configuration steps in the order displayed on the left side of the figure. To do this, click on the respective step and assign the required configuration objects in the dialog box that appears:

1. In the first configuration step, specify the component view (see Section 3.3.1). In this case, we keep the component view that is already selected, ABAP_Proxy_2_ABAP_Proxy.

2. In the second configuration step, assign a service to each application component. The dialog box that appears displays the first application component Agency. Assign the business system service U6X_105 to it. Use the blue navigation arrow to switch to another application component Airline. Assign the services U6X_106 and U6X_107 to it.

3. The third configuration step deals with connections (see Figure 6.7). Each receiver service requires a communication channel to enable the Integration Server to forward the respective message to the technical system. On the sender side, on the other hand, it is not necessary to configure a communication channel for the XI adapter (this is discussed in detail in Section 6.5).

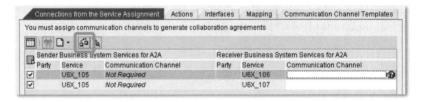

Figure 6.7 Configuring Connections

Let's concentrate for the moment on how to select a communication channel. In Section 6.2.2, we learned that a *collaboration agreement* is required to select a particular communication channel at runtime. This example deals with a *receiver agreement* for the message to the *receiver* business system U6X_106 or U6X_107. There are two different cases:

▶ If there is no existing receiver agreement that matches the receiver business system and the inbound interface, you must assign the required communication channel using the input help. An appropriate receiver agreement is generated later. Figure 6.8 shows the dialog box where you make this selection. All communication channels that are available for the receiver service are displayed.

▶ If a receiver agreement already exists for your receiver, you can use the function circled in red in Figure 6.7 to automatically define the channel. In this case, the dialog box displays only the communication channel defined by the receiver agreement in the communication channel selection. If the receiver agreement is for all inbound interfaces of the receiver system (referred to as a *generic* receiver determination), you can expand the communication channel selection by creating a *more specific* receiver determination, that is, one that is intended for a specific inbound interface. Section 6.3.2 addresses generic and specific configuration objects.

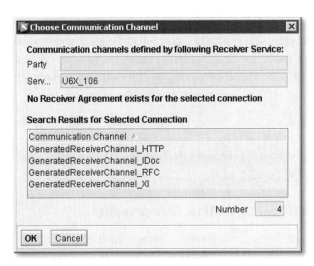

Figure 6.8 Selecting a Communication Channel

4. Finally, once you have made these preparations, you can have the integration scenario configurator generate all the remaining configuration

objects. You can restrict this generation to particular object types. To check the generation without creating new configuration objects, you can also simulate the procedure. In both cases, the Integration Builder shows the results in a detailed generation log. Figure 6.9 shows a screenshot of the log. The traffic lights in the log represent generation steps with errors (red traffic light), incomplete generation steps (yellow traffic light, as in Figure 6.9), and complete generation steps (green traffic light). If a generation step is incomplete, this means that you may have to add information that cannot be generated automatically, for example, routing conditions.

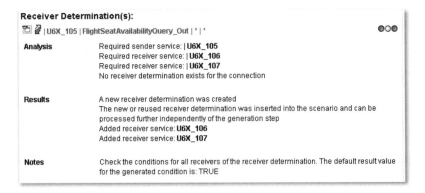

Figure 6.9 Generation Log

The Integration Builder automatically adds all generated and reused objects to the object list of your configuration scenario. You can also use the context menu for the connection to display the configuration objects belonging to each connection in the component view.

To finish the configuration, work through the generation log by navigating directly from the log to the corresponding objects and adding the missing information. The next section deals with the background knowledge necessary to complete the configuration.

6.3.2 Overview of Configuration Object Types

We've already looked at the configuration objects of the collaboration profile: party, service, and communication channel. Before examining other configuration objects, let's see how all the objects are related to one another.

Key Fields

Unlike the objects in the Integration Repository, the objects here are not organized using software component versions. Therefore, all configuration objects become globally visible in the Integration Directory as soon as they are released and are simultaneously activated for the runtime environment. Consequently, it's worth taking a closer look at the key fields of the objects. To simplify this overview, the objects are separated into three tables according to their use.

Key Fields	Object Type		
	Party	Service	Communication Channel
Service	(X)	X	
Communication Channel	(X)	X	X

Table 6.1 Key Fields for Objects of the Collaboration Profile

There is little more to say about the key fields of the objects of the collaboration profile in Table 6.1. There are services without a party, but no parties without a service. In objects without a party, the key field remains initial. The communication channel consists of the key fields of the higher-level service and its own name. As we have already determined, you choose the objects of the collaboration profile during the remaining configuration steps and determine the relationships between them. Therefore, the key fields of the service are always part of the key of the other configuration objects.

Key Fields	Object Type	
	Sender Agreement	Receiver Agreement
Sender party	(X)	(X)* (Header mapping)
Sender service	X	X* (Header mapping)
Outbound interface	X	
Namespace of the outbound interface	X	
Receiver party	(X)*	(X) (Header mapping)

Table 6.2 Key Fields for Sender and Receiver Agreements

Key Fields	Object Type	
	Sender Agreement	Receiver Agreement
Receiver service	X*	X (Header mapping)
Inbound interface		X*
Namespace of the inbound interface		X*

Table 6.2 Key Fields for Sender and Receiver Agreements (cont.)

Table 6.2 focuses on collaboration agreements. To ensure that the information in the table is complete, we added the following additional information to the table:

▶ The values from four fields of the receiver agreement can be mapped to other values using a header mapping. We'll examine the reasons for doing this in the cross-company scenarios in Section 6.4.

▶ Key fields marked with an asterisk (*) can be filled *generically*. Don't confuse these fields with the input fields in the Integration Builder that are marked with a red asterisk. The latter are *required* fields.

Generic and Specific Fields

You use generic fields to define the configuration for multiple cases by entering an asterisk in the field. For example, you can create a receiver agreement independently of a specific inbound interface. During message processing, the Integration Server checks for receiver determinations with matching key fields and selects the most specific. In some constellations, the Integration Builder cannot determine this due to overlapping. The Integration Builder checks this and notifies you during creation if this is the case. You must also be aware that generic configurations are valid globally in the Integration Directory. If several configuration scenarios use the same generic object, any changes to this object will result in side effects for all these scenarios.

The remaining two configuration objects are for logical routing. The key fields are displayed in Table 6.3. The virtual receiver is relevant to only cross-company communication, which we will look at in Section 6.4. If you don't specify a virtual receiver when creating a receiver determination, the Integration Builder inserts an asterisk for both fields (in other words, the receiver determination is independent of a virtual receiver).

We will now expand on this brief overview and look at the individual object types and their uses in more detail.

Key Fields	Object Type	
	Receiver Determination	Interface Determination
Sender party	(X)*	(X)*
Sender service	X*	X*
Outbound interface	X	X
Namespace of the out-bound interface	X	X
Receiver party	(X)* (Virtual receiver)	(X)*
Receiver service	X* (Virtual receiver)	X*

Table 6.3 Key Fields for Objects of Logical Routing

Collaboration Agreements

Senders and receivers of a message use a collaboration agreement to agree on the communication channel to be used to exchange messages. The obvious question here is what is meant by *sender* and *receiver*, since the Integration Server sends and receives messages, as do the application systems. Logically speaking, the Integration Server is situated between the application systems, therefore we need not just *one,* but *two* communication channels: one between each application system and the Integration Server. For this reason, there are collaboration agreements that define the channel on the sender side, and those that define the channel on the receiver side. Figure 6.10 illustrates this symmetry and the corresponding sender and receiver agreements.

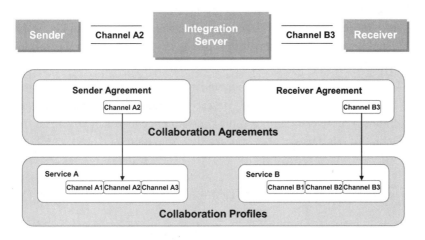

Figure 6.10 Sender and Receiver Agreements

You can see from the key fields of collaboration agreements in Table 6.2 that both the sender agreement and the receiver agreement have the sender service and the receiver service in their key. They are always intended for a communication pair, but each configures just one side of the communication with the Integration Server.

Sender and Receiver Agreement

Receiver agreements are *obligatory*, since the Integration Server must know which adapter to forward the message to. The situation is different on the sender side, because the sender adapter can use information from the SLD to determine the address of the Integration Server. In Section 6.5, we examine in more detail when sender agreements are necessary and why. The communication channel for the sender is also not absolutely necessary if the adapter can find the required configuration data itself.

Security Settings

The RNIF, CIDX, XI, and marketplace adapters also support security settings (signatures, authentication). The corresponding attributes are part of the respective communication channel, where you define whether and which security settings are supported. You configure these settings for a specific connection in the collaboration agreement.

Receiver and Interface Determination

The remaining task is to configure the logical routing. Logical routing has two steps:

▶ You use a *receiver determination* to define one or more receiver services for a message. You can define a condition for each receiver service in XPath or with context objects (see Section 4.4.3). There is no guaranteed receiver sequence for receiver services, and this is not important in stateless message processing. You encounter such requirements using integration processes, which are discussed in Chapter 8.

▶ You use an *interface determination* to define one or more inbound interfaces as receiver interfaces for the message. In this case, you define a receiver sequence using the sequence in which you enter the inbound interfaces in the interface determination.

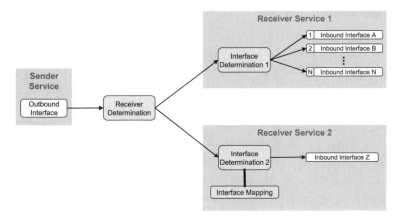

Figure 6.11 Example of Logical Routing

In the example in Figure 6.11, there are two receiver services, which are configured using a receiver determination for a sender service and an outbound interface. If conditions are specified in the receiver determination for the forwarding of the message, it is not a problem if these overlap. The Integration Server copies[3] the message for each true condition, generating a new message ID for each receiver service.

Copying Messages

Whether an interface determination is required depends on the configuration scenario. If a mapping is necessary, you definitely need an interface determination to configure the selection of mapping programs. We saw in Section 5.1.2 that you can bundle mapping programs for an interface pair by using an interface mapping. If you need to use a mapping, specify the interface mapping in the interface determination. If you use an integration scenario to generate the configuration, the interface mapping is entered automatically.

Configuring Mapping Programs

A mapping is not always necessary, because the sender and receiver both use the same interface technology, for example IDoc-IDoc communication or RFC-RFC communication using the Integration Server. In these cases, the name and namespace of the interface remain the same throughout the entire message transfer, and it is therefore not necessary to determine an interface. Outbound and inbound *message* interfaces, however, are located in different namespaces or have different names, which means that an interface determination is always necessary (even if no mapping is needed).

---

3 Somewhat misleadingly, this process is sometimes referred to as a *message split*, even though the message cannot be divided into smaller messages at this point. To split or merge messages, you need an integration process.

Configuration Overview

Besides the configuration scenarios, which bundle all the configuration objects of a scenario together, the Integration Builder also provides a *configuration overview*. This overview focuses on all objects that are required to process and forward messages to the receiver once the inbound processing in the Integration Server is complete: the receiver determination, the interface determination, and the receiver agreement. The Integration Server first uses the sender information in the message header to determine the configured receiver or receivers (receiver determination), then the configured inbound interface or interfaces and a corresponding interface mapping (interface determination), and finally, the communication channel (receiver agreement). Figure 6.12 illustrates this relationship. Information that arrives after the receiver determination is shown in gray.

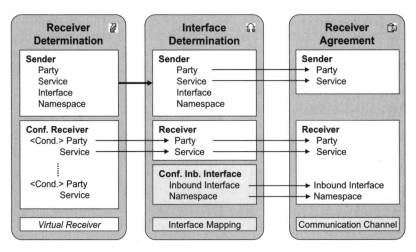

Figure 6.12 Configuration Based on Receiver Determinations

Since the processing steps proceed from the receiver determination, this is where the configuration overview is located. You can add configuration information to this table and navigate directly to the configuration objects listed there by double-clicking them.

The concepts that we have introduced so far are essentially sufficient to configure internal company configuration scenarios. However, even within a company it may be the case that the sender and receiver identify the same object in different ways. If this is the case, the receiver would then interpret the corresponding values in the message payload incorrectly. The next section explains how to handle such ambiguity using SAP XI.

6.3.3 Value Mapping

If the same objects are identified differently at the sender and receiver sides, you need a value mapping. As we saw in Section 5.1.1, SAP XI has a value-mapping table for all value mappings. Before we explain how to enter the source and target values of an object in the table, let's take a closer look at a table entry in Figure 6.13. To illustrate this point, we have taken a fictitious table entry from the Business-to-Business (B2B) world. This example involves a long-serving SAP employee, who orders from an online music store (Thomann) in his free time. At SAP, he is identified uniquely by his *employee number* (D000002). The online music store is not aware of any employee numbers and instead identifies the same person with a *customer number* (05940). Though unlikely, if SAP were to offer a service whereby its employees could place orders with the online music store using a B2B application and have the payments deducted from their salaries, these values would have to be mapped to each other.

Agency	Identification Scheme	Value	Agency	Identification Scheme	Value
SAP	EmployeeId	D000002	Thomann	CustomerId	05940
...	...	...	...	...	...

Source Values   Target Values

Figure 6.13 Entries in the Value-Mapping Table

A person is identified differently at SAP than at Thomann. We talk about different *representations* of the same object. The important thing is that the person in our example can be identified by the following trio:

Identifying Representations

▶ An *issuing agency*, which defines how an object (in our example a person) is to be uniquely identified. In our example, the issuing agency is the company SAP or the online music store.

▶ The agency uses an *identification scheme* to identify the object. In our example, this is the employee number or the customer number.

▶ The actual *value* for identification, according to the conventions of the identification scheme.

You use this trio (agency, identification scheme, value) to identify the *representation* of an object. It is up to you which representations you use in the value-mapping table, and depends on how the value of the representation is defined. The above example addresses cross-company communication. In the case of internal company communication, the following cases are possible:

▶ The issuing agency of the representation can be determined by the application components that exchange messages with each other, for instance APO or CRM.

▶ In a productive landscape, you can identify objects by their technical unit. In this case, the agency is the name of the business system and the identification scheme is determined by the object type (for example, the `Customer` object type for a business object).

If you want to execute value mappings within a Java mapping or a message mapping, you reference the values to be mapped by specifying the agency and the identification scheme in the mapping. Therefore, you need to consider how to identify values that are to be mapped at design time. You can enter the values in the value-mapping table in the following ways:

▶ Use the Integration Builder (Configuration) to enter all representations of an object in a **Value-Mapping Group**. Create a value-mapping group and enter all representations of the same object. To display the resulting value mappings, choose **Tools · Value Mapping...** in the main menu.

▶ Use the message interface `ValueMappingReplication` that is defined in the software component version `SAP Basis 6.40` in the namespace *http://sap.com/xi/XI/System*. SAP ships a Java server proxy for this inbound message interface, which executes the mass filling of the value-mapping table. For this filling, you implement the outbound side and configure the communication in exactly the same way as for any other configuration. Choose adapter type **XI** for your communication channel and specify the Java proxy runtime that runs on the same SAP Web AS on which the Integration Server is running.

The advantage of the first method is that it has object versioning and a transport connection for value-mapping groups. In the latter case, you access the value-mapping table in the runtime cache of the Integration Server directly. Therefore, you cannot call and edit entries made in this way in the Integration Builder.

The agency and identification scheme are not only relevant to value mappings, but also to cross-company communication, because there can be different representations for communication parties in B2B applications as well. This is discussed in more detail in the next section.

6.4 Configuring Cross-Company Processes

So far, we have focused on internal company processes. When configuring cross-company processes, you must consider the following additional configuration requirements:

▶ The companies must be able to be addressed as the sender and receiver of messages.

▶ Each company has an internal system landscape, which must not be revealed during communication with business partners.

▶ More importance is placed on standard protocols than in internal company communication.

As we have already seen in Section 6.3.1, using an integration scenario from the Integration Repository simplifies configuration considerably. The same is true for cross-company configuration scenarios. The only prerequisite is that you must identify the application components of your business partner as B2B components in the integration scenario (see Section 3.3.1). Similarly to internal company communication, the Integration Builder guides you through the configuration procedure and generates the missing objects automatically. Therefore, Section 6.4.1 just looks at the additional steps and differences in cross-company communication, and does not cover the individual configuration steps. It is assumed that both business partners are using SAP XI.

B2B Configuration Using Integration Scenarios

If your business partner does not have SAP XI, this does not make any difference to the configuration on your side of the communication. Your business partner has the following options:

▶ The business partner supports a standard protocol that SAP XI also supports, for example RNIF 2.0. Section 6.6 looks at adapters for industry standards.

▶ The business partner uses the Partner Connectivity Kit (PCK), which provides a limited selection of SAP XI features and is a more cost-effective alternative for smaller business partners. Section 6.4.2 looks at the PCK in more detail.

Furthermore, the Integration Server in SAP XI 3.0 understands the message protocol of the Integration Server in SAP XI 2.0. Figure 6.14 shows an overview of the possible variants.

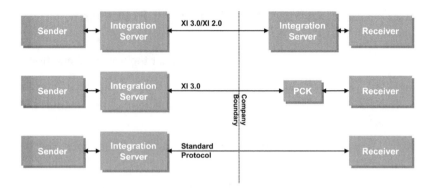

Figure 6.14 Variants of Cross-Company Communication

6.4.1 From Internal to Cross-Company Communication

In internal company communication, you work with services in the configuration that reference either business systems or integration processes. In cross-company communication, the company itself must also be addressed. To consider this in the configuration, we first have to clarify how to identify companies independently from SAP XI.

Identifiers for Companies

If two business partners want to exchange messages, they can simply agree on corresponding technical names (SAP, Bosch, ALDI). This is further simplified if all involved parties have a central agency issue an ID for their company. To do this, contact the agency to identify a company for the purposes of electronic message exchange. Unfortunately, this tried and tested method has one drawback: There are several agencies issuing such IDs on a worldwide scale, so the IDs alone are not unique. The following are examples of *issuing agencies*:

▶ 016: Dun & Bradstreet Corporation

▶ 009: EAN—International Article Numbering Association

▶ 166: NMFTA—National Motor Freight Traffic Association

As you can see from the list, issuing agencies are also numbered. Fortunately, there is only one agency that issues IDs for issuing agencies,[4] so this does not cause an additional problem. Therefore, each company has an *issuing agency* identify it via the *identification scheme* used by the agency and a *code*. (This is exactly the same as the trio that we encountered in value mapping in Section 6.3.3.) This trio is referred to as an *identifier*.

---

4 All issuing agencies are listed in the code list DE3055, which is managed by UN/EDIFACT (*www.unece.org/trade/untdid/welcome.htm*).

Normalization to XI Party

During configuration in the Integration Builder, you address companies by using the *communication party* object. The name of this object is required only within SAP XI and must be unique there. You specify *alternative identifiers* for this communication party (for example, `Bosch`), which can be used to identify the company. This makes the following conversion possible:

▶ **Normalization**
If the Integration Server receives a message with an identifier for a company (for example, a DUNS number), it can map it to the communication party in SAP XI.

▶ **Denormalization**
During configuration, you can stipulate which identifier the Integration Server writes in the message header before it forwards the message. In this way, the communication party in SAP XI is mapped to an identifier in the message header.

You choose which identifier to send in the communication channel for the receiver (**Identifiers** tab page). This conversion means that you have to reference the communication party object only when configuring a cross-company process, and all possible identifiers are automatically included.

However, some protocols have exceptions or enhancements, and these are listed below:

▶ In IDoc communication, you can work with IDoc partners. These must, in turn, be mapped to the communication party (see Section 6.5.2).

▶ Marketplaces based on the MarketSet Markup Language (MML) message format use a document destination ID (DDID) to address senders or receivers. The configuration object **communication party** is not needed in this case. Instead, you map the DDID to a service in the Integration Directory by entering it using the editor menu **Service · Adapter-Specific Identifier.**

We will now return to the general procedure and examine how you can provide services to your business partner without revealing details about your internal system landscape.

Business Services for Business Partners

To address services independently of the respective system landscape, you work with *business services*. Like all services, you can define business services with or without a party. The important thing is that the business service assumes the role of an alias for the business system service. If business partners exchange messages using SAP XI, you simply reference the business service. The names of the business services then appear in the message header instead of the names of the internal systems.

How do you configure this alias? As shown in Figure 6.15, each business partner has its own configuration area. Let us consider the configuration for the configuration area of `Party A`. `Party B` makes the configuration settings in the same way on the other side (when we refer to Party A and Party B in the following, we are referring to the person making the configuration settings, and not the configuration object).

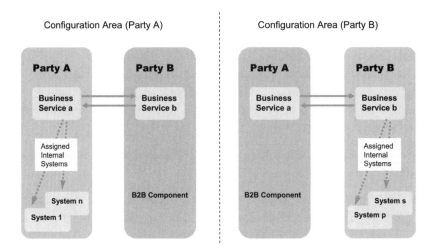

Figure 6.15 Configuration Areas

Party A uses business service a to mask its internal systems and exchanges messages with the business service b of Party B. Therefore, it must create both business services in its Integration Directory (Party B configures business services *with the same name* in its configuration area). To set the alias to the internal systems, it assigns business service a to one or more business system services during configuration.[5] It must also configure the

---

5 This is only possible when using an integration scenario. If there is no integration scenario, Party A must make the settings described below manually.

technical details of the message exchange by using communication channels:

▶ Since business service a has been assigned to the business system services, you can use the communication channels of these services.

▶ Party B must let Party A know how to access business service b (address of the Integration Server or PCK). Party A uses this information to create a communication channel of adapter type **XI**. Party A can also enter all relevant interfaces in business service b.

Let us assume that Party A sends a message to Party B and receives a message from Party B. Table 6.4 shows the attributes that the Integration Builder generates in the receiver agreement, and the receiver determination for the B2B-specific configuration.

Virtual Receiver and Header Mapping

Step	Configuration Object: Attribute(s)	Use
Send	**Receiver agreement**: Header mapping	Converts the *sender* business system service to the business service a and the communication party `Party A`.
Receive	**Receiver determination**: Virtual receiver	Logical routing of business service b to the internal business system services (receiver-dependent routing)

Table 6.4 Converting Business Services and Business System Services

You may have looked at the overview of the key fields and asked yourself why you can enter receiver information in the key of the receiver determination (see Table 6.3). You specify a *virtual* receiver in the key in the receiver determination to hide the *actual* receiver from outside parties. When sending, on the other hand, you must adapt the message header with a header mapping.

Moreover, if the payload contains the business service and the communication party, you can configure the header mapping in such a way that the values are read from the payload at runtime. This is just one way to enhance the static routing configuration dynamically. In Section 7.3, we'll see that the proxy runtime provides other methods for this purpose.

Payload-Based Routing

Header mapping and denormalization both modify the message header in the following order: First, you can use the header mapping to modify sender and receiver information, which you can then denormalize to an alternative identifier. Whether you need to do both depends on the

Header Mapping and Denormalization

application case. Besides the mapping of business system services to business services, you also use header mappings to delete or insert a communication party in the header, depending on whether or not the receiver adapter type requires this modification. If you don't use a header mapping or normalization, the Integration Server leaves the sender information as is when it receives the message.

We have now covered the central concepts of configuration. Of course, you may still have questions relating to specific configuration scenarios, but the sections in this chapter thus far have provided you with an understanding of how to use the individual configuration objects. Before we turn our attention to the differences between the various adapter types in Section 6.5, we will look at the Partner Connectivity Kit (PCK) as an addition to the central functions of XI.

6.4.2 Partner Connectivity Kit

SAP XI is a comprehensive solution for exchanging messages. However, in some cases, the advantages of SAP XI don't justify the costs and effort required to install and run it:

▶ A large company has a head office and several smaller branch offices, which are separate organizational units in different geographical locations. At the head office, systems are integrated using SAP XI. The branch offices need to exchange messages only with the head office.

▶ A large company that uses SAP XI would like to exchange messages with a smaller company. To make this message exchange possible, the smaller company needs only a selection of the SAP XI functions.

SAP provides the PCK as a supplementary solution for such cases.[6] SAP XI and the PCK are based on the same technology, although the features of the PCK are limited to smaller areas of operation:

▶ The PCK always forwards messages to an Integration Server and receives messages from an Integration Server. Therefore, you cannot use the PCK to exchange messages directly between two application systems.

▶ The PCK has the same interface as the Integration Builder, but the features are restricted to mappings (message, XSLT, and Java mappings) and the necessary configuration objects. No SLD is required.

---

6 The PCK is a separate product; it is not part of SAP XI and is therefore subject to separate licensing provisions.

▶ The PCK does not contain any routing logic. Each message can have only one receiver: either the Integration Server (send) or an application system that is connected using an adapter supported by the PCK. Mappings are supported in the PCK.

▶ The PCK offers the following adapters: file/FTP, JDBC, JMS, SOAP, RFC, BC, and mail adapter (see also Section 6.5.1). Customers can license additional SAP adapters or non-SAP adapters. The PCK uses the SAP XI adapter (SAP XI 3.0 protocol) to communicate with the Integration Server.

▶ If you have a development license, you can use the PCK to develop your own adapters for your system landscape.

Figure 6.16 gives you an idea of how to configure communication with the PCK. Due to the limited features in the PCK, you work with fewer configuration objects: communication party, business service, communication channel, mapping objects, and sender and receiver agreement. To simplify matters, you can specify the inbound interface and a mapping program in the receiver agreement in the PCK. Since the PCK does not support routing, the receiver agreement determines the receiver of the message directly. Therefore, the receiver determination and the interface determination that you know from the configuration of the Integration Server are not required in the PCK.

Configuration Objects in the PCK

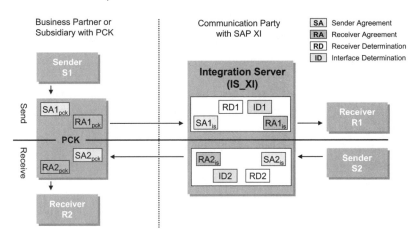

Figure 6.16 Configuration with the PCK

Let's take a brief look at configuration in the PCK with the help of the configuration objects in Figure 6.16. To understand the configuration procedure in the PCK, it helps to imagine the Integration Server as the receiver application system, and the PCK as the Integration Server. You configure the sender and receiver agreement between sender S1 and the Integration Server IS_XI accordingly (in this and the following step, whether you need the sender agreements SA1$_{pck}$, SA1$_{is}$, SA2$_{is}$, and SA2$_{pck}$ or not depends on the adapter type and on the encryption requirements). To understand the configuration in the Integration Server on the other hand, it helps to imagine the PCK as an application system and to make the configuration settings for forwarding the message normally using the receiver and interface determination. If you do this, a message from sender S1 is forwarded to the receiver R1 using the PCK and the Integration Server. Since there are the two intermediate stations (PCK and Integration Server), the specification of senders and receivers in the respective collaboration agreement is a little more complicated. Therefore, we have summarized the specifications in Table 6.5 (to keep matters simple, we have limited the table to the specification of S1, R1, S2, R2, and IS_XI instead of using the communication party and service). The direction is from the perspective of the PCK.

Direction	Collaboration Agreements	Sender	Receiver
Send	SA1pck, RA1pck	S1	IS_XI
	SA1is, RA1is	S1	R1
Receive	SA2is, RA2is	S2	R2
	SA2pck, RA2pck	S2	R2

Table 6.5 Sender and Receiver for Each Configuration Area

It is notable that the PCK specifies the Integration Server (in bold) as the communication party when sending to the Integration Server, but not in the receive direction. This is because the Integration Server sets the receiver in the message header, but leaves the sender unchanged. Furthermore, the Integration Server and the PCK address each other using a corresponding communication channel.

Now that we have covered the PCK, let's examine the details of adapter configuration.

6.5 Adapter Configuration

Adapters convert a transport protocol and a message format to XI proto-col, and vice versa. We will not look at every attribute of the individual adapters in this section, but instead focus on a few common features that are relevant to the configuration in the Integration Builder.

6.5.1 Overview

We already discussed adapter architecture and strategy in Section 1.2.1. The open architecture allows partners and customers to develop their own adapters and configure them centrally in the Integration Builder. This poses the question of how to describe the interface for configuring such adapters in the Integration Directory, because after the SAP XI installa-tion, the Integration Builder does not yet *know* these adapters. You enter the relevant information in the Integration Repository, and it is evaluated in the Integration Directory. You use adapter metadata to define the attributes that the adapter can handle and how the corresponding config-uration interface looks. SAP provides adapter metadata for adapters that are shipped by SAP.[7]

Adapter Type	Transport Protocol(s)	Message Protocol(s)
XI	HTTP(S)	XI 2.0, XI 3.0
IDoc	Sender adapter: tRFC, file Receiver adapter: tRFC (no sender channel configuration)	IDoc-XML
RFC	RFC	RFC-XML
SOAP	Sender channel: HTTP Receiver channel: HTTP, SMTP	SOAP 1.1
HTTP	HTTP(S) (no sender channel configuration)	XI payload in HTTP body
File	File system (NFS), FTP	File
JDBC	JDBC 2.0	XML insert format, XML SQL format, native SQL string

Table 6.6 Adapter Types

---

7 With SAP XI 3.0 in software component version *SAP BASIS 6.40* in the namespace *http://sap.com/xi/XI/System*.

Adapter Type	Transport Protocol(s)	Message Protocol(s)
JMS	SonicMQ MS Provider, WebSphereMQ (MQ Series) JMS Provider, JNDI JMS Provider Lookup, JMS Provider Administrator Objects via File, generic JMS Provider	JMS1.x
Marketplace	HTTP(S), JMS Sonic MQ35	MML
RNIF	HTTP(S)	RNIF 2.0
Mail	Sender channel: IMAP4, POP3 Receiver channel: SMTP, IMAP4	XIALL, XIPAYLOAD
BC (Business Connector)	HTTP(S)	RFC-XML with envelope

Table 6.6 Adapter Types (cont.)

We'll limit our focus to the adapter types that SAP ships with SAP XI. Table 6.6 gives an overview of the adapters shipped together with the SAP XI 3.0 Feature Pack. Let's now take a more detailed look at some of the configuration aspects that apply to several of the aforementioned adapter types.

Central and Non-Central Adapter Engine (All Adapter Types Except IDoc)

With the exception of the IDoc adapter, all adapters in Table 6.6 run on the Adapter Engine, which you install centrally on the Integration Server or deploy non-centrally on a separate SAP J2EE Engine. The latter case is recommended when you want or need the Adapter Engine to run in close proximity to the business system, whether for organizational or technical reasons (for example, operating-system requirements for back-end-specific drivers such as JDBC or JMS, or performance or memory requirements). You select the Adapter Engine in the communication channel. The Adapter Engine will be responsible for inbound or outbound processing on the Integration Server.

Obligatory Sender Agreement (File/JMS/JDBC)

In order to process a message at the inbound channel of the Integration Server, the Integration Server retrieves the required information from the message header at runtime and evaluates the existing configuration data. To do this, the Integration Server needs information about the sender interface and the interface namespace, among other things. However, sender file, sender JMS, and sender JDBC adapters cannot provide this information, because the protocols don't require an interface. Therefore, the corresponding fields in the message header are empty. To enable messages to be exchanged, you must therefore configure the missing information in the Integration Directory:

▶ A sender channel that has exactly one sender agreement.

▶ A sender interface (name and namespace) and a sender service in the sender agreement. You are free to choose these values. The remaining fields in the sender agreement are optional.

The aforementioned entries are mandatory to configure the sender file, sender JMS, and sender JDBC adapters. All other adapter types in Table 6.6 provide the necessary information in the message header. An example of when the sender channel and sender agreement are necessary for these adapters is when you need to make message security settings on the sender side.

It is not absolutely necessary to have an interface for outbound processing in the Integration Server. Therefore, you can enter an asterisk (*) as a generic interface in the receiver agreement instead, so that the receiver is determined only by the service. However, if you want to execute a mapping before outbound processing, this changes matters. Since mapping programs are referenced using interface mappings, you need an interface on the receiver side (see Section 5.1.2) at design time. Because no such interface exists for the file, JMS, and JDBC adapters, you can use an abstract message interface to help you. This interface type is an option, because the interface is intended only for interface mapping and not for implementation in an application system with proxies, which don't exist for these adapter types.

Configuring Outbound Processing

Security Settings

There are various areas in the configuration of security settings. Most adapters support authentication in the receiver system using logon data (XI, SOAP, RNIF, RFC, Marketplace, Mail, JDBC, HTTP, BC). Some adapters also support HTTPS and, in some cases, message security.

HTTPS (XI, HTTP, Marketplace, RNIF, BC)

HTTPS is HTTP with the additional support of a *secure sockets layer* (SSL) and relates to security on the transport level. HTTPS is part of the transport protocol, and is therefore configured in the communication channel. If you select **HTTPS** as the **Transport Protocol** in the receiver channel, you must specify a corresponding HTTPS port in the **Service Number** input field of the channel. You also have to configure this HTTPS port in SAP Web AS (for the Integration Server) and in the receiver to be able to use the required certificates.

You enter an HTTP destination for receiving and sending messages in the HTTP adapter, and you must specify whether HTTP or HTTPS is to be used for this destination.

HTTPS in the Sender Channel When you look at the other adapters, at first it may strike you as odd that, apart from the RNIF adapter, you cannot specify HTTPS as the transport protocol in the sender channel, although you can do so in the receiver channel. Does this mean that the other adapters can only send HTTPS and not receive it? The answer is no. To help you understand, let's compare the SAP XI adapter with the RNIF adapter:

▶ For the SAP XI adapter, it's always a SAP Web AS that sends messages to the Integration Server. Because SAP Web AS supports the HTTPS protocol (ICF framework), you configure it there as well.

▶ The standardized message exchange of RNIF requires the RNIF adapter to respond to an external partner with a signal as soon as a message arrives at the Integration Server. To send this signal using HTTPS, you choose **HTTPS** in the sender agreement in the RNIF adapter. The sender channel of the RNIF adapter therefore has an outbound semantic for sending this signal.

With HTTPS, security can be guaranteed only at the transport level, that is, for the transfer path. The message content continues to be visible to the receiver (in a trace, for example).

Message Security (XI, RNIF)

The next level of security settings is at the message level. To configure message security, you specify whether it is required in the SAP XI or RNIF communication channel. Since signatures and encryptions are always agreed upon by the sender and receiver, you specify the actual certificates, views, and so on in the collaboration agreement. Therefore, the configuration settings in the communication channel represent a sort of declaration of intent, and the collaboration agreement references the algorithms to be used.

To explain all the properties of the individual adapters would exceed the scope of this book. Therefore, the next section focuses on a few special features of the RFC and IDoc adapters. Since the RNIF adapter is conceptually different from all other adapter types, it is addressed separately in Section 6.6.

6.5.2 Special Features of the RFC and IDoc Adapters

The RFC adapter converts an RFC call to RFC-XML and sends it to the Integration Server. Conversely, the RFC adapter receives RFC-XML from the Integration Server and then generates an RFC call at the receiver. Correspondingly, in communication with the IDoc adapter, the Integration Server sends and receives IDoc-XML.

This section does *not* explain how to configure the RFC and IDoc adapters to exchange messages with the Integration Server. Instead, it looks at how the adapters map the information to the configuration objects of the Integration Directory in an RFC or IDoc. It will become clear from this explanation just how you can configure the message exchange with these adapters in the Integration Directory.

Mapping Logical Systems to Services

During configuration in the Integration Directory, you work with services. The Integration Server expects information in the message header about which service has sent the message and uses the configuration data to assign a receiver service. But how does the name of the service get into the message header?

In the last section, we saw that you must configure a sender channel and a sender agreement for sender file, sender JMS, and sender JDBC adapters, to add to the message header. This is not necessary in RFC and IDoc adapters, because the adapters can determine the service name by using an *adapter-specific identifier*. The following identifiers exist for RFC and IDoc adapters:

Adapter-Specific Identifiers

▶ **SAP system ID and client**
SAP systems set the system ID (for example, U6X) and the client (for example, 105) in the RFC or IDoc control record.

▶ **Logical system**
This field can be set arbitrarily by external IDoc senders. The field is not evaluated if SAP systems are communicating with the Integration Server.

The RFC and IDoc adapters can access these identifiers and map them to service names as follows:

1. The SAP system ID, client, and logical system are available in the sender SAP system as well as in the SLD. They are attributes of the business system that you have configured (see Section 6.2.1). When a business system is assigned to a business system service, the Integration Builder transfers the identifiers from the SLD to the Integration Directory. To view which identifiers have been transferred from the SLD for the service, choose **Service · Adapter-Specific Identifiers...** in the menu.

2. Sender SAP systems set the SAP system ID and the client in the RFC or IDoc control record at runtime. External IDoc senders set the logical system.

3. RFC and IDoc adapters read the adapter-specific identifiers from the Integration Directory and compare them with the information from the RFC or IDoc control record. The adapter determines the service name in this way, and writes it in the message header.

To map the identifiers to the service, it is sufficient to have entered the business system in the SLD. Therefore, the adapter-specific identifiers in the Integration Builder are read-only. By using the menu options from the first step, you can not only view the identifiers for the RFC and IDoc adapters, but also enter a DDID identifier for the marketplace adapter. This identifier cannot be entered in the SLD and fulfils the same purpose as the identifiers for the RFC and IDoc adapters.

Mapping IDoc Partners to XI Parties

We saw in Section 6.4.1 that the Integration Server normalizes identifiers from external business partners to the XI party so that it only has to reference this XI party in the configuration. In the IDoc world, you can use partner types for a message exchange using EDI, for example, logical system (LS), customer (KU), or vendor (LI). If IDoc communication is to take place using the Integration Server, the following differentiation is important:

▶ IDoc partners of type LS exchange messages with the Integration Server at the service level. In this case, the IDoc adapter leaves the communication party field in the message header empty. The mapping to the service was covered in the previous section.

▶ For all other IDoc partner types, the IDoc adapter generates an alternative identifier for the external party in the message header, according to the following rules:

▶ The name of the sender service (determined as described in the previous section) determines the *issuing agency*. For example: U6X_106.

▶ The name for the *identification scheme* is formed from the partner type and, optionally, the partner role, thus ALE#<Partner type> or ALE#<Partner type>#<Partner role>. For example: ALE#KU.

▶ The partner number of the IDoc is taken as the partner name. For example: 0000010053.

To map IDoc partners of this latter type to XI parties, proceed as described under *Normalization to XI Party* in Section 6.4.1. Enter the alternative identifier generated by the IDoc adapter in the XI communication party to which the IDoc partner is to be mapped. You select the identification scheme that is to be sent in outbound processing of the Integration Server in the communication channel later.

XI Party with Business System Service

An additional factor to consider is that, unlike external business partners, partner types in IDoc communication are used for internal company scenarios. If you map IDoc partners to XI parties, you must therefore assign a business system service to the XI party by creating the business system service at the XI party. (This is one of the few cases where a business system service and communication party are required in the key in configuration.) In Figure 6.17, the business system service U6X_106 is assigned to XI party IDocPartner. The key of this service therefore comprises both fields.

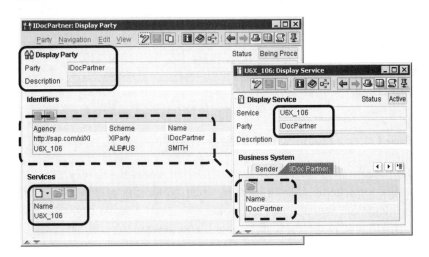

Figure 6.17 Business System Service with XI Party for IDoc

The Integration Builder uses the alternative identifiers in the XI parties to determine which XI parties reference the service U6X_106 and lists them on the **IDoc Partner** tab page of the service (in this example, IDocPartner).

Example In the example[8] in Figure 6.18, two IDoc partners with a partner type other than LS (logical system) exchange IDocs using the Integration Server. In B6M_000, the sender party is registered as user SMITH, and in XID_112 it is registered as a customer with the customer number 0000010053. To map the sender parties to one another, proceed as follows:

1. Create a communication party Party_One in the Integration Directory and assign the business system service B6M_000 to this party.

2. Enter the alternative IDoc partners for the sender under **Alternative Identifiers** for the communication party Party_One: B6M_000 | ALE#US | SMITH and XID_112 | ALE#KU | 0000010053. This enables the Integration Server to recognize during inbound processing that the message with the sender information B6M_000 | ALE#US | SMITH | B6M_000 belongs to the communication party Party_One | B6M_000 (normalization).

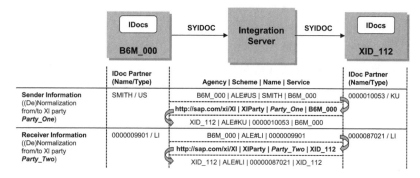

Figure 6.18 Case Example for (De)normalization with IDocs

3. In the receiver channel for the connection, select the agency XID_112 and the scheme ALE#KU for the sender. As a result of this setting, the Integration Server writes the sender XID_112 | ALE#KU | 0000010053 | B6M_000 in the message header (denormalization).

---

8 For more information about these and other IDoc configuration scenarios, see SAP Service Marketplace at *service.sap.com/netweaver* • *SAP NetWeaver* • *Media Library* • *How-to Guides* • *Exchange Infrastructure* • *How To Sample IDoc Scenarios within XI3.0*.

In the same way, you must create a communication party `Party_Two` for the mapping of the receiver parties. Select scheme `XID_112 | ALE#LI` in the same receiver channel as in Step 3.

The sender and receiver in our example are identified by different IDoc partners. To conclude this section, we draw your attention to a similar IDoc scenario: If the receiver in our example was an IDoc partner of type `LS` (logical system), you would have to delete the sender and receiver party from the message header for the receiver system `XID_112`. In this case, instead of denormalizing using the receiver channel, you would use a header mapping (receiver agreement) to map these fields to empty values.

IDocs Without Partners

Once again, we see that the functions in the Integration Builder support as many configuration scenarios as possible. Unfortunately, we can't describe them all in this book. Before we turn our attention to the transport of configuration data in Section 6.7, the next section addresses one final scenario: using the RNIF adapter to support the RosettaNet industry standard.

6.6 Adapters for Industry Standards

If two business partners want to exchange data with one another, they must use the same data exchange format. The business partners must also negotiate on aspects such as data security and the data exchange procedure until they reach an agreement. Coordinating these issues can involve considerable costs and, consequently, an increasing number of industries are cooperating to agree on standards for data exchange.

In the high-tech industry, RosettaNet is a consortium of world-leading companies in the information technology, electronic component, semiconductor manufacturing, and telecommunication sectors. This self-funded consortium produces industry-wide, open e-business process standards for harmonizing processes between supply-chain partners worldwide. This section examines the RosettaNet standards adopted by this consortium and how they are supported in SAP XI.[9]

RosettaNet

---

9   SAP XI 3.0 SP09 also supports the CIDX standard of the chemical industry.

6.6.1 RosettaNet Standards

RosettaNet has adopted the following specifications (presented here in a simplified version) to define standards:[10]

▶ **Partner Interface Processes (PIPs)**
RosettaNet models processes in a supply chain based on PIPs. A PIP specifies how business partners interact in different roles (for example, buyer and seller). This specification includes the sequence and content of the messages to be exchanged, as well as the duration, security settings, and authentication of the interactions.

▶ **RosettaNet Implementation Framework (RNIF)**
PIPs are *executed* using the RosettaNet Implementation Framework. The RNIF specification determines the message exchange protocol at the transport, routing, packaging, and transaction level, *irrespective of the content* of the messages to be exchanged. There are two RNIF versions: 1.1 and 2.0. The RNIF adapter supports RNIF 2.0.

The RosettaNet standards do more than merely define a message protocol; a PIP also determines the sequence of multiple messages. Before we examine the implications for using RosettaNet with SAP XI, let's take a closer look at PIPs.

PIPs A PIP describes a *business transaction* that is part of a higher-level process. For organizational purposes, PIPs are divided into clusters and segments representing the corresponding business areas. Figure 6.19 shows an example for PIP3A4. Various different PIPs are required to execute a higher-level process. Therefore, the complexity of a PIP is relatively low.

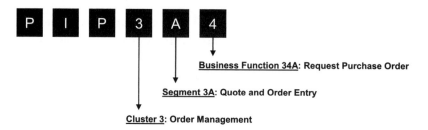

Figure 6.19 Naming Conventions for PIPs

RosettaNet defines the content of a PIP using document type definitions (DTDs), which belong to the PIP. A PIP also describes the sequence of

---

10 For more information, see the RosettaNet homepage at *www.rosettanet.org*.

messages for the particular business case. There are two types of messages:

▶ **RosettaNet action messages**
These messages are defined and are part of the PIP. They contain the business data, for example, for a purchase order.

▶ **RosettaNet signal messages**
These messages are confirmations of RosettaNet action messages. As a rule, they are asynchronous.

The message sequence always follows the same pattern, specified in RNIF 2.0: There are synchronous and asynchronous *single-action* and *two-action* patterns. Figure 6.20 shows the model for the exchange of asynchronous messages. Communication parties that support RNIF must be able to assume the role of both initiator and responder.

Single-Action Asynchronous

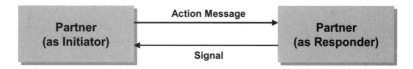

Two-Action Asynchronous

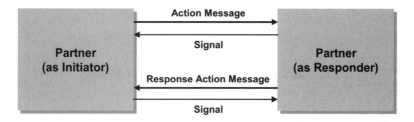

Figure 6.20 Asynchronous Single-Action and Two-Action Patterns

Keeping these basic points in mind, let's look at how SAP XI supports the execution of PIPs.

6.6.2 RosettaNet Support with SAP XI

To start with, let's clarify what it means for an SAP customer to have SAP XI support the RosettaNet standards. Figure 6.21 shows the implementation of RosettaNet communication with SAP XI as an extension of Figure 6.20.

► From the point of view of the business partner, it exchanges messages using RosettaNet standards. To do this, it communicates using the RNIF adapter of the Integration Server as if it were any other communication party that supports RNIF 2.0.

► A customer that uses SAP XI can offer a business partner message exchange using RosettaNet for certain SAP applications. The SAP application must meet the following requirements:

  ► It must provide interfaces that can be mapped to the interfaces specified by the corresponding PIP.

  ► It must provide the mapping programs required for this mapping.

Any message protocol can be used between the SAP system and the Integration Server, but it must be converted to RNIF for the business partner. To date, SAP XI supports only asynchronous single-action or two-action process types.

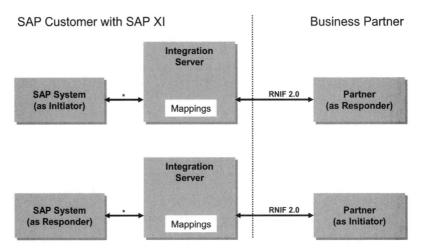

Figure 6.21 RNIF Communication with SAP XI

SAP Business Package

With regard to the basic principle, additional design objects are required as well as the RNIF adapter to support a RosettaNet standard. It is SAP's responsibility to develop these design objects and ship them as process integration content of the Integration Repository. For this purpose, SAP offers its customers *SAP business packages*, which contain the following:

► Integration scenarios for selected PIPs. We'll look at this in more detail below.

► Interfaces and mappings of the SAP application that customers use to implement the RNIF communication for selected PIPs.

▶ Communication channel templates, which simplify the configuration of the RosettaNet scenario considerably.

Table 6.7 lists all PIPs that are contained in the first SAP business package.

PIP	Business Transaction
PIP3A4	Request Purchase Order
PIP3A7	Notify of Purchase Order Update
PIP3A8	Request Purchase Order Change
PIP3A9	Request Purchase Order Cancellation
PIP3B2	Notify of Advance Shipment
PIP3C3	Notify of Invoice
PIP3A6	Distribute Order Status
PIP3C6	Notify of Remittance Advice[12]

Table 6.7 PIPs of the SAP Business Package for Industry Standards

Now we'll use an example to illustrate how RNIF communication is modeled using integration scenarios in the SAP business package. Each PIP has three integration scenarios:

▶ One integration scenario in which the RosettaNet standard is modeled. These integration scenarios are located in the software component version ROSETTANET 1.0.

▶ One integration scenario for modeling an SAP application in the role of initiator and one for the role of responder. These scenarios are located in the software component version ROSETTANET R3 1.0, which references the underlying software component version ROSETTANET 1.0. This enables these scenarios to use the basis objects of the RosettaNet standard.

Figure 6.22 shows an example for PIP3B2 and an SAP application in the role of responder (R3 MM as Receiver). In the same way, SD in the second integration scenario (not shown) PIP3B2_Shipper from ROSETTA-NET R3 1.0 assumes the role of initiator.

---

11 While working on this book, PIP3C6 was not yet released for the business package.

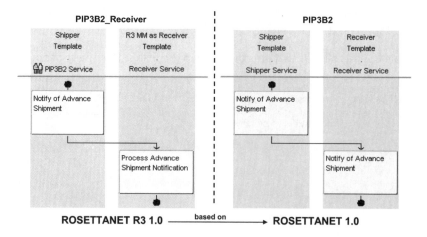

Figure 6.22 PIP3B2 as Integration Scenario

During configuration, you reference the integration scenario from the software component version ROSETTANET R3 1.0 in each case. These integration scenarios reference the interface mappings for RNIF communication.

Abstract Message Interfaces One final point to mention is that all actions of the integration scenarios of ROSETTANET 1.0 reference abstract message interfaces. The reason behind this is that the RosettaNet methodology does not make any differentiation between outbound and inbound, and therefore the interfaces modeled in RosettaNet can be used for both directions.

This concludes the description of the configuration concepts. In the next section, we'll consider how to transport configuration objects between different Integration Directories.

6.7 Transports Between the Test and Productive Landscape

Section 3.2.3 discussed transports between different Integration Repositories. These transports are important for the organization of a development and a shipment landscape.

The Integration Directory contains the configuration for runtime. Therefore, we recommend that you test the configuration in a test landscape before transporting the configuration data to a productive landscape. SAP XI provides the same transport options for this purpose as for Integration Repositories. Of course, there are some differences, as design and configuration objects serve different purposes and are organized in a singular way:

▶ **Transport units**

Since configuration objects are not shipped, there are no software component versions in the Integration Directory. You can either transport all configuration objects or use a configuration scenario (see Section 6.1) or the object hierarchy (see Figure 6.23) to specify a selection.

▶ **Versioning**

The transport between Integration Directories is not concerned with keeping object versions of different Integration Repositories consistent. When an object is transported to a target directory, the Integration Builder always creates a new object version. Therefore, the import sequence is important.

▶ **Adaptations**

To avoid messages being sent from the productive landscape to the test landscape, the Integration Builder limits the transportable attributes of the configuration objects. The adapter metadata from the Integration Repository specifies which attributes in the communication channel are transportable and which are not. (Non-transportable attributes are not exported.) Once the import in the Integration Directory is complete, you have to revise the imported configuration. For this reason, the Integration Builder puts configuration objects in a change list after import. You can make any necessary changes to these objects before you release them for runtime.

The transport environment converts some attributes of the configuration objects automatically. For example, the address of a non-central Adapter Engine is converted to the Adapter Engine of the Integration Server, because the non-central address is no longer valid in the target landscape. Furthermore, the names of the technical systems also change in the target landscape. It would be an arduous task to assign the new technical names to all business systems in the SLD. Instead, SAP XI provides a mechanism that converts the names of business systems automatically during transports to a target directory:

Conversions

1. The system data in the central SLD refers to your whole system landscape. You enter the technical systems and business systems there, for both the source and target landscape.

2. To keep business systems from the source and target landscape separate, you define a group for each landscape in the SLD. You then create a business system group for the respective Integration Server of the landscape (in the **Business Landscape** area of the SLD). All business

Business System Groups

systems that are assigned to the Integration Server are automatically part of this group.

3. To convert the business systems, you must assign a business system from the target landscape group to each business system from the source landscape group. To do this, you specify the transport target directly in the business system of the source landscape (see Figure 6.23).

In Figure 6.23, the business systems BS1 and BS2 belong to the Test group. The business system BSA is entered in the SLD as the transport target for BS1, and BSB is entered as the transport target for BS2. The Integration Builder thus converts the names of the business systems from the Test group to the names of the business systems from the Productive group during directory transports. This also works with more than two Integration Directories: You can therefore transport configuration objects from a test directory to a consolidation directory, and from there to a productive directory, and convert the names of the business systems using the corresponding groups in the process.

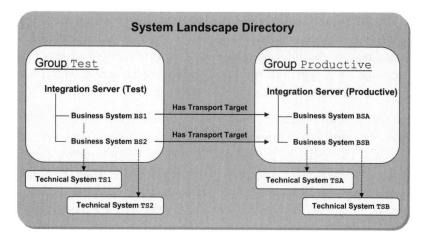

Figure 6.23 Mapping Business Systems Using Transport Targets

This chapter has provided a comprehensive description of configuration in the Integration Directory. In the next chapter, we look at the runtime components of SAP XI. We'll see that programming with proxies does not overwrite the configuration; rather, it enables you to enhance the configuration in a dynamic way.

7 Runtime

This chapter looks at the runtime components of SAP XI and how you can check them in monitoring. The focus of the chapter will be on the Integration Engine as the most important Integration Server component, and the proxy runtime as the runtime environment for programming with ABAP and Java proxies.

7.1 Introduction

In the last chapter, we learned that you can use adapters to connect many different application systems to the Integration Server. Of course, each adapter has its own protocol and programming model in the application, which exceeds the scope of this book and therefore is not included. For this reason, Section 7.3 covers only the new programming model for message interfaces from the Integration Repository. Since the interfaces here are based on Web Service Definition Language (WSDL), Section 7.3.2 explains the role played by proxies for Web services, and vice versa. However, to better understand how messages are processed, we'll begin by concentrating on the technical aspects of the Integration Engine in Section 7.2. Finally, in Section 7.4, we'll provide you with an overview of monitoring.

7.2 Integration Server and Integration Engine

All messages that are processed by SAP XI pass through the Integration Server. The Integration Server is implemented in ABAP on SAP Web AS 6.40 and uses its middleware technology, for example, the Internet Connection Framework (ICF). In this section, we provide you with an overview of the configuration of the Integration Engine (and the Integration Server) and look at message processing. Unlike configuration in the Integration Directory, the technical configuration described in this section is predominantly the system administrator's task.

7.2.1 Basics

Once you've installed SAP Web AS, you create clients for the ABAP side. **Clients** Each client can have the role of either a sender or receiver. Note the following two cases:

► You want to use the RFC or IDoc adapter to exchange messages with the Integration Server. In this case, the IDoc adapter and the Adapter Engine, respectively, are responsible for messaging with the Integration Server.

► You want to use proxies to exchange messages with the Integration Server. In this case, a local Integration Engine on SAP Web AS looks after messaging. When we look at the receivers and senders of messages in Section 7.2, we will concentrate on communication using ABAP proxies.

Configuration as the Integration Server
We now know that the local Integration Engine of the business system is responsible for messaging tasks when communicating with the Integration Server. To configure an SAP Web AS as the Integration Server, you must specify a client in which the Integration Engine is configured as the central Integration Server. Therefore, the client for the Integration Server uses the same runtime component as clients to which you give the role of an application system: the *Integration Engine*. The difference is that besides the messaging logic for receiving and sending messages, you can use the Integration Engine that is configured as the Integration Server to call additional services (for example, routing and mapping). For each SAP Web AS, there can be only one client in which an Integration Engine is configured as the Integration Server. Figure 7.1 shows an example. The local Integration Engines can exchange messages only by connecting to the Integration Engine that is configured as the Integration Server. If a client on the SAP Web AS is configured as the Integration Server in a productive system landscape, you must not use any other Integration Engines on that SAP Web AS.

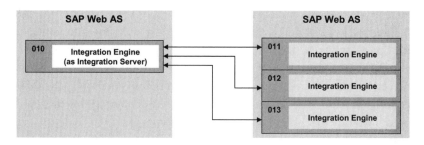

Figure 7.1 Integration Engines on SAP Web AS

Global and Specific Configuration Data
In the original status of a client, the Integration Engine is configured neither as a local Engine nor as the Integration Server. To define the role of a business system, you must configure the *global configuration data* in the

relevant client. To do so, in transaction SXMB_ADM, choose the entry **Integration Engine Configuration**. The Integration Engine cannot function without the global configuration data. In the same transaction, you can construct *specific configuration data* to optimize the exchange of messages or to tailor it to meet your requirements. The global and specific configuration data is client-specific, and the transaction saves it in a customizing table.

The processing steps of the message are collected in a *pipeline* for each Integration Engine. Each processing step is handled by a pipeline element, which calls a pipeline service. In this way, pipeline services can be called by different pipeline elements. The composition of the pipeline element here is strictly defined by SAP. XI runtime creates a separate instance of the pipeline for each message to be processed; this pipeline is then used exclusively to process the message until all pipeline elements have been worked through. The term *pipeline* is used because runtime processes the *sender pipeline*, the *central pipeline* (the pipeline for the Integration Engine configured as the Integration Server), and the *receiver pipeline* one after the other.

Structure of the Integration Engine

We'll end this section with a look at how a message that is processed by the Integration Engine is structured. The XI message protocol is based on the World Wide Web Consortium (W3C) note *SOAP Messages with Attachments*.[1] The Integration Server expects the message to be structured as shown in Figure 7.2. Therefore, all sender adapters convert a call or message from the sender to this format; the proxy runtime creates this format directly. The SOAP header of a message contains all the important information that the Integration Server requires to forward the message, while the *payload* contains the actual business data. In proxy communication, you can also append an unlimited number of attachments to the message before it is sent. Attachments typically comprise non-XML data, for example, pictures, text documents, or binary files. The information in the message header must have the correct format for the message to be processed on the Integration Server. The payload is not touched unless the data needs to be mapped. When you view messages in message monitoring, you will recognize the structure of the message from Figure 7.2.

Structure of a Message

Building on what we have learned so far, in the next section we'll look at how the Integration Engine processes messages.

---

1 For more information, see *www.w3.org/TR/SOAP-attachments*.

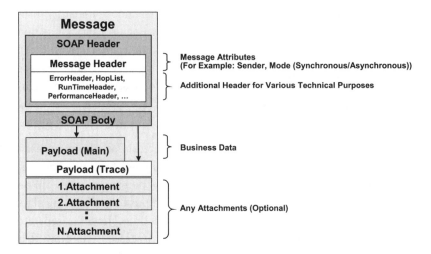

Figure 7.2 Message Format of the XI Message Protocol

7.2.2 Processing Steps of a Message

Quality of Service The way that the Integration Engine processes messages depends on the *quality of service* (QoS). Together, the proxy runtime (ABAP and Java), local Integration Engine, and Integration Server support the following qualities of service:

▶ **Best Effort (BE)**
Synchronous message processing; the sender waits for an answer before continuing with processing.

▶ **Exactly Once (EO)**
Asynchronous message processing; the sender does not wait for an answer before continuing with processing. The Integration Engine guarantees that the message is sent and processed exactly once.

▶ **Exactly Once In Order (EOIO)**
The same as EO quality of service, except that the application can serialize messages by using a queue name. The Integration Engine delivers the messages in this queue in the sequence in which they were sent from the sender system.

Since the local Integration Engine exchanges messages with the Integration Server when proxies are used for communication, all qualities of service mentioned above are supported for proxy communication. Which adapter supports which quality of service depends on the adapter. In this case, Adapter Engine messaging ensures the relevant quality of service and executes the inbound or outbound processing on the Integration Server.

To make things easier, we'll focus on message processing using ABAP proxies in the following example. We'll begin by looking at how the Integration Engine processes asynchronous messages. In both the EO and EOIO QoS cases, the Integration Engine accesses the *qRFC inbound scheduler* on SAP Web AS. The following qRFC queues are used:

Asynchronous Processing

▶ Queues for sending and receiving messages. For EO QoS, the Integration Engine distributes the messages to different queues. The various different queues have fixed prefixes that correspond to the way in which they are used. The name suffixes are used to distribute the messages to different queues that are used in the same way.

For EOIO QoS, all messages share a queue; the suffix of this queue must be set explicitly in the application program by a *serialization context* before the client proxy is called (see also Section 7.3). This means that the EOIO queue acts as a blocker queue. For EO, the Integration Engine distributes the messages at random. If an EO queue contains a message with errors, whether or not the message is removed from the queue depends on the type of error (whether subsequent messages are more or less likely to terminate with the same error also depends on the type of error).

▶ Queues for returning acknowledgments for asynchronous messages to the sender. To ensure that acknowledgments are sent back along the same path as the corresponding request message but in the opposite direction, the Integration Engine uses the hoplist of the message header and *backward pipelines*.

▶ A queue that is specially reserved for unusually large EO messages. By using specific configuration parameters, you can define the minimum size of messages that are processed separately in this queue.

Before you can exchange asynchronous messages at the sender, at the receiver, and on the Integration Server, you must first register the qRFC queues in transaction SXMB_ADM.

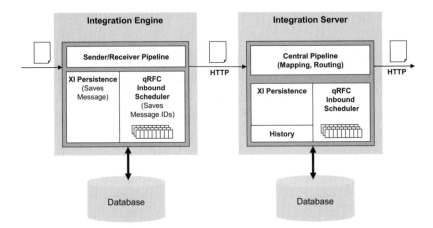

Figure 7.3 Asynchronous Message Processing

We will now use Figure 7.3 to follow the processing of an asynchronous message. We'll start with processing in the local Integration Engine at the sender:

1. A proxy call in the application program (not shown in Figure 7.3) provides the local Integration Engine with the payload, attachments, and other details for the message header, which the Integration Engine uses to structure the message as illustrated in Figure 7.2. At the same time, a message ID is created for the message.

2. The Integration Engine persists the entire message by using an XI persistence layer, and schedules processing in the qRFC inbound scheduler via a function module. The function module merely references the message ID.

3. Processing of the application program continues after the next COMMIT WORK statement.

4. The qRFC inbound scheduler processes the scheduled function module calls by using the round-robin algorithm: The queues have the same time slot in the default setting, therefore, the scheduler takes the same amount of time to process each queue. If you require prioritized message processing, you can increase the time slot for particular queues and distribute messages to these queues via a filter.

5. As soon as the qRFC inbound scheduler calls the scheduled function module, the latter reads the message from the XI persistence layer. The sender pipeline then sends the message by using HTTP.

Prioritized Message Processing

The sequence of steps is similar at the inbound channel of the Integration Server, except for the following differences:

▶ On the Integration Server, the caller that sends the messages to the Integration Engine is not the proxy from the application program, but the local Integration Engine at the sender.

▶ The qRFC inbound scheduler on the Integration Server schedules messages for processing in the central pipeline. The *history* is a table in which the Integration Engine saves the message ID and the status of the message at the end of each processing step. In this way, the Integration Engine can still guarantee the Exactly Once quality of service, even if the message has already been deleted or archived from the XI persistence layer.

▶ New message IDs are created only if multiple receivers are determined for the message during logical routing. In this case, the Integration Engine generates a new message with a new message ID for each receiver, and then persists each one.

The process repeats with the local Integration Engine at the receiver. When processing messages asynchronously, the Integration Engine works *as much as possible* like a tRFC (for EO) or a qRFC (for EOIO): Temporary application data and Integration Engine calls are written to the database together (as an atomic action) in a COMMIT WORK. However, unlike tRFC or qRFC, different Integration Engine calls within a transaction are also sent in different messages. Each Integration Engine call generates a separate independent message. The logical unit of work (LUW) that encompasses the individual calls is not transported to the target of the call.

Commit Handling

Unlike the course of action that occurs during asynchronous processing, synchronous calls are not put in the queue for the qRFC inbound scheduler; instead, they act as blockers for the relevant callers (the application program and Integration Engine). If the request message is processed successfully at the receiver, a new message ID is generated for the response message. The connection between the latter and the original request message is not lost, because the runtime references the message ID of the request message in the header of the response message (in the header field RefToMessageId). As far as the database commit (DB_COMMIT) is concerned, the Integration Engine functions in exactly the same way as it does during a synchronous RFC call.

Synchronous Processing

Additional Configuration Options

Finally, we'll give you an overview of how you can influence message processing in other ways:

▶ **Time-Controlled Message Processing**
You can postpone the processing of messages with QoS EO and EOIO. To do so, you must define a filter for the messages concerned, as well as a job that schedules processing of the filtered messages.

▶ **Logging**
Logging logs the status of the message to be processed prior to the first processing step (inbound message) and after each call of a pipeline service. The Integration Engine persists for the entire message as does the information attained about the processing status so that you can monitor message processing in message monitoring. Logging for synchronous messages is deactivated in the default setting.

You can activate logging in different grades: for an Integration Engine (at the sender, Integration Server, or receiver), for all Integration Engines, for specific pipeline services, or for a specific field in the message header. In the latter case, the logging information is saved in the message header even if logging is explicitly deactivated in the configuration settings.

▶ **Tracing**
At runtime, various XI runtime components write information to the trace to document each processing step as it is executed. As described in Sections 5.1.2, 5.2.1, and 5.3.2, you can also write information to the trace during a mapping program. The level of detail of the information about message monitoring that is written to the trace varies according to the trace level configured (i.e., 0: no trace; 3: all processing steps traced).

Similar to logging, there are different grades of trace that you can activate: for the Integration Engine, for all Integration Engines involved in message processing, and for a particular message in the message header.

▶ **Deleting and Archiving Messages and Retention Periods**
Correctly processed messages are deleted in the default setting. However, in transaction SXMB_ADM, you can configure how long the Integration Engine retains messages as well as history entries, before they are deleted.

You must archive all messages that are not to be deleted. Messages that have been modified or cancelled manually are archived automatically. To archive messages, first specify the interfaces of the messages that you want to archive, and then schedule one job to write the messages to the archive, and another to delete the archived messages. If you want to delete the messages only periodically, you simply need to schedule one job, however. These mechanisms stop the database tables from overflowing.

From this overview of the Integration Engine forward, we will examine the programming model for proxy communication more closely.

7.3 Proxy Runtime

We already gave reasons for the outside-in approach in Section 4.2. Starting with a message interface in the Integration Repository, you generate a proxy in an application system to enable messages to be exchanged with the Integration Server.

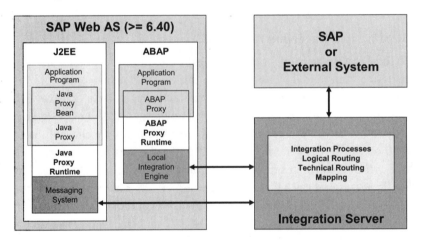

Figure 7.4 Communicating Using the Java or ABAP Proxy Runtime

Figure 7.4 shows which runtime components enable proxy communication with the Integration Server:

Components in Proxy Communication

▶ In terms of software logistics, proxies are part of the application. Therefore, you must compile and transport the proxy objects together with the application program. On a technical level, a proxy is a class (outbound) or an interface to be implemented (inbound).

▶ The *proxy runtime* is part of SAP XI. Note that the ABAP proxy runtime is a component of SAP Web AS (Release 6.40 and higher) and that the Java proxy runtime must be installed together with SAP XI. From the data transferred to a client proxy, the proxy runtime creates the message to be sent or reads the received messages to call a corresponding server proxy.

Local Integration Engine

▶ The *Local Integration Engine*, which was introduced in the last section, is also part of SAP XI. Along with the Integration Server, the Integration Engine guarantees messaging—the sending and receiving of messages, including the selected quality of service and status management for messages. When communicating using ABAP proxies, the Integration Engine is part of SAP Web AS. To communicate using Java proxies, SAP ships a *messaging system* with SAP XI; the messaging system performs the tasks of the local Integration Engine on the SAP J2EE Server.

In the following section, you'll learn how to program with proxies in an application program. We'll start by looking at concepts that apply to both ABAP and Java.

Sending and Receiving Messages

To send a message to the Integration Server, you must first define its contents and then send it by using a proxy call. You define the contents in the application program by using the generated proxy objects. In Java, you use the access methods of the generated objects; in ABAP, you assign the required values to the generated structures and fields. Finally, you use a method call for the generated class to transfer the data to the proxy runtime, which then creates the message from the data (proxy call). The proxy runtime automatically writes the sender in the message header; the receiver information is extracted from the configuration in the Integration Directory.

Synchronous and Asynchronous Communication

The proxy call thus corresponds to the sending of a message. If, at design time, you created a synchronous message interface, the program is stopped until a response message is received and the proxy runtime transfers the values of the message to the application program via the return parameters. There are, of course, no return parameters in asynchronous communication. In the default setting, the proxy runtime delivers such messages by using the Exactly Once quality of service. This means that it is immaterial in which inbound and outbound queues of the Integration Engine the messages are processed. The Integration Engine distributes the messages to different queues to optimize performance.

However, if the Exactly Once In Order quality of service is selected, the messages are all processed in one queue to ensure that they are processed in the order in which they were received. You must enter the queue name in the application program of the proxy runtime as a *serialization context* prior to the proxy call. The Java proxy runtime transfers asynchronous messages directly to the messaging system, whereas in the ABAP application program, you bundle together asynchronous messages in multiple proxy calls and then send the messages by using a closing COMMIT WORK statement.

Both the ABAP and Java proxy runtimes provide you with options for transferring information to the proxy runtime or querying information at the receiver in addition to the payload. We will mention only the most important options:

▶ **Exactly Once In Order and Acknowledgments**
In addition to the serialization context for Exactly Once In Order mentioned before, the proxy runtime can also process *acknowledgments* for asynchronous messages, which enable the receipt of a message (system acknowledgment) and successful processing of the message at the receiver (application acknowledgment) to be confirmed. From SP9 on, all receiver adapters mentioned in Section 6.5.1 support system acknowledgements; integration processes and proxy runtime also support application acknowledgments.

▶ **Setting the Receiver**
You specify the receiver of a message in the application program. This does not replace logical routing in the Integration Directory; rather, it enhances it. The routing runtime sends a message to the specified receiver only if there is a valid routing rule in the receiver determination in which it is specified that the receiver must be taken from the message header.

▶ **Message Attachments**
The proxy runtime enables any text or binary files to be appended to the message or queried at the receiver.

▶ **Querying the Payload**
You can query the payload of the message, for example, to archive it.

▶ **Querying the Message ID**
Once you have sent the message, you can query the message ID, for example, to write it to an application log.

At the receiver, the application developers implement the ABAP Objects or Java interface created by proxy generation. When the local Integration Engine forwards a message to the proxy runtime, the message header does not contain this interface, but instead contains the message interface that was created at design time. The proxy runtime must determine the implementing class and the method to be called for this message interface. For this reason, you must register receiver message interfaces with the proxy runtime. (We have already seen this briefly in Section 4.2.2) Once the message has been processed successfully at the receiver, the ABAP proxy runtime triggers a COMMIT WORK. Before we delve into more detail in subsequent sections, let's look at error handling in proxy communication.

Error Handling

The proxy runtime can react to two types of errors:

► System Errors

These errors occur when transporting the message and are triggered by an XI runtime component, for example, when no receiver could be determined. The sender must use the exception class CX_AI_SYSTEM_FAULT (ABAP) or SystemFaultException (Java) to catch this kind of error. At the receiver, the proxy runtime persists system errors for monitoring (asynchronous communication) or returns the error to the sender (synchronous communication).

► Application Errors

These errors occur at the receiver and are application-specific. An example of such an error is when a query at the receiver cannot be answered, because the customer number given is not known in the target system. This type of error is primarily important for synchronous communication; the runtime persists fault messages for monitoring in asynchronous communication.

You define the structure of fault messages in the Integration Repository. They always consist of a standard part and, optionally, an application-specific part. You put all the essential information about the error in the standard part, for example, the error text, type of error, and possibly a URL to link to further information. You define the structure of the application-specific part via a data type that you assign to the fault message type. Proxy generation creates an exception class for each fault message type, which the sender uses to catch the error in the application program via a try-catch block. Figure 7.5 shows an example with a J2EE application as the sender.

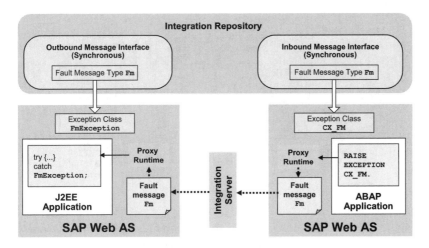

Figure 7.5 Error Handling with Fault Messages

All exception classes have the same superclass: CX_AI_APPLICATION_FAULT (ABAP) or ApplicationFaultException (Java).

7.3.1 Special Features for Java Proxy Communication

The Java Proxy Runtime (JPR) supports J2EE applications on the SAP J2EE Engine by using Enterprise JavaBeans (EJB) 2.0. Java proxy generation creates the following classes for this purpose:

▶ Proxy classes that send or receive messages by using the Java proxy runtime and Java classes for the data types used.

▶ Bean classes as an outer shell that conform to the J2EE standard. The bean classes call the proxy classes for communication. The bean classes are the home, remote, local home, and local interfaces commonly used in bean programming.

You program the message exchange in the J2EE application with the generated bean classes, which you then deploy along with the application, as you do with the Java classes.

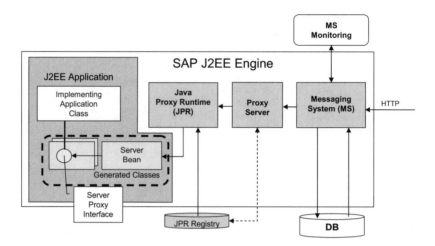

Figure 7.6 Java Proxy Runtime as Receiver

Figure 7.6 shows the processing of an inbound message. As we've already seen, the proxy runtime must be able to determine the remaining service to be called from the message interface in the message header. Therefore, when dealing with J2EE applications, you must register a server bean and the name of the corresponding bean method in the *JPR registry* for each message interface. SAP XI provides a *proxy server* servlet to access the JPR registry in the J2EE cluster environment synchronously. You usually register interfaces just once during the initial configuration of the runtime; however, you can also register new interfaces or deregister existing interfaces at runtime. The proxy server rereads the registry each time it is changed, without having to be restarted. All commands that you send to the proxy server servlet have the following structure:

```
http://<host>:<port>/ProxyServer/<command>
```

For example, the command `listAll` lists all registered message interfaces in alphabetical order. The command `jprtransportservlet` causes the proxy server servlet to perform a self test.

Lastly, we should mention a few general points regarding the Java proxy runtime:

▶ **Co-located Beans**
Since the JPR supports EJB 2.0, you can use `co-located` beans. These beans are deployed in the same EJB container system and are executed on the same Java Virtual Machine (JVM); performance is therefore

improved. To differentiate `co-located` beans from `remote` beans, use the `localejbs/` prefix.

▶ **Indirect Outbound Communication**
In addition to being able to be called by a J2EE application, the client proxy bean can also be called by a J2SE application. In this case, you must register the bean with the J2EE server by using the file `jndi.properties`.

Perhaps you're wondering to what extent do proxies or SAP XI support the use of Web services, particularly since message interfaces are based on Web Service Description Language (WSDL). This point is discussed in more detail in the next section. In SAP NetWeaver '04, programming or communication via Web services or SAP XI, which is the subject of Section 7.3.2, has been harmonized for ABAP proxies. In the Java world, however, proxy generation still involves many different tools and a programming model that is yet to be adopted. Besides the programming model, the next section also addresses Web service calls using the Integration Server.

7.3.2 ABAP Proxies and Web Services

So far on the subject of proxy communication, we have concentrated on the exchange of messages with the Integration Server. In fact, ABAP proxy generation supports two different scenarios:

▶ **XI Runtime**
Using the XI Runtime enables you to exchange messages by using the Integration Server. Here, you use the Integration Builder to configure the receiver (or receivers) of the message centrally in the Integration Directory so you can access routing, mapping, and integration processes.

▶ **Web Service Runtime**
The Web service runtime is part of SAP Web AS. You can use the Web service runtime to call point-to-point services independently of SAP XI. The idea behind Web Service Runtime is that business partners publish a language-independent description of this service as a WSDL document. To call this type of service, generate an ABAP client proxy.

In the following paragraphs, we describe the ABAP proxy runtime from the point of view of SAP XI. We assume that proxy communication takes place via the XI Runtime and will examine which enhancements are required to use the Web service runtime. The programming model is otherwise identical. Figure 7.7 shows both scenarios. If the integration logic of the Integration Server is not required, you can, in principle, switch between the two runtime environments. In this case, the application can use only those functions of the XI Runtime that are also supported in the Web service runtime, and vice versa. One significant difference is that the Web service runtime currently supports only synchronous communication.

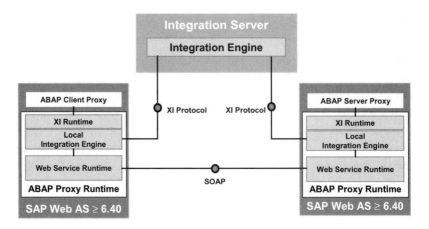

Figure 7.7 XI Runtime and Web Service Runtime

Logical Port When a proxy call is made using the XI Runtime, you don't need to enter a receiver, because all receivers are determined by the configuration in the Integration Directory. When communicating using the Web service runtime, use transaction LPCONFIG to configure the receiver in the sender system via a logical port. Besides the address of the receiver, the port settings also contain options for logging and tracing as well as security settings, for example. In the application program, you enter this port when you instantiate the proxy, for example:

```
CREATE OBJECT
    lo_clientProxy('LOGICAL_PORT_NAME').
```

Specification of the port when communicating using the XI Runtime is optional. If you do specify the port, on the **Runtime** tab in transaction LPCONFIG, specify whether you want to use the XI or Web service runtime. If you don't specify the port during instantiation, the XI Runtime is selected.

Point-to-Point Connections If two communicating ABAP proxies don't require any of the services that are provided by the Integration Server, you can use the logical port to switch to the Web service runtime, and thereby accelerate the rate of message exchange. In addition to the logical port, you also require a virtual interface and a Web service, which has been released in transaction WSADMIN, for the generated server proxy. To address the receiver at the logical port, create an HTTP destination to the released Web service and enter the destination in the logical port.

The only other difference between the programming models is the protocols that are available. Because the XI Runtime supports Exactly Once In Order quality of service, there is, for example, an asynchronous protocol available that enables you to set the serialization context. You access the protocol the same way in both cases: Using the GET_PROTOCOL method of the proxy, you get a protocol instance that provides the required attributes and methods for the protocol. If the active runtime does not support the protocol, an exception is triggered.

As illustrated above, you can switch from XI communication using ABAP proxies to communication using Web services. However, the reverse is not possible because message interfaces support only a subset of the range of WSDL commands, as mentioned in Section 4.2.1. For example, the XI protocol expects a predefined structure for fault messages, whereas a fault message can have any structure in WSDL.

In addition to a point-to-point connection using the Web service runtime or a connection using the XI Runtime, there is also a third option. Since the Integration Server can process SOAP messages, you can also call a Web service by using the Integration Server. The Integration Server receives the SOAP message from the caller and forwards it to a receiver in accordance with the configuration in the Integration Directory (here, too, only synchronous calls are currently possible). Therefore, the receiver does not have to be a proxy. Because you can use the services of the Integration Server for this Web service call, it is known as an *enhanced* Web service. The following steps are required to define an enhanced Web service:

1. To be able to generate a WSDL description for the caller, you require a message interface. This can be either an outbound or an inbound message interface. The message interface is not necessarily required for further configuration because it describes only the signature for the caller.

2. In the Integration Builder for configuration, call the menu **Tools · Define Web Service....** You create a WSDL description by entering the following details in the wizard:

Protocols (margin note)

WSDL and Message Interfaces (margin note)

Enhanced Web Services (margin note)

- The address of the Integration Server or another Web server that is to receive the SOAP call
- The message interface from the first step to publish the call signature via the WSDL document
- Details about the sender of the SOAP message (party, service, and outbound interface)
- When the Integration Server receives the SOAP message, it requires these details to evaluate the configuration data. You enter the details about the sender in logical routing or interface mapping and in the collaboration agreements.

3. The caller can use the generated WSDL description to generate a client proxy, and then send the SOAP message to the Integration Server by using the Web service runtime. You configure the receiver for the SOAP message on the Integration Server.

This concludes the overview of programming with proxies. In the next section, we look at the options for message monitoring.

7.4 Monitoring

As we have already seen in this chapter, besides the sender and receiver systems, cross-system message exchange involves a whole series of runtime components. This section gives an overview of the options available for monitoring these runtime components.

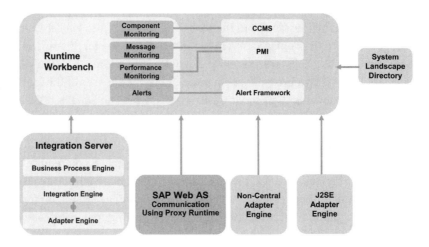

Figure 7.8 Monitoring Areas

The monitoring components are shown in Figure 7.8 at the top. The *Runtime Workbench* is a Java-based tool that uses a Web interface to access all monitoring areas centrally; you open the Runtime Workbench from the XI start page in the same way as the Integration Builder. The Runtime Workbench uses existing monitoring components of the SAP Web AS: the Computer Center Management System (CCMS), the Process Monitoring Infrastructure (PMI), and the Alert Framework. Among other things, process monitoring of the PMI enables you to monitor a continuous process that encompasses multiple components; therefore, PMI is not intended to support the monitoring of an integration process. The last point is discussed in more detail in Section 8.4.

Runtime Workbench

Monitoring with the Runtime Workbench enables you to monitor all XI Runtime components (*component monitoring*), message processing both on the Integration Server and across all (*end-to-end*) XI Runtime components (*message monitoring*), as well as the speed and throughput of message processing (*performance monitoring*). Additionally, administrators can use alerts to be informed about any errors that occur (*Alert Framework*).

For the purposes of end-to-end monitoring and performance monitoring, the Runtime Workbench evaluates data from the PMI. For this purpose, you must define the monitoring level of each component that you want to monitor in the **Configuration** area of the Runtime Workbench. All the other runtime components (Integration Server, Adapter Engine, Proxy Runtime) can determine their data without your having to make any configuration settings in the Runtime Workbench. In **Cache Monitoring,** you can also display the Integration Engine or Adapter Engine cache. In this way, you can display the value-mapping groups as well as which mapping programs or software component versions are in the cache. The next section has a more detailed look at the remaining monitoring areas.

Data for Monitoring

Component Monitoring

You use Component Monitoring to monitor all XI Runtime components. Figure 7.9 shows the status overview for the Integration Server. The status of the Adapter Engine is *ok* (green), the status of the Integration Engine is *error* (red), and the status of the Business Process Engine and the mapping runtime is *undefined* (gray). A gray status means that no information is available for the component in question; this is possibly because monitoring is not activated for this component. To display more details, click on the status. Depending on the runtime component, you can do the following in

Status overview

the lower area of the Runtime Workbench: execute a self-test, call configuration data for the component, or send a test message to the component.

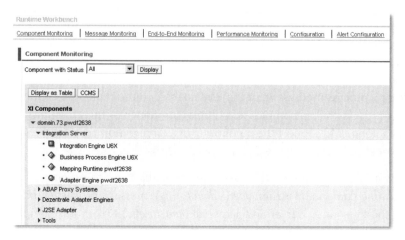

Figure 7.9 Overview of the Status of XI Runtime Components

CCMS To resolve a component problem, start CCMS, which is integrated in the Knowledge Workbench via the *SAP GUI for HTML*. With CCMS you can monitor all systems in your system landscape, call statistical information for your systems, start or shut down systems, and much more. Figure 7.10 shows the system status for the system on which the Integration Server is installed. The queues with the prefix XBTI* in client 105 of the qRFC inbound scheduler, which we first encountered in Section 7.2.2, are blocked. You can navigate to the qRFC monitor directly from here to display more information.

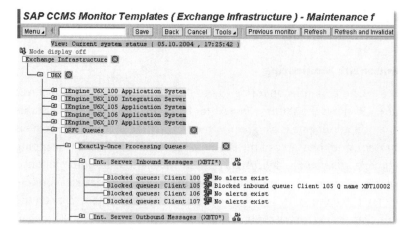

Figure 7.10 Working with CCMS from the Runtime Workbench

In CCMS, you can define an automatic alert notification that informs administrators by email, pager, or fax about problems with a component. In the next section, we'll examine the options for monitoring message processing offered by the Runtime Workbench, and then take a look at the alerts that you can configure in the Runtime Workbench specifically for this purpose.

Alerts

Message Monitoring

You monitor the processing of messages in message monitoring. The level of detail that the information in message monitoring contains varies according to the settings you made in logging and tracing for the relevant runtime component. For example, in the default setting, synchronous messages that have been processed without errors are not shown in monitoring.

Once you have selected **Message Monitoring**, you must restrict the number of processed messages. To do so, first select a runtime component and then restrict the messages to be selected via the processing date and time and other fields in the message header. For example, by selecting the **Status** field, you can display all the messages with errors for a particular period of time. In the list of messages that is then displayed, you can perform the following actions for individual messages:

Selecting Messages

▶ You can manually resend messages with errors to the intended receiver, for example, if the receiver was temporarily not available.

▶ To display more information about a selected message in the list, choose **Details**. Here you can view the message in the course of processing by the Integration Engine:[2] The split screen enables you to display and compare different pipeline processing steps simultaneously.

▶ Because a message is passed between numerous runtime components in its journey from sender to receiver, you can also navigate directly to end-to-end monitoring from the list in message monitoring. The prerequisite for this is that you have activated PMI in the **Configuration** area of the Runtime Workbench for all runtime components involved.

You can also call end-to-end monitoring directly in the Runtime Workbench. The following information is displayed whether you specify a sender or receiver:

End-to-End Monitoring

---

2 The monitoring transactions in the Integration Engine can also be accessed in the system from transaction SXMB_MONI.

- ▶ **Process Overview**
  The total number of processed messages (with errors) for all components. As soon as processing by a component results in one or more
  messages with errors, the status of the component changes from green
  to red.

- ▶ **Instance View**
  The instance view shows the route of a particular message through the
  components involved (in other words, this pertains to the message
  instance). Figure 7.11 shows an example in which message processing
  was terminated on the way to the receiver. The relevant component is
  shown in red.

In addition to performance data, the **Statistics Data** frame shows the
number of open messages, messages with errors, and successfully processed messages. To display these messages, click the respective status
category. Using this same approach, you can also update the graphical
overview for a message in the list (see Figure 7.11).

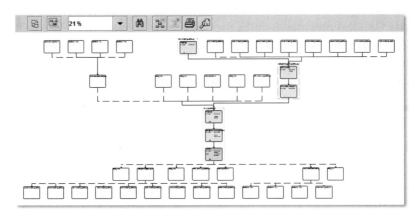

Figure 7.11 Overview in End-to-End Monitoring

To conclude this section, let's look at the notification options that are
available to administrators when problems arise.

Alerts

Configuration   Alerting in SAP XI uses the Alert Infrastructure (CCMS) of SAP Web AS;
however, you can now also configure message-oriented alerts. To be notified by email, fax, or SMS about an error during message processing, use
the **Alert Configuration** in the Runtime Workbench. Put simply, the con-

figuration converts a selected error code into a notification (alert). Alerts are classified by *alert categories*.

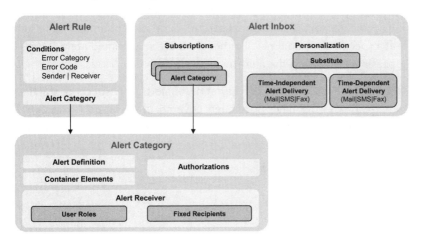

Figure 7.12 Configuring Alerts

Figure 7.12 gives an overview of the configuration of alerts. The configuration enables alerts to be distributed to various users or user groups, who can subscribe to a particular category of alerts. The assignment of an alert to a user requires a few steps:

1. First, you need to define the alert itself. To do so, create an alert category with the following information:

User Assignment

   ▶ The general attributes for the alert, for example, the maximum number of times it is to be sent.

   ▶ The notification text (not shown in Figure 7.12). Furthermore, you can use **Container Elements** to include information from the message header in the alert.

   ▶ Finally, you assign a *user role for authorization*. This authorization is required by all users who later want to subscribe to the alert category in the **Alert Inbox** of the Runtime Workbench. If a user does this, the system automatically enters him or her in the *fixed recipients list*. Alternatively, you can assign the alert category to all users of a particular role. Independently of this, the users must also be assigned the aforementioned authorization role.

2. To convert error codes into alerts, you must define an **Alert Rule**. You describe the conditions under which an alert is to be triggered, and then assign the rule to an alert category.

3. If an alert rule for an alert category is true, all users who have subscribed to the category in their alert inbox are notified. The alerts are always sent to the **Alert Inbox**, but they can also be sent to the receiver by email, fax, or SMS (**Personalization**). Time-dependent alerts are sent at a specific point in time; all other alerts are sent immediately. It is also possible to forward the alert to a substitute.

This chapter ends with the configuration of alerts. All aspects of stateless message processing have now been covered in Chapters 1 through 7. *Stateful* message processing means that information about a cross-system process is stored on the Integration Server. We will look at *integration processes* in the next chapter.

8   Integration Processes

SAP XI not only enables message exchange, it also lets you use integration processes, which allow you to account for semantic connections between messages and control message processing accordingly, in other words, via Business Process Management.

8.1   Introduction

The previous chapters explained how you use messages to integrate application components. The systems exchange messages by using the Integration Server. The Integration Server ensures that the messages are transferred correctly, but does not save any information about semantic connections between the exchanged messages or the status of the collaborative process. This stateless message processing is fine for most integration tasks. Chapter 10 describes one such customer scenario where this is the case.

However, some situations require you to consider the semantic connections between messages and control the process flow accordingly. A practical example of such a requirement is the collection and bundling of messages. Related messages, such as purchase order items, are collected and assembled into a purchase order. The entire purchase order, instead of the individual purchase order items, is sent to the receiver. The opposite case can also arise: You need to partition a message into individual submessages and send them to different receivers.

Controlling processing in this way requires stateful processing of messages, where the status of the process or message processing is saved on the Integration Server. In SAP XI, stateful processing is realized by using integration processes. Chapter 9 describes a customer scenario using integration processes.

Stateful Processing

8.1.1   What Is an Integration Process?

An integration process specifies how messages are processed on the Integration Server at runtime. To define an integration process, you use a graphical editor to assemble the individual *steps*. The graphical editor provides predefined step types for this purpose. These include step types for processing messages, such as the *receive step* for receiving messages,

Step Types

and the *send step* for sending messages. There are also step types for controlling the process flow, such as a loop or switch.

For each step, you define the relevant properties and the data that the step will process. For example, for a receive step, you specify the message that the step is to expect. The editor displays error messages and notes to enable you to identify problems and errors during definition.

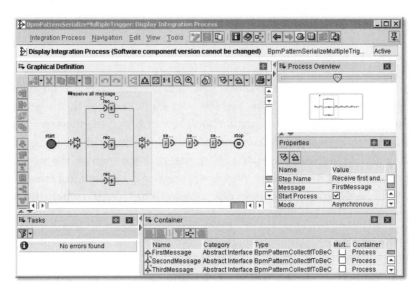

Figure 8.1 Integration Process in the Graphical Editor

Integration Processes in SAP XI

The definition, configuration, and execution of integration processes are completely integrated into SAP XI: You define an integration process in the Integration Repository, you configure it in the Integration Directory, and it is executed at runtime. To define the process, you use the graphical process editor in the Integration Builder, as shown in Figure 8.1. In the Integration Directory, a wizard guides you through the configuration. The Business Process Engine, which runs on the Integration Server, is responsible for executing the integration process. Additional functions for monitoring the Business Process Engine are available in monitoring.

Predefined Integration Processes

In reality, some integration process requirements arise repeatedly. To avoid having to start from scratch every time, SAP ships predefined processes for such cases. These are located in the Integration Repository under **SAP Basis SAP Basis 6.40** in the namespace *http://sap.com/xi/XI/System/Patterns*. You can simply add the definitions of these shipped processes to your own processes, and adapt and enhance them to meet your needs.

These predefined processes are also a good starting point for defining integration processes if this is new to you. The majority of the figures in this chapter show these predefined integration processes.

8.1.2 Integration Processes and Other Processes

Processing business processes is also referred to as *Business Process Management* (BPM). You can execute business processes within an application or system, or across systems.

Business processes within applications usually require user interaction. A *leave request* is a simple yet typical example. An employee makes a leave request, which is forwarded to his or her manager. If the manager approves the request, the employee receives a corresponding notification and the leave is updated in the system. If the manager rejects the request, the employee receives a corresponding notification and can edit the request. This type of process must usually consider the organizational structure: In our example, it is essential that the employee's manager or stand-in receives the leave request. To implement such processes that run within applications in SAP NetWeaver, you use *SAP Business Workflow* to define workflows.

Workflows Within Applications

In addition to these standardized work processes, which you model using workflows, you may also have to deal with processes that arise less frequently or are less structured. Here, too, you want to be able to track the status of the process at any time and determine who is currently working on which part of the process. To implement these processes in such a way that they are both transparent and traceable, end users in SAP Enterprise Portal can use wizards to define their own *collaboration tasks* "on the fly."

Collaboration Task

Unlike workflows, integration processes are not executed within an application, but across applications. Integration processes control the message exchange between systems, but don't support user interaction. This topic is also referred to as *cross-component Business Process Management* (ccBPM).

Integration Processes for Cross-Component Processes

SAP NetWeaver offers a comprehensive BPM approach, including predefined workflows, collaboration tasks, and cross-component integration processes. All three approaches are closely linked and integrated. If user interaction is required at a particular stage in an integration process, you can start a workflow from the integration process. Conversely, a workflow can send a message to an integration process to start the integration process, for example. Similarly, a user can start a collaboration task from a

Integration

business workflow, for example, to incorporate greater flexibility for particular subprocesses.

Now that we have an overview of the BPM approach in SAP NetWeaver, we will redirect our attention to integration processes within SAP XI.

8.2 Designing an Integration Process

Before we look at how to define integration processes in detail, let's first consider a few basic design aspects. This will make it easier for you to select the correct design elements later on and translate your practical requirements into error-free integration processes.

Block-Oriented Design

Similar to when writing procedural programming languages, you use *blocks* to structure integration processes. A block can contain steps and additional blocks. Furthermore, the integration process itself is the outermost block of all blocks in the integration process.

This block structure helps you to design a transparent and traceable process, and automatically prevents certain design errors. Furthermore, the block structure has other functions, for example, to determine the visibility and validity of the data processed within a process. We will look at these individual functions in more detail in the next sections.

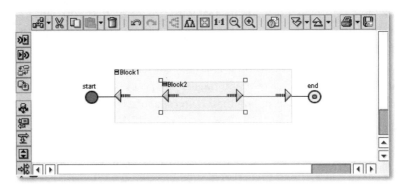

Figure 8.2 Process with Two Blocks

8.2.1 Data of an Integration Process

If a received message is not to be simply forwarded, but processed in some way, the integration process must work with the data. For example, it must be able to receive, collect, and convert messages, increase counters, or check conditions. There are special *step types* for each of these tasks. To ensure that these step types process the various data correctly, you must describe which data is relevant in each case. To do so, you must define the data as *container elements*.

Container elements are comparable to variables in a programming language. You define the required container elements at design time; at runtime, they contain references to the respective data.

Container Elements

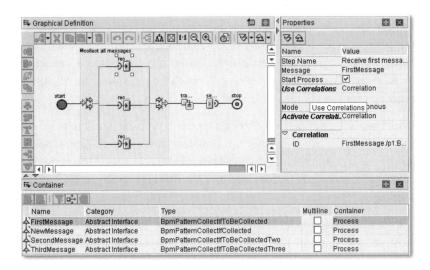

Figure 8.3 Receive Step and Associated Container Element

In Figure 8.3, the selected receive step is to receive a particular message. We have defined the container element `FirstMessage` to describe this message. To enable the receive step to use this container element to receive the message, we enter the container element name as the **Message** property in the **Properties** area. At runtime, the container element `FirstMessage` references the corresponding message. In this case, the container element is defined globally (in the case of global container elements, **Process** is specified as the container in the **Container** area of the editor). This means that it can be used in all blocks of the integration process. If the integration process is complex, it may be necessary to define *local container elements*, to exclude naming conflicts, for example. A local container element is visible in the block in which it is defined and in all lower-level blocks of the same block.

| Categories and Types of Container Element | Various categories and types are available to enable you to describe different data. For example, if a container element is to reference a message at runtime, use the **Abstract Interface** category and specify the message type. If a container element is for a counter, select the **Simple Type** category and the corresponding xsd data type, which for a counter is **xsd:integer**. |

Categories and Types of Container Element — Various categories and types are available to enable you to describe different data. For example, if a container element is to reference a message at runtime, use the **Abstract Interface** category and specify the message type. If a container element is for a counter, select the **Simple Type** category and the corresponding xsd data type, which for a counter is **xsd:integer**.

Multiline Container Elements — You can also define a container element as a list of container elements of the same type. This is necessary if you want to collect messages in a container element, for example, in order to bundle them into a collective message at a later time. To define a list of this type, select the **Multiline** checkbox for the container element.

Using Container Elements — Once the data is defined as container elements, you can use it in the steps of an integration process. Enter the container element in the corresponding property of the step. If a receive step is to receive a message, enter the container element name that describes the message to be received as the **Message** property.

Setting Values — If a counter is to be increased or a list is to be created at runtime, you must set the value of the corresponding container element. You use a special step type to do this—the *container operation*. A container operation enables you to assign a value for a counter, for example, or append a message to a list of messages.

8.2.2 Processing Messages

We already discussed receive and send steps briefly. Both step types receive or send messages respectively in the integration process by using only abstract message interfaces. Altogether, all the message interfaces used describe a process signature. Since you use container elements to access data in the integration process, you proceed in exactly the same way when you want to access data of a message. You use a container element of the type **Abstract Interface,** you specify the container element in the respective step, and, in this way, you can access the message type in the step. Let us now look at the two basic step types for sending and receiving in more detail and examine the other options for processing messages.

Receive Step — At runtime, an integration process is always started by a receive step, which pertains to exactly one message. In practice, however, you may want to start an integration process by using different messages. In this case, you assign several receive steps in parallel, as shown in Figure 8.3.

To do this, you must insert the receive steps in a *fork*. Section 8.2.3 describes this step type in more detail.

Sending Messages from the Integration Process

In addition to one or more receive steps, an integration process usually contains at least one send step as well, which sends a received and processed message to a service (a business system, another integration process, or a service outside your own system landscape).

There are different ways to determine the receiver of the message. The send step provides the following options for the **Receiver From** property:

Receiver Determination

▶ **Send Context**

You normally configure the receiver determination in the Integration Directory and specify a *send context* in the send step. The send context enables you to address different receivers for the same message interface by assigning different send contexts for the respective steps. You reference the respective send context during configuration.

▶ **Receivers List**

In the send step, you can reference a foregoing receiver determination step that uses the receiver determination in the Integration Directory to compile a list of receivers. You can use a **ForEach** (discussed at the end of the next section) to distribute the messages to the various receivers.

▶ **Response to Message**

A send step can respond directly to a previously received message. In this case, the receiver is determined from the message, and you don't need a receiver determination from the Integration Directory.

You can send a message from an integration process asynchronously or synchronously. If sending asynchronously, the send step does *not* wait for a response message from the receiver. If sending synchronously, the send step waits until the response message has been received from the receiver.

Asynchronous or Synchronous

Transforming Messages

We have now seen how an integration process can receive and send a message. However, it is often insufficient to forward a message in its original format. For example, if the original message is a catalog and the receiver system can process only individual items, the original message must be divided so that the receiver system can process it.

If this is the case, you use a transformation step, which can separate a message into several messages or bundle several messages into a single message. You can also use a transformation step to convert a message for another interface. You define a corresponding interface mapping (see Section 5.1.2) for all these transformations and specify it in the transformation step.

Correlating Related Messages

Often, several related messages are processed in an integration process, for example, a purchase order and a purchase order response, or a booking and a booking confirmation. You describe the relationship between these messages by using correlations. But why do we need correlations? Let's examine this question using an example.

You defined an integration process that processes ordering transactions: A receive step receives a purchase order, sends it to the corresponding receiver, and waits for a purchase order response. We will refer to this process as an *ordering process* and examine what happens when the process receives several messages for different purchase orders (see Figure 8.4):

1. A purchase order for a desk arrives and starts the ordering process for the desk. The Business Process Engine generates a process instance, which holds the status of the ordering process on the Integration Server. Once the purchase order has been sent, the process instance waits for the purchase order response.

2. A second purchase order arrives, this time for a computer. The Business Process Engine starts the ordering process again for the computer. It generates a second process instance of the ordering process. Once the purchase order has been sent, this process instance also waits for the purchase order response.

3. The purchase order response for the desk arrives.

How can you tell which of the two waiting process instances the purchase order response relates to? You would probably look for the purchase order number in the purchase order response and check which of the two instances contains a request for an article with this purchase order number.

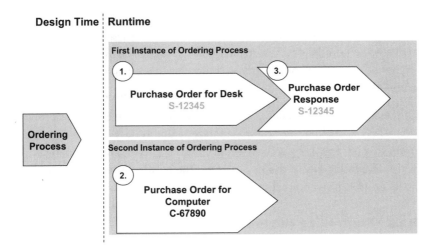

Design Time ┊ **Runtime**

First Instance of Ordering Process

1.

Purchase Order for Desk
S-12345

3.

**Purchase Order
Response**
S-12345

**Ordering
Process**

Second Instance of Ordering Process

2.

**Purchase Order for
Computer
C-67890**

Figure 8.4 Ordering Process

The Business Process Engine does exactly this. All you have to do is describe the two messages involved and specify which element of these messages contains the purchase order number. In other words, you define a *correlation*. A correlation specifies how the Business Process Engine can identify related messages. To define a correlation, you enter the involved messages and the XML element in which the messages match. In more complicated cases, you can also use several XML elements to define a correlation. In this case, the values of all specified elements of the involved messages must match.

Correlation

⇆ Correlation Editor				
Correlation Name	BookingConfirmation 🖾			

Correlation Container		**Involved Messages**		**Properties**

Name	Type	Name	Namespace	Name	Value
AgencyID	xsd:string	FlightBookingOrderReque...	http://sap.com/xi/XI/...	▽ **FlightBookingOrderR**	
OrderNumber	xsd:string	FlightBookingOrderConfir...	http://sap.com/xi/XI/...	AgencyID	Interface./p1:FlightBoo...
				OrderNumber	Interface./p1:FlightBoo...
				▽ **FlightBookingOrderC**	
				AgencyID	Interface./p1:FlightBoo...
				OrderNumber	Interface./p1:FlightBoo...

Figure 8.5 Defining a Correlation in the Correlation Editor

The correlation in Figure 8.5 is defined using the elements `AgencyID` and `OrderNumber`. Therefore, the two messages specified must have the same values for these two elements. The location of the two elements in the two messages is specified on the right side of the window (XPath specification).

Activating and Using Correlations

All that is left to do is define which steps the correlation is to be used in. In our example, the receive step that accepts the purchase order must *activate* the correlation. This means that the system generates a unique key when a purchase order arrives, and saves this key as the value of the correlation.

The receive step that gets the purchase order response *uses* this correlation. This means that the system generates a unique key when a purchase order response with a purchase order number arrives, and compares this with the existing key. If the key matches the existing one, the message is assigned to the same process instance.

8.2.3 Controlling the Process Flow

So far, we have concentrated on processes comprising single steps executed one after the other. However, it is often necessary to execute steps more than once or execute steps only when a particular condition is met. To model such situations, you can use loops and other control structures in an integration process that is similar to the way in which a programming language works. This is discussed below.

Fork

We have already seen in the receive step that several receive steps can be arranged in a *fork* so that the process can wait for different messages at the same time. You can also use forks for any other steps that are executed simultaneously, for example, for send steps that send independently to different receivers. In addition, you can specify whether the process has to complete all branches, or just a specific number. Furthermore, you can define an end condition for the entire fork.

Switch

Similar to the fork arrangement of steps, several processing branches can be defined with a *switch*. You specify a separate condition for each branch. In this case, processing does not continue in all branches simultaneously, as it does with a fork, but in the branch that first provides a *true* result for the condition. If none of the conditions are met, processing continues in the *Otherwise* branch, which is created automatically.

While Loop

You've probably encountered loops in programming languages. Loops enable steps to be repeated within the loop. The steps in the loop are executed as long as the end condition for the loop produces a *true* result (while loop).

Executing Steps for Multiple Elements

Let's assume that you have several processing steps that you want to execute not just for *one* message, but for several messages. To do this, you can define corresponding processing branches of a fork. However, this solution is rather complicated, and requires you to already know the number of messages at definition time. A preferable solution is to use blocks with *dynamic processing*.

In Section 8.2.1, we learned that you can define multiline container elements referencing container elements of the same type. Dynamic processing means that the Business Process Engine executes the steps within a block for all lines of a multiline container element of this type. For example, you can collect messages in a loop and use a container operation to append them to a multiline container element. **Dynamic Processing**

If you want to process all elements of the multiline container element concurrently, use the **ParForEach** mode. For example, use this mode to send a message to multiple receivers in parallel. **ParForEach**

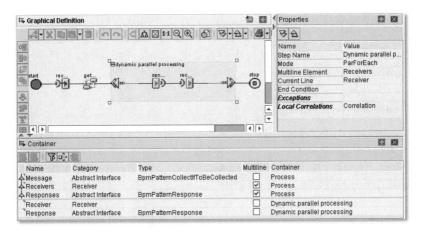

Figure 8.6 Send Step in a Block with ParForEach

In Figure 8.6, a send step within a block with **ParForEach** sends to all receivers in a receiver list in parallel. A subsequent receive step receives the response from each receiver.

If you want to process the individual elements of the multiline container element one after the other, use the **ForEach** mode. For example, use this mode to send a message to multiple receivers continuously. **ForEach**

Local Correlation Note that there is a special feature in relation to correlations in dynamic processing. A correlation is usually valid for the entire process. If a request message and a response message are correlated via a purchase order number, as in Figure 8.5, only one purchase order number can be processed using this correlation for each process instance. However, in dynamic processing, a separate purchase order number should be processed each time a block is executed. To do this, define the corresponding correlation as a local correlation. This means that it is valid only for the block and can process a separate value for each block instance.

8.2.4 Time Control and Exception Handling

The time aspect is important when controlling integration processes. At the beginning of this chapter, we learned that the status of a process is saved. This means that a process can wait several hours, days, or even weeks to receive a message without the process being canceled. However, it is often necessary for certain processes or process steps to be executed or completed at a specific point in time.

Exception handling is closely related to time control. An integration process can contain exception or error situations other than exceeding a deadline. You can define how the system is to react to such situations in exception handling.

Deadline Monitoring

If you want to monitor whether the Business Process Engine has executed selected steps by a particular moment, you define a *deadline*. To do so, insert the steps to be monitored in a block and then define a deadline branch for the block.

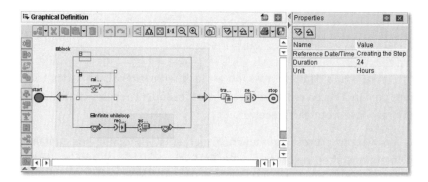

Figure 8.7 Block with Deadline Branch (Middle Branch)

Figure 8.7 shows a block with deadline monitoring. If the block has not been completed 24 hours after generation, processing continues in the deadline branch; in this case, in the middle branch in the figure.

Deadline Branch

A deadline branch is a processing branch that is executed when a deadline expires. You can put any steps in this branch; these steps are executed when the deadline expires. A deadline does not affect the other steps in the block. You can decide yourself what should happen when a deadline expires.

If you want the process to be canceled, for example, add a control step for canceling the process to the deadline branch. If, on the other hand, you simply want a particular user to be informed, add a **Throw Alert** control step. This throws an alert for SAP Alert Management, which enables you to ensure that the user responsible is informed of the process status by email or SMS, for example, so that he or she can then take the necessary measures.

Specifying the Start Time of a Step

Another time control aspect of an integration process is the *start time* of a step. You can define the start time of a step in an integration process by inserting a delay before the step. To do this, use a wait step, for which you define the delay as a moment or period of time.

Exception Handling

We encountered an exception situation in the previous section—the expiry of a deadline. An integration process can contain other exceptional or erroneous situations, such as system errors or exceptional business situations.

An example of a system error is when a message cannot be sent from a process. In this case, the process *can no longer* continue normally. An example of an exceptional business situation is when one of the involved receivers does not have a required material. In this case, the process *should* no longer continue normally. Instead, normal processing should be canceled, a warning given if necessary, or alternative processing steps executed.

Exceptions and Exception Handlers

You account for such situations by defining exception handling when you define the process. First, you define an *exception* for the event that the process cannot or should not continue normally. Exceptions for system errors, for example, can be thrown by a send step or a transformation step. You throw exceptions for business errors with a control step. You then insert the control step at the corresponding point in the process definition and specify the name of the exception that is to be thrown.

If the system error occurs at runtime or the process reaches the control step for the business exception, an exception is thrown. The exception triggers the process not to continue normally, but instead to continue in another processing branch—the *exception handler*. The active steps of the block for which the exception handler is defined are canceled, and processing continues in the exception handler instead. You can use all step types when defining the exception handler. This gives you great flexibility when defining the reaction to an exception. Once the exception handler has been processed, the process continues normally after the block.

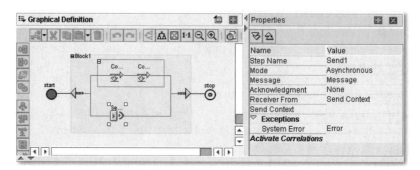

Figure 8.8 Block with Exception Handler Branch

In Figure 8.8, a system error causes the send step in the lower processing branch to throw the exception `Error`. This exception is assigned to the exception handler (upper processing branch). If a system error occurs during sending at runtime, processing continues in the exception handler. The first control step throws an alert for SAP Alert Management; the second control step cancels the process.

8.2.5 Importing or Exporting Integration Processes

If you want to use SAP XI to execute integration processes that you have developed using third-party software, you can import them to the graphical editor. Therefore, you don't have to define new processes, but can add existing processes to the Integration Repository by using a wizard. The opposite is also possible: You can export integration processes and use them in other systems.

BPEL4WS   The graphical editor supports the exchange format BPEL4WS 1.1 (*Business Process Execution Language for Web Services*) for import and export.

BPEL4WS is an initiative of BEA Systems, IBM, Microsoft, SAP AG, and Siebel Systems for improving interoperability of service-based processes.

8.3 Configuring Integration Processes

The configuration of integration processes does not differ a lot from the configuration of other collaborative processes. Therefore, we won't discuss the entire configuration topic in this section; rather, we'll focus on only the special features.

8.3.1 Overview

At runtime, the Business Process Engine uses the services of the Integration Engine to send and receive messages. This interplay is shown in Figure 8.9:

1. The Integration Engine receives a message from any sender. In this example, the Integration Engine uses a receiver determination in the Integration Directory to determine an integration process as the receiver. If the interface determination references an interface mapping, the Integration Engine executes the referenced mapping programs.

2. After outbound processing, the Integration Engine forwards the message to the Business Process Engine. The Business Process Engine first determines whether the message is correlated with other messages, and whether a matching instance of an integration process is waiting for the message (see Figure 8.4). Of course, the message can also start a new process.

3. If the Business Process Engine reaches a send step during execution of the process, it transfers the message to the inbound channel of the Integration Engine, where the same steps are performed as in the first step.

4. Finally, the Integration Engine determines a receiver that is not an integration process, and forwards the message accordingly.

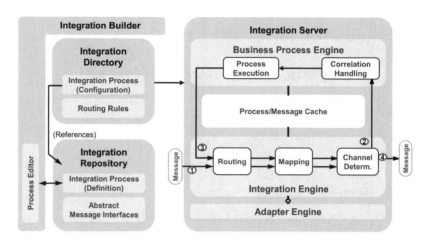

Figure 8.9 Integration Engine and Business Process Engine

As we have already seen in Section 8.2.2, you need the receiver determination from the Integration Directory when sending messages (unless the message is to be returned as a response to a message received during the process). You configure the receiver of the message that you are sending from the integration process in the Integration Directory in the normal way. To do this, specify the integration process as the sender service in the receiver determination and assign one or more receivers to it. But what do you do if the receiver you want to use is dependent on the send step in the process? In this case, you use the send context of the send step to differentiate between different send steps of the same integration process. Let's use an example to illustrate this point.

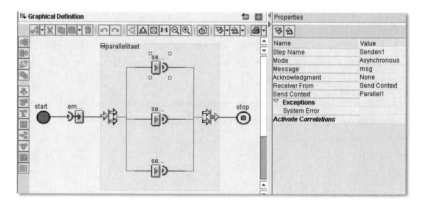

Figure 8.10 Parallel Send Steps with Individual Send Contexts

The integration process in Figure 8.10 has a fork with three send steps. You want to send a message to different receivers, depending on which branch is processed at runtime. To account for this in the configuration, you assign a different send context to each send step, for example `Parallel1`, `Parallel2`, and `Parallel3`. You then use the send context in the condition in the receiver determination to reference the respective send step of the integration process (see Figure 8.11). To reference a process step, use the technical context object `ProcessStep`. Context objects are discussed in Section 4.4.3.

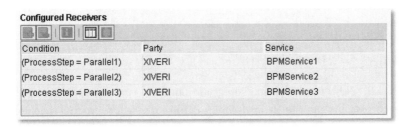

Configured Receivers

Condition	Party	Service
(ProcessStep = Parallel1)	XIVERI	BPMService1
(ProcessStep = Parallel2)	XIVERI	BPMService2
(ProcessStep = Parallel3)	XIVERI	BPMService3

Figure 8.11 Configured Receivers in the Receiver Determination

Now that we have discussed the dependencies between the Integration Engine and the Business Process Engine, we'll look at the configuration process flow using integration scenarios in the next section.

8.3.2 Configuration Using Integration Scenarios

As we have already seen in Section 6.1, it is not absolutely necessary to define an integration scenario in the Integration Repository. However, using an integration scenario does make configuration considerably easier since you can use a configuration wizard when using an integration scenario in the Integration Repository.

The following procedure is recommended for defining a corresponding integration scenario in the Integration Repository:

Creating an Integration Scenario

1. Define an action for each use of a message interface in the integration process.

2. Create the integration scenario.

3. Insert the actions in the corresponding application component in the integration scenario.

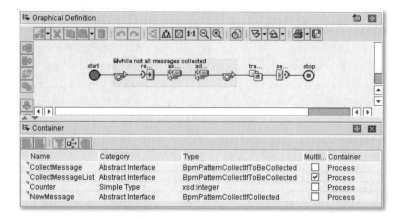

Figure 8.12 Example Integration Process

Figure 8.12 shows an example integration process, and Figure 8.13 shows the corresponding integration scenario. The integration process receives messages in a loop, bundles them into a collective message, and sends it. The first action in the integration scenario represents the sending of the messages by the sender, the second represents the receiving and bundling of the messages in the integration process, the third represents the sending by the integration process, and, finally, the fourth represents the receipt of the messages in the receiver system.

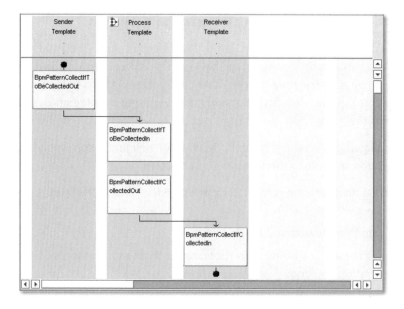

Figure 8.13 Integration Scenario for the Process in Figure 8.12

Once we have created the integration scenario, we can start the actual configuration in the Integration Directory. You must take the following steps:

1. Create a service without a party for the integration process.

2. Define a service without a party for each business system of the integration scenario.

   In the example in Figure 8.13, for instance, you must define a service for the sender system and one for the receiver system.

3. Create a configuration scenario that references your integration scenario from the Integration Repository.

4. You can now call the integration scenario configurator, which guides you through the necessary steps.

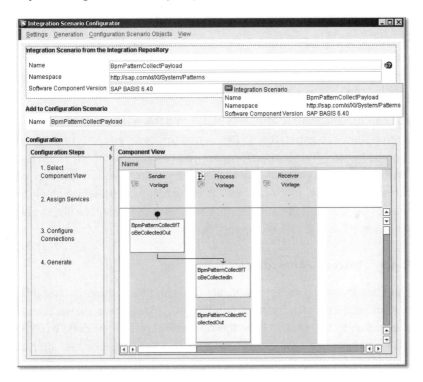

Figure 8.14 Configurator for the Scenario in Figure 8.13

We encountered the integration scenario configurator in Section 6.3.1. Therefore, we'll skip the steps in the configurator and turn our attention to the monitoring of integration processes in the next section.

8.4 Monitoring the Execution of an Integration Process

At runtime, the Business Process Engine executes an integration process. You can monitor the execution of integration processes by using the monitoring functions of the Business Process Engine. Of course, you can also use the monitoring options in SAP XI, as described in Section 7.4; however, this chapter focuses on the special features when monitoring integration processes. Since the Business Process Engine runs on the same client of SAP Web AS that is configured as the Integration Server, the following options pertain to this client.

8.4.1 Analyzing the Runtime Cache

If an integration process has not been started, you can check whether a runtime version of the process has actually been generated. The runtime version of an integration process is generated from the definition of the integration process in the Integration Repository and the entries for the service and party in the Integration Directory. This is done as soon as you activate the change list in the Integration Directory.

You can use the transaction SXI_CACHE to determine whether the runtime version was generated. If this is not the case, you can update the runtime version. This transaction gives you detailed reports of errors that have occurred. If you want to analyze the runtime version further, you can display it either in XML format or as a graphical representation in the Process Builder. You can also save the XML representation as a file, should you want to send it to SAP support, for example.

8.4.2 Process Monitoring

There are many transactions available for analyzing and monitoring integration processes. The starting point for accessing these transactions is transaction SXMB_MONI_BPE. This transaction gives you access to other transactions for selecting, diagnosing, and restarting processes, after an error, for example. Most of these transactions take you to the workflow log, where you can perform a detailed analysis.

Process Builder The Business Process Engine and the Workflow Engine of SAP Business Workflow are closely related. At runtime, the Business Process Engine uses the integration process to generate work items corresponding to the steps of the integration process. You can display these work items in the

Process Builder and see at a glance how far the process has been executed and where problems may have arisen.

In addition to the graphical display in the Process Builder, you can display the workflow log as a view with technical details. In addition, you can display and analyze the details for each step of the execution, and branch to the work item container and navigate to the processed messages.

Workflow Log

8.4.3 Message Monitoring

In message monitoring, you can use transaction SXMB_MONI to display a selection screen where you can filter all messages that are processed by the Business Process Engine. You can navigate from the message to the workflow log, which displays all steps or work items and their status. In addition, you can display the work item container, should you want to analyze a message before and after processing by a particular step, for example.

This brings us to the end of the conceptual part of the book. In the second part of the book, we look at how SAP XI is used in the context of two customer scenarios.

In the next chapter, we continue our discussion of integration processes, using a practical case study to further illuminate the concepts already introduced.

9 Cross-Component Business Process Management at the Linde Group

Cross-Component Business Process Management (ccBPM) is available in Release 3.0 of SAP Exchange Infrastructure. Linde uses this function to collect, sort, regroup, and merge XI messages.

9.1 Business Background of the Scenario

With its three brands, Linde, STILL, and OM Pimespo, and strategic partner Komatsu, the Linde Group (business area Material Handling, MH) is one of the largest manufacturers of industrial trucks in the world.

The authorized dealerships of Linde Material Handling (UK) Ltd can create warranty claims decentrally on an SAP R/3 4.6C system. However, the warranty claims are processed on the central SAP R/3 Enterprise. The data is exchanged between the systems via SAP XI 3.0.

The warranty claims scenario at the Linde Group consists of three communication steps:

The dealership associated with Linde MH (UK) Ltd registers every fork lift sold on the local SAP R/3 system at the Basingstoke (UK) branch; this data is later used to process the warranty claims. The data is sent through SAP XI to the central SAP R/3 Enterprise system via IDoc-to-IDoc communication. The data container used is an IDoc of type ZFSSUB1, which is developed by Linde.

Registering the Fork Lifts

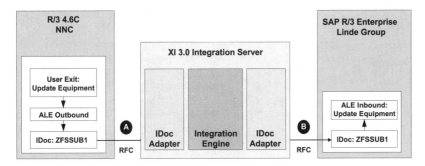

Figure 9.1 Registering the Fork Lifts

The dealerships in the UK (NNC, National Network Companies) create every warranty claim in the SAP R/3 system at the Basingstoke branch. The warranty claims are sent to SAP XI, which then forwards them to the central SAP R/3 Enterprise system. During the technical realization of the scenario, the emphasis was put on reusing as much of an existing file interface as possible. For this reason, a file containing the data for one or more warranty claims is saved on an FTP server every day for each dealership. The files are read by a sender FTP adapter, converted to one XI message per warranty claim, and then sent to SAP XI. The XI messages are mapped to an XI message that is defined by the IDoc type ZWRANTY02. Finally, the message is sent to the central SAP R/3 Enterprise system via the IDoc adapter.

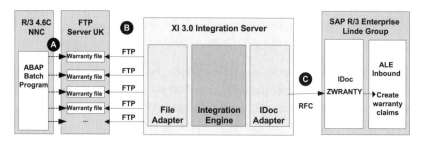

Figure 9.2 Creating the Warranty Claims

Once the warranty claims have been processed in the Linde Group's central SAP R/3 Enterprise system, the result is sent back to the local SAP R/3 system in the UK. In the process, all the returned warranty claims for one day are collected and sorted and merged by dealership. Because this scenario uses an interesting example of a cross-component integration process, we will look at it in more detail throughout this chapter.

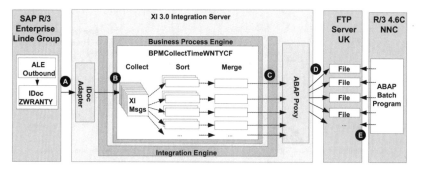

Figure 9.3 Returning the Warranty Claims

9.2 Technical Description

9.2.1 Sending the Responses to the Warranty Claims

Once the warranty claims have been processed, one IDoc per warranty claim is sent from the Linde Group's central SAP R/3 Enterprise system back to the local SAP R/3 system in the UK as part of an ALE scenario. The IDoc type ZWRANTY02, which is Linde's enhancement of the basis IDoc type WRANTY02, is used as the data container.

ALE Scenario

9.2.2 Arrival of the Messages on the Integration Server

The IDocs of type ZWRANTY02 are first sent to the Integration Server by using the IDoc adapter. Acting as the link between the SAP R/3 Enterprise system and the Integration Server, the IDoc adapter has two tasks: it enables the technical connection between the IDoc/RFC protocol and the XI pipeline, and, it converts the data in native IDoc format to an XML representation of the IDoc (IDoc-to-XML). The result is that the IDoc is converted to an XI message of type ZWRANTY02.

IDoc Adapter

9.2.3 Cross-Component Business Process Management

Once the Integration Server has received this XI message, it is forwarded to the integration process BPMCollectTimeWNTYCF by logical routing. The integration process itself can be divided into three sections that are processed sequentially:

Starting the Integration Process BPMCollectTimeWNTYCF

1. Collect XI messages
2. Sort warranty claim responses
3. Merge and send messages

Collecting the XI Messages

The integration process is started by an XI message. The message interface StartInterface was defined and an ABAP proxy was created specifically for this purpose. The message ensures that the first part of the integration process—the collecting of messages—will begin exactly when this message is received.

All IDocs of type ZWRANTY02 sent to SAP XI are caught and processed by the block CollectWranty. This block corresponds to the example step combination BpmPatternCollectMessage. The *Collect* pattern is one of a series of example step combinations that are shipped together with SAP

Example Step Combinations

XI 3.0. The patterns provide examples of frequently occurring tasks to ease process modeling. The patterns are part of the software component SAP BASIS and are located in the integration processes of the namespace http://sap.com/xi/XI/System/Patterns.

BpmPattern-CollectMessage Within this Collect pattern, all IDocs sent to SAP XI are individually put in an endless loop by a receive step. A container operation then collects the messages in a multiline process container. The latter contains the contents of all IDocs received since the process started.

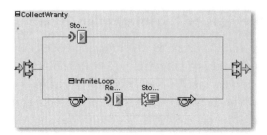

Figure 9.4 Block CollectWranty

Fork Since the endless loop with the receive step and the container operation was created as a branch of a *fork* in the block CollectWranty, it can be stopped by using a defined message (in this case, the message interface StopInterface). The message interface StopInterface is used only to stop the collection of IDoc messages at a specified point in time. Apart from this, it does not serve any other function. An ABAP batch process starts daily at 0:05 am and sends StopInterface to the integration process via a proxy.

Correlation The XI message of type ZWRANTY02 is connected to the running integration process via a correlation, which comprises the date and the name of the message type. The Collect pattern causes all IDoc messages of this type to be collected every day until 11:55 pm and then transferred to the second section of the integration process.[1]

Sorting the Responses to the Warranty Claims

The second section of the integration process sorts the responses to the warranty claims collected in the first step by dealership.

---

1 IDoc messages that are sent to the Business Process Engine after the arrival of the end message enter a new instance of the integration process.

In this second section, a loop reads the IDoc data collected in the first step. This loop is created as part of the block `SortWrantyCfBlock` in mode **ParForEach**. The loop reads the multiline element that was created in the first section and that contains the content of the collected IDocs. Each step in the loop fills a new container, which contains the data of the individual IDocs.

ParForEach

Using the process step *Switch*, these containers are then distributed to the individual, dealership-specific branches. The messages are partitioned by using the partner number of the dealership, which is part of the container content. Each branch processes the messages that are intended for precisely one dealership.

Switch

A counter (process step *Container Operation*) determines the number of warranty claim responses accrued for a particular dealership (note that we are in a program loop here). Then, the second process step of the branch (type Container Operation) collects the individual, dealership-specific container content in a new container. At the end of the loop, these dealership-specific containers are transferred to the third section of the integration process before being sent.

Container Operation

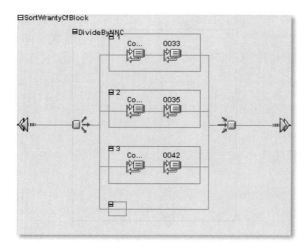

Figure 9.5 Block SortWrantyCfBlock

Merging and Sending the Messages

The third section of the integration process starts with a process step of type Fork. In this process step, each dealership has a separate branch to enable messages to be sent simultaneously. The process step Switch checks each individual branch to determine whether this process cycle

Fork

contains any messages for the relevant dealership. The counter from the second section is used for this purpose.

Transformation If there are one or more responses to warranty claims, the multiline elements of the container are put in one message for each dealership via a process step of type *Transformation*. This is performed as part of a multi-mapping. If there are no messages for a specific dealership, the default branch of the switch, which contains no further process steps, is executed.

Sending Finally, the responses to the warranty claims, which have been collected and put in a single message, are sent to the individual dealerships.

Chapter 8 contains a detailed introduction to integration processes and process steps.

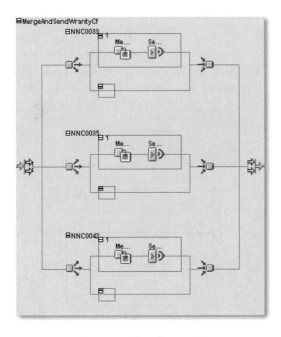

Figure 9.6 Fork MergeAndSendWrantyCf

9.2.4 Message Outbound Channel

The send step in the integration process transfers the messages to the Integration Server pipeline. A receiver agreement determines the communication channel of type XI. This means that when the message leaves the pipeline, it is sent to the receiver by using the XI protocol. In this scenario, the receiver is a local Integration Engine of SAP Web AS. From there, the messages are transferred to an ABAP proxy. The proxy creates a file on an FTP server for each outbound message, that is, for each dealership.

The decision to include the FTP server was made to incorporate a file interface that existed prior to the installation of SAP XI. By using a specific background job, the dealerships can import their messages to the R/3 NNC system from the FTP server and process them there.

This concludes the technical overview of the scenario. Now we'll take a more detailed look at the configuration steps necessary to define the scenario.

9.3 Implementing the Scenario at the Linde Group

The scenario is implemented in three sections, with each section building on the previous one.

1. First, the business systems that are involved in the integration scenario are created in the System Landscape Directory (SLD). Since Linde develops its own SAP XI objects within the scenario, certain software components must be defined in the SLD to accommodate these objects.

2. The building blocks of the integration scenario—such as data types, interfaces, mappings, and the integration process—are developed in the Integration Repository.

3. In the final step, the business systems created in the SLD and the building blocks of the integration scenario from the Integration Repository are assigned to routing rules in the Integration Directory. Once activated, these are then available in the XI Runtime to ensure that the messages sent to SAP XI are forwarded to the correct receiver.

9.3.1 System Landscape and Software Catalog

Objects in the Integration Repository are assigned to software component versions; the latter first need to be created in the SLD software catalog and then imported to the Integration Repository. All the objects required for the warranty claims scenario at Linde were developed as part of the software component NNC, Version 1.0. This, in turn, is a part of Version 1.0 of product NNC.

Software Component Versions

Business System	SAP XI uses the parameters *party*, *service*, *interface*, and *namespace* to form the key for the routing rules that are to be defined. In the case of the service parameter, you can choose between *business service* (with or without a party), *integration process*, and *business system*. The business system represents a separate application system within the customer's system landscape, and is therefore created in the SLD.

Two steps are required to define the SAP R/3 Enterprise 4.70 business system in the SLD:

The technical system D01 of type *Web AS ABAP* is created. This requires the installation number, the host of the central message server, and the instance number to be entered. The system can be assigned additional application servers. In our scenario, client 200 was created on the technical system, and it was assigned to the product Linde MH.

Business System D01BS200	Then, the business system D01BS200 can be defined. It is assigned to client 200 and the central Integration Server DXI.

Business System XI_Proxy_Client	The XI messages in the outbound channel of the Integration Server are sent to the FTP server via an ABAP proxy; an additional client (100) was set up on the technical system (which also accommodates the Integration Server) for this purpose. This is assigned the business system XI_Proxy_Client, which is also used to send the messages for starting and ending the integration process (see Section 9.2.3).[2]

9.3.2 Designing the Integration Objects in the Integration Repository

Before development of the objects can begin, Version 1.0 of software component NNC must be imported to the Integration Repository from the SLD.

Software Component Version in the Integration Repository

Importing Interfaces	Because the warranty claims scenario includes the definition of message mappings based on IDoc structures, Linde enables the import of RFCs and IDoc interfaces in software component Version NNC 1.0. This means that you can use existing RFC and IDoc structures from SAP systems rather than having to create them again. In Figure 9.7, you can see the

---

2 Note that SAP does not recommend installing the Integration Server and a business system on the same SAP system (see also Chapter 7).

connection data to SAP system D01, client 200. The entry in the **Message Server** field has been blacked out for security reasons.

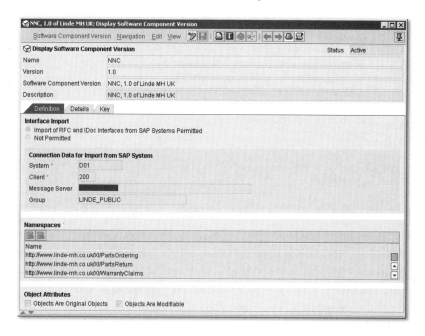

Figure 9.7 Connection Data and Namespaces of Version 1.0 of Software Component NNC of Linde MH UK

New integration objects that are created in the Integration Repository are assigned to namespaces. The namespaces are defined in the Integration Repository in the relevant software component version. By extending the company's Uniform Resource Locator (URL), you can ensure that a namespace is unique globally. The namespace `http://www.linde-mh.co.uk/XI/WarrantyClaims` is defined for all SAP XI objects that are created as part of the warranty claims scenario.

Namespace

Since system D01 is the Linde Group's XI development system, the object properties—**Objects Are Original Objects** and **Objects Are Modifiable**—are set.

Object Properties

Once the changes to the software component version have been saved, the entries for the namespaces and imported objects are displayed in the overview tree (see Figure 9.8).

Development of the objects can now begin in the Integration Repository.

Figure 9.8 Overview of Namespaces Created in Version 1.0 of Software Component NNC of Linde MH UK

Definition of Messages Involved in the Integration Process

Both IDocs and ABAP proxies are used to exchange messages with the integration process. For IDoc communication, the relevant structures are imported from the Linde Group's SAP application system. For ABAP proxy communication, the data structure is defined as a message interface in the Integration Repository. The following messages are involved in the integration process:

Importing IDoc Structures

▶ **Importing the Structure of IDoc ZWRANTY02**
The warranty claims are returned by using the IDoc ZWRANTY02. Because the IDoc structure is required for the definition of mappings and as a template for abstract interfaces, it is imported from the SAP system D01.[3] Figure 9.9 shows how the structure of the IDoc ZWRANTY02 is displayed in the Integration Repository.

Starting and Stopping

▶ **Defining the Messages for Starting and Stopping the Integration Process**
The processed warranty claims must be collected and sorted by cross-component Business Process Management (ccBPM) within a defined period of time. Because the time when the integration process is to start and end is controlled by a non-SAP system in this scenario, you must define both a start and a stop message. Since both messages are sent to XI from the business system XI_Proxy_Client (as we will see later), the message interfaces StartInterface and StopInterface are created with the attributes **asynchronous** and **outbound**.

---

3 The sender or receiver SAP system does not have to be identical to the system from which the structure is imported. However, the IDoc structure must be the same in both systems.

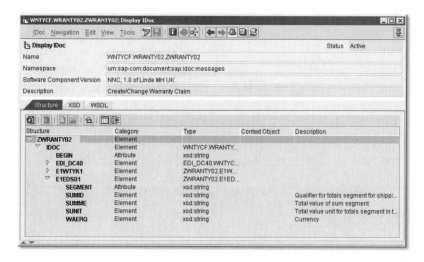

Figure 9.9 Message Structure of IDoc Type ZWRANTY02 in the Integration Repository

Figure 9.10 shows the message type `StartMessage` for the interface `StartInterface`, which is used to start the integration process.

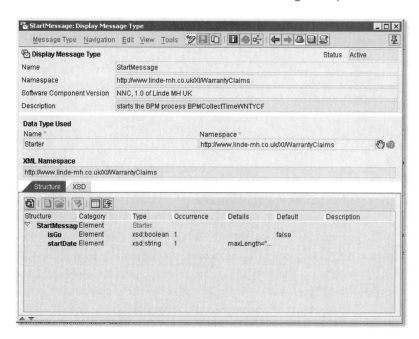

Figure 9.10 Message Type StartMessage

▶ **Message Interface for Sending Collected and Processed Warranty Claims**

After the warranty claims have been collected and sorted by the ccBPM process, they are sent to the local SAP system of the Linde dealership in the UK via an ABAP proxy. The asynchronous inbound interface NNCWarrantyClaimsConfirmation_BPM is defined in the Integration Repository for this purpose. Figure 9.11 shows the message type NNCWarrantyClaimsConfirmation, which is referenced by the interface; it defines the structure of the messages that are sent to the dealership.

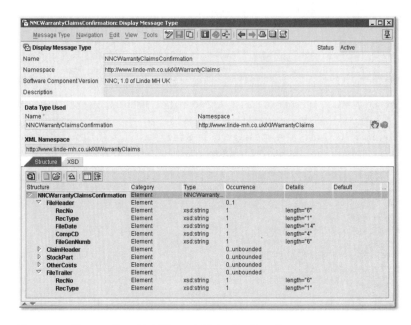

Figure 9.11 Message Type NNCWarrantyClaimsConfirmation

▶ **Signature of the Integration Process**

All message interfaces that are sent to or from an integration process define the signature of the integration process. In the case of our integration process, the signature is defined *unambiguously* by the message interfaces above: The integration process receives messages from the message interfaces ZWRANTY02, StartInterface, and StopInterface, and sends messages of type NNCWarrantyClaimsConfirmation_BPM.[4]

---

4 As shown in Section Configuration in the Integration Directory, we need to differentiate between the message interfaces of the sender and receiver services and the abstract interfaces of the integration process. Because no mapping is required in any of the four cases in this scenario, the structures are identical.

Now let's look at the individual configuration steps of the integration process in more detail.

Integration Process BPMCollectTimeWNTYCF

Figure 9.12 shows a graphical overview of the integration process BPM-CollectTimeWNTYCF, with the three sections for collecting, sorting, and sending the messages. The configuration of the process steps 1–14 is explained in more detail in the rest of this chapter. Note that the current solution is implemented at three dealerships. This is indicated by the three branches in the sorting and sending sections.

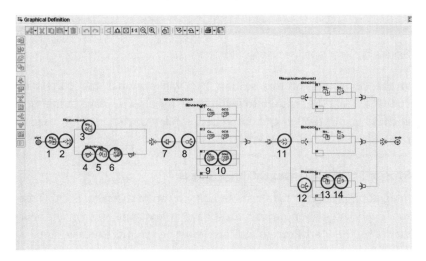

Figure 9.12 Overview of the Integration Process BPMCollectTimeWNTYCF

Defining the Correlations CorrelationA and CorrStartAndStop

To be able to selectively incorporate other messages in the process in additional receive steps, correlations need to be defined and activated.

Figure 9.13 shows the entries for the correlation CorrStartAndStop used by Linde in the warranty claims scenario.

Once the correlation has been activated, the correlation container TimeStamp of type String saves its key value. The correlation involves the messages StartMessage_BPM_Abstract and StopMessage_BPM_Abstract. The fields of the messages that fill the correlation container at runtime—or whose contents will be compared with the contents of the correlation container to incorporate the message in the process—are defined in the properties. For the correlation container TimeStamp, the fields are startDate and stopDate.

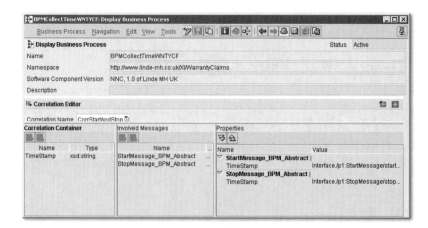

Figure 9.13 Correlation CorrStartAndStop

In the remainder of this section, we will see that the correlation `CorrStartAndStop` is used to incorporate the stop message in the runtime instance of the integration process, while `CorrelationA` is used to receive IDocs of type `ZWRANTY02`.

Step 1: Start the Integration Process

Receive Step Integration processes can be started only by an XI message. For this reason, every integration process must have at least one receive step. Furthermore, the **Start Process** indicator must be set in the receive step.

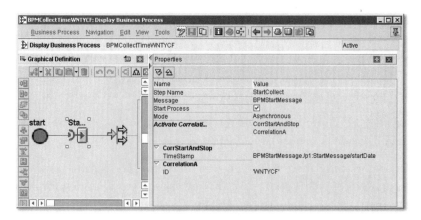

Figure 9.14 Receive Step StartCollect

In the integration process BPMCollectTimeWNTYCF, this role is performed by the asynchronous receive step StartCollect (Figure 9.14). The container element BPMStartMessage is filled with the data from the start message. For this to happen, the container element must reference the abstract interface StartMessage_BPM_Abstract. In the description of the configuration steps in the Integration Directory, we'll see how the outbound interface StartInterface, which is sent to SAP XI, is transferred to the abstract interface StartMessage_BPM_Abstract.

Typically, the following cascading reference applies when an XI message is transferred to the container of an integration process: The container element to be filled references an abstract interface. This dependency is defined in the container definition of the integration process editor. This abstract interface must, in turn, be defined by an interface determination when an XI message is sent to the integration process.

Besides starting the integration process and filling the container, the receive step StartCollect activates the correlations CorrStartAndStop and CorrelationA. The correlation container TimeStamp (of correlation CorrStartAndStop) is given the value of the field startDate from the container BPMStartMessage (and therefore the message StartMessage_BPM_Abstract), while the correlation container ID (of correlation CorrelationA) is assigned the constant WNTYCF. These correlations are now the keys for future receive steps.

Activating the Correlations

We already encountered the example step combination BpmPatternCollectMessage in Section 9.2.3. Now let's look at exactly how it is used in practice in the integration process BPMCollectTimeWNTYCF. In our scenario, it covers steps numbers two to six.

Step 2: Fork CollectWranty

The fork CollectWranty defines the stopping criterion for the receipt of the IDocs of type ZWRANTY02. In Figure 9.15, you can see that the number of necessary branches is one. This means that the fork will end and the integration process will move on to the next step as soon as one of the two branches is successfully processed.

Stopping Criterion

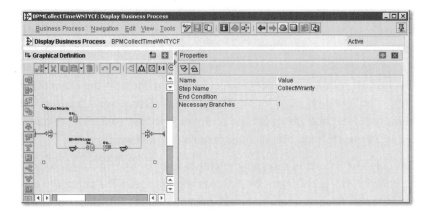

Figure 9.15 Fork CollectWranty

Step 3: Receive Step StopCollect

The properties of receive step `StopCollect` are shown in Figure 9.16. Again, the association with the message to be received of type *abstract interface* is indirect: The container `BPMStopMessage` is created with a reference to the abstract interface `StopMessage_BPM_Abstract`. The messages of this interface that are sent to SAP XI will enter the process only if the condition in the correlation `CorrStartAndStop` is satisfied. To satisfy the condition, the value in the field `stopDate` in the message must be the same as the value in the correlation container `TimeStamp` in an existing process instance.

Figure 9.16 Receive Step StopCollect

The receive step `StopCollect` is on one of the branches of the fork `Col-`
`lectWranty`. Consequently, it is capable of stopping the fork; indeed that
is its task. Later, we will see that it is not possible for the second branch to
be processed successfully. The receive step `StopMessage` therefore
"switches off" the fork `CollectWranty`.

Step 4: Loop InfiniteLoop

A loop in an integration process will continue to be executed as long as
the defined condition returns true. In this integration process, an endless
loop is created by ensuring that two constants are set equal to the value 1.

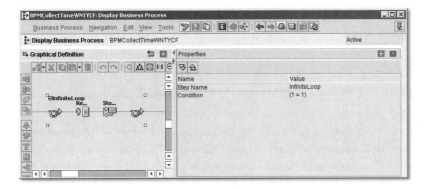

Figure 9.17 Loop InfiniteLoop

Step 5: Receive Step ReceiveIDOCs

The receive step `ReceiveIDOCs` receives IDocs of type `ZWRANTY02`, and
transfers their contents to the container element `WarrantyConfirma-`
`tionIn`. Here too, the link between the XI message and the container
element is enabled by the fact that the container element references the
abstract interface `WNTYCF_BPM_Abstract` in the container definition. The
abstract interface, in turn, references the imported IDoc type `ZWRANTY02`.
In Figure 9.18, you can see that the receive step uses the correlation `Cor-`
`relationA`. It ensures that the only messages that enter the process
instance are those in which the field `MESTYP` in the payload is equal to the
constant `WNTYCF` (see also Step 1).

Receiving IDocs

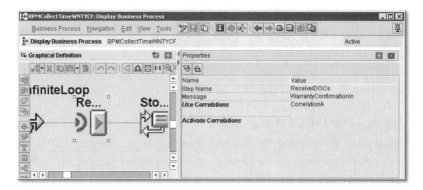

Figure 9.18 Receive Step ReceiveIDOCs

Since the receive step is in the infinite loop, IDocs can continue to be received until the end of the fork `CollectWranty`.

Step 6: Container Operation StoreMessage

Collecting IDoc Contents

Each time the receive step `ReceiveIDOCs` receives an IDoc, it fills the container element `WarrantyConfirmationIn`. A container operation is used to collect the contents of each IDoc in a multiline container element before the next IDoc arrives and overwrites the container contents. This ensures that the contents of none of the IDocs are lost.

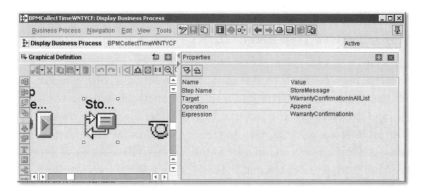

Figure 9.19 Container Operation StoreMessage

Figure 9.19 shows how such a collect step is created. It is important that the single-line container `WarrantyConfirmationIn` and the multiline container `WarrantyConfirmationInAllList` reference the same abstract interface and therefore have the same structure. The operation **Append** then collects the data.[5]

Step 7: Block SortWrantyCfBlock

Sorting Container Contents

In the previous steps, the contents of all IDocs of type ZWRANTY02 sent to SAP XI in the period of time between the receipt of the messages StartInterface and StopInterface were collected in the container element WarrantyConfirmationInAllList. The contents of this container now have to be sorted by dealership.

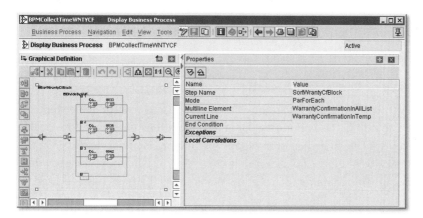

Figure 9.20 Block SortWrantyCfBlock

Again, this is achieved by using a loop, which in this case is defined by a block in mode ParForEach. The loop runs through the individual lines of the multiline container element WarrantyConfirmationInAllList and transports its contents line by line to the container WarrantyConfirmationInTemp once for each loop. This container can now be operated on within the block.

Step 8: Switch DivideByNNC

Figure 9.21 shows that within the loop, a specific branch is executed for each dealership. In our example, the sort mechanism was implemented for three dealerships. The branch criterion is defined by the field PARNR (party number) in container WarrantyConfirmationInTemp.

---

5 Remember that this process step is part of an infinite loop.

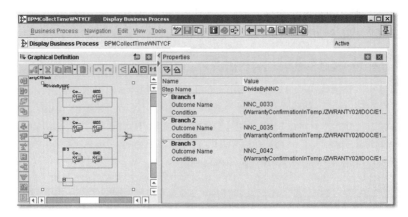

Figure 9.21 Switch DivideByNNC

Step 9: Container Operation Count_0035

Counting the
Warranty Claims
Responses

First, the number of warranty claims responses for each dealership is to be counted. This is done by container operations on each of the dealership-specific branches in the loop. A container element MsgCount_NNC_ ⟨PARNR⟩ of type xsd:integer is created for this purpose for each dealership. This container counts how many times the branch is executed.

Figure 9.22 shows how the step is defined for the dealership with the party number 0035. Each time the process step is called, the value 1 is added to the contents of container MsgCount_NNC_0035.

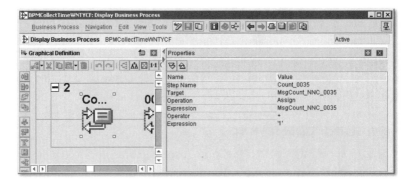

Figure 9.22 Container Operation Count_0035

Step 10: Container Operation 0035

Collecting the
Responses

Until now, we operated on the single-line container element Warranty-ConfirmationInTemp within our loop. Now, however, the warranty claims responses for each dealership must be collected in separate containers. This is done by using a container operation, similar to collecting the IDocs in Step 6. Each time a dealership branch is executed (for example, PARNR=0035), the single-line container WarrantyConfirmationIn-Temp is appended to the multiline container WarrantyConfirmation_NNC_0035 (see Figure 9.23).

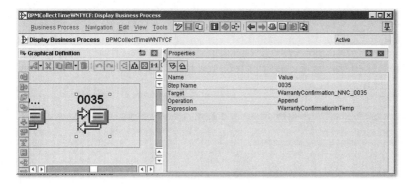

Figure 9.23 Container Operation 0035

Once all the warranty claims responses have been distributed to the containers of the individual dealerships, they can be sent to each dealership as messages.

Step 11: Fork MergeAndSendWrantyCf

In our example, the responses to the warranty claims are sent to three dealerships. A fork with three necessary branches is used to ensure that the containers with the sorted responses reach the correct dealership (see Figure 9.24).

Sending the Responses

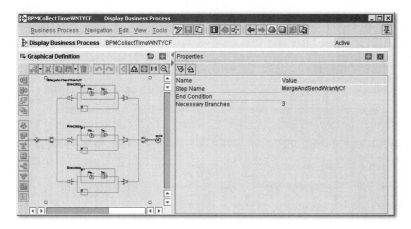

Figure 9.24 Fork MergeAndSendWrantyCf

Step 12: Switch NNC0035

Checking Number of Responses To ensure that no messages are sent to the dealerships without any warranty claims responses, the responses determined in Step 9 are queried for each dealership. The switch has two branches: If the parameter MsgCount_NNC_0035 does not equal 0, the upper branch is executed and the responses are sent to the dealership. However, if the counter equals 0, the *empty* lower branch is executed without any additional process steps.

Figure 9.25 shows the settings required to define a switch for one dealership as an example.

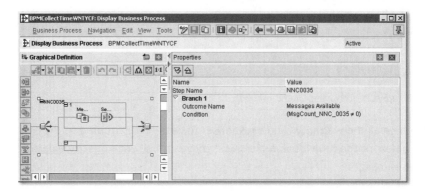

Figure 9.25 Switch NNC0035

Step 13: Transformation Merge_0035

Mapping Thus far in the integration process, all container elements that contain data about warranty claims responses reference the abstract interface WNTYCF_BPM_Abstract. The latter is based on the structure definition of the IDoc ZWRANTY02. However, the messages that will be sent to the dealerships must have the structure shown in Figure 9.11, which means that a mapping is required before the messages can be sent.

Aggregation In addition to the conversion of the structure, the contents of the container also need to be aggregated. This is done with a *multi-mapping*. The multiline container WarrantyConfirmation_NNC_0035 from Step 10 is applied to the transformation step. However, the container that leaves the step (WarrantyConfirmationOut_0035) is a single-line container.

Figure 9.26 illustrates some dependencies of the message mapping created in the Integration Repository. This message mapping is called from the interface mapping `WNTYCF2Warranty_ClaimsConfirmation_BPM` as a mapping program.

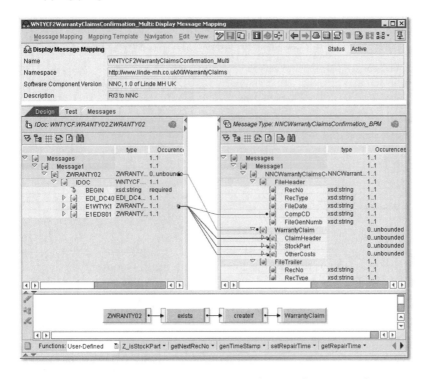

Figure 9.26 Message Mapping WNTYCF2WarrantyClaimsConfirmation_Multi

We now have everything we need for the transformation and can create the process step. Figure 9.27 shows the necessary settings. Note that you must enter both the names of the abstract interfaces and of the corresponding containers for the source and target messages.

Creating the Process Step

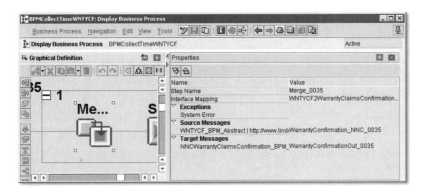

Figure 9.27 Transformation Merge_0035

Step 14: Send Step Send_0035

Sending the Responses

In the final step, the collected, sorted, and aggregated responses to the warranty claims are sent to the dealerships.

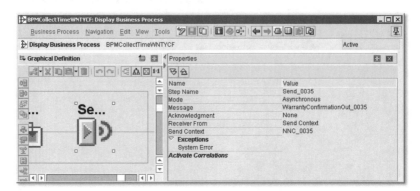

Figure 9.28 Send Step Send_0035

Figure 9.28 shows the settings that are required. The contents of the container `WarrantyConfirmationOut_0035` from the previous transformation step are sent asynchronously in send context NNC_0035. Therefore, the message is transferred to the pipeline of the Integration Engine, which then sends the message.

Before we look at the settings in the Integration Directory, we'll summarize the containers and their references that are involved in the integration process in the following overview table. The container elements are shown chronologically in the order in which they appear in the integration process.

Container Element	Abstract Interface	Message Type/IDoc Structure
BPMStartMessage	StartMessage_BPM_Abstract	StartMessage
WarrantyConfirmationIn	WNTYCF_BPM_Abstract	ZWRANTY02
WarrantyConfirmationIn AllList	WNTYCF_BPM_Abstract	ZWRANTY02
BPMStopMessage	StopMessage_BPM_Abstract	StopMessage
WarrantyConfirmationIn Temp	WNTYCF_BPM_Abstract	ZWRANTY02

Table 9.1 Containers and References in the Integration Process

Container Element	Abstract Interface	Message Type/IDoc Structure
WarrantyConfirmation_ NNC_<PARNR>	WNTYCF_BPM_Abstract	ZWRANTY02
WarrantyConfirmationOut_ <PARNR>	NNCWarrantyClaimsConfirmation_ BPM_Abstract	NNCWarranty ClaimsConfirm ation_BPM

Table 9.1 Containers and References in the Integration Process (cont.)

9.3.3 Configuration in the Integration Directory

In this chapter, we have already seen what settings were made in the SLD and Integration Repository in Linde's SAP XI system. Therefore, all the building blocks required for the scenario have been created and can now be assigned to the actual application systems. The necessary configuration steps, such as defining services, logical routing, and communication channels, are performed in the Integration Directory.

Configuration Scenario

Using configuration scenarios, all the configuration objects in the Integration Directory can be grouped into logical entities. In the Linde scenario, the configuration scenario NNC_WarrantyClaimConfirmation_To groups together all the Integration Directory objects that are required to send the responses to the warranty claims.

Services

In SAP XI, services represent the technical or business sources and targets of the XI messages. Therefore, they are the start and end points for all configuration steps.

In the Linde scenario, services without a party of type *integration process* and *business system* are used. (For a description of the different types of services, see Section 6.2.6.)

In Section 9.3.1, we saw the steps that were necessary to create the business systems D01BS200 and XI_Proxy_Client in the SLD. Before they can be used to define logical routings, they first need to be imported into the Integration Directory from the SLD. While being imported, they are assigned to the configuration scenario NNC_WarrantyClaimConfirmation_To, and are then added to the navigation tree under the relevant node (see Figure 9.29).

Business Systems D01BS200 and XI_Proxy_Client

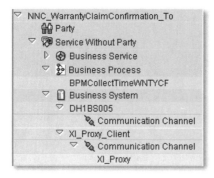

```
▽  NNC_WarrantyClaimConfirmation_To
     ▦ Party
   ▽ ▦ Service Without Party
     ▷ ⊕ Business Service
     ▽ ▣ Business Process
          BPMCollectTimeWNTYCF
       ▽ ▯ Business System
         ▽ DH1BS005
              ⚒ Communication Channel
          ▽ XI_Proxy_Client
            ▽ ⚒ Communication Channel
                 XI_Proxy
```

Figure 9.29 Services of the Integration Scenario NNC_WarrantyClaimConfirmation_To

Integration Process Service BPMCollectTi- meWNTYCF Section 9.3.2 showed the steps that are necessary to create the integration process BPMCollectTimeWNTYCF in the Integration Repository. For the integration process to be able to receive and send XI messages at runtime, an integration process service needs to be created in the Integration Directory. This, in turn, references the actual process definition in the Integration Repository. Note that both the integration process in the Integration Repository as well as the integration process service in the Integration Directory have the name BPMCollectTimeWNTYCF. However, these are two different entities. Figure 9.30 shows the reference to the integration process in the Integration Directory and the signature of the messages to be received.

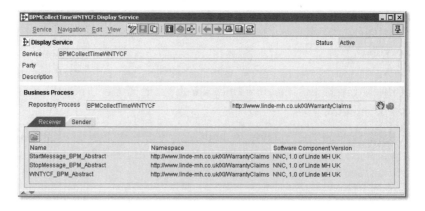

Figure 9.30 Receiver Interfaces of the Integration Process Service BPMCollect-TimeWNTYCF

All services involved in the scenario are now defined, and we can begin to create the logical routings based on them.

Logical Routing and Communication Channels

In Section 9.3.2 we saw that the messages ZWRANTY02, StartInter-face, and StopInterface are sent to the integration process, while the system for the Linde dealerships receives messages of type NNCWarrantyClaimsConfirmation_BPM. These correspond to the abstract interfaces WNTYCF_BPM_Abstract, StartMessage_BPM_Abstract, StopMessage_BPM_Abstract, and NNCWarrantyClaims-Confirmation_BPM_Abstract of the integration process signature. Consequently, four receiver determinations and four interface determinations have to be created in the Integration Directory:

1. Sending the start message from the proxy client to the integration process service

Receiver and Interface Determinations

2. Sending the responses from the application system to the integration process

3. Sending the stop message from the proxy client to the integration process

4. Sending the sorted and bundled responses to the proxy client

In Figure 9.31, you can see the configuration settings that are required to ensure that the start message finds its way to—and is received by—the integration process service BPMCollectTimeWNTYCF. The settings are as follows: If a message with the key fields[6] **Sender Service** = XI_Proxy_Client, **Interface** = StartInterface, and **Namespace** = http://www.linde-mh.co.uk/XI/WarrantyClaims is sent to the Integration Engine, it is forwarded to the receiver service BPMCollect-TimeWNTYCF (the integration process service).

Sending the Start Message

The newly determined receiver service is now part of the key and is used for the interface determination. Figure 9.32 illustrates how the receiver interface StartMessage_BPM_Abstract is derived from the newly formed key. Because the sender and receiver interface reference the same message type, no interface mapping is required.

Since the receiver service is an integration process service, no communication channel needs to be defined for it.

---

6 These *key fields* are filled automatically by the sender ABAP proxy.

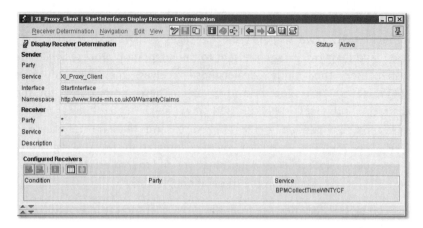

Figure 9.31 Receiver Determination for the Outbound Interface StartInterface

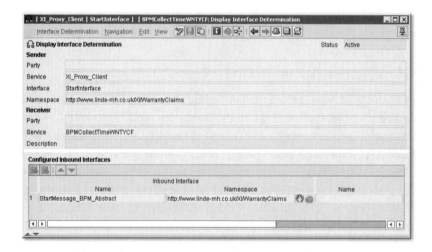

Figure 9.32 Interface Determination for the Outbound Interface StartInterface

Sending the Responses

In Figure 9.33, you can see the settings for the receiver determination and interface determination for the IDocs of type ZWRANTY02 that were sent to SAP XI from business system D01BS200. Note that only messages that have the key *UK* are sent to the receiver service BPMCollectTimeWN-TYCF (the integration process). Neither an interface mapping nor a receiver agreement is required in this case.

However, it is still not guaranteed that the contents of the IDocs can also be transferred to the relevant container in the integration process. As described in Section 9.3.2, the relevant receive step uses the correlation

CorrelationA. The message will be accepted by the integration process only when the condition in the correlation is satisfied.

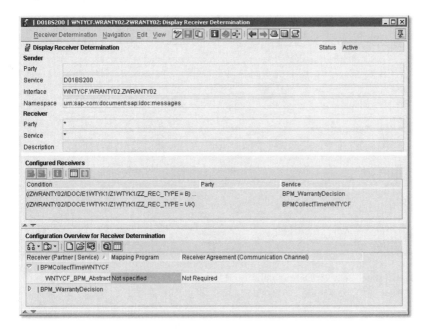

Figure 9.33 Receiver Determination and Interface Determination for the Outbound Interface ZWRANTY02

With the exception of the interfaces, the configuration settings are the same as those used for the start message (see Figures 9.31 and 9.32). The message is also sent by the business system XI_Proxy_Client, and again the receiver service BPMCollectTimeWNTYCF acts as the receiver.

Sending the Stop Message

A fourth logical routing is required to make the messages from the integration process available to the various dealerships. The receiver in this case is the business system XI_Proxy_Client, which is also used to send the start and stop message. The necessary settings are summarized in Figure 9.34.

Sending the Sorted and Bundled Responses

Unlike those instances whereby the integration process acts as a message receiver, here a receiver agreement is required. The receiver agreement XI_Proxy contains a reference to a receiver communication channel of the same name. Figure 9.35 shows the settings required to send a message to the local Integration Engine of client 100. The entries for the target host and the service number have been blacked out for security reasons.

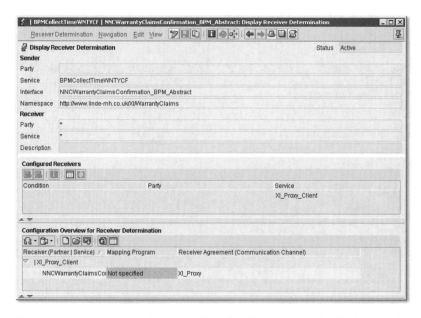

Figure 9.34 Receiver Determination and Interface Determination for the Outbound Interface NNCWarrantyClaimsConfirmation_BPM_Abstract

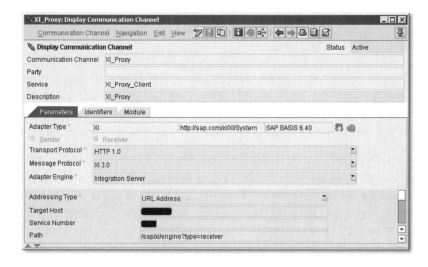

Figure 9.35 Communication Channel XI_Proxy

The ABAP proxy implemented on the Integration Engine receives the messages and makes them available on an FTP server UK (see Figure 9.3). These files are then imported into the local SAP R/3 system in the UK.

The logical routings for the responses to the warranty claims have now been created. Once the changes are activated, the XI Runtime can be used to sort and merge the responses and then make them available to the Linde dealerships.

9.4 Summary

The Linde Group demands that all messages that contain individual responses to warranty claims are collected and returned to the respective dealership in the form of a dealership-specific message within 24 hours. SAP XI, with its integrated ccBPM function, provides the Linde Group with a tool for this purpose that enables the dependencies and associations between messages to be defined. Therefore, this scenario is a typical example of how cross-component Business Process Management can be applied.

10 Cross-Company Communication Using SAP XI

A global food manufacturer uses SAP XI as a central hub for exchanging business data with its partners. It uses the enhanced B2B functions of Version 3.0.

10.1 Business Background of the Scenario

This SAP XI customer uses the Internet to exchange business data with its partners. The role that SAP XI 3.0 plays here is that of a central gateway for connecting the internal system landscape of the company with the services of its business partners.

This chapter explains how connections are implemented between an SAP Customer Relationship Management (SAP CRM) 4.0 system and the UCCnet™ Data Pool Service. We will pay particular attention to those functions provided by SAP XI 3.0 for Business-to-Business (B2B) communication.

B2B Communication

UCCnet enables product data to be published on the Internet, thus making it available to business partners at a central location. The product information is sent as catalog messages to UCCnet, where it is saved in a standardized format. This enables potential business partners to access the catalog data. The UCCnet Data Pool Service enables information to be collected at a central location and made available in a standardized form, thus providing a foundation for electronic commerce.

UCCnet

10.2 Technical Description

Our example focuses on integration that goes beyond the boundaries of the internal system landscape of the SAP XI customer. Therefore, this chapter concentrates on the following components and functions of SAP XI 3.0:

1. **B2B functions in the Integration Repository**
   In SAP XI, you can use integration scenarios to model cross-application collaborative processes. These integration scenarios are like blueprints, representing sample message flows between applications. Later in this chapter, Figure 10.4 shows an example of such an integration scenario. You assign actual business systems and services to these blueprints to create logical routings in the Integration Directory. To enable the

Integration Scenario

parameters required for B2B communication to be set automatically as well, the **External Party with B2B Communication** checkbox must be selected under **Communication Type** during definition of the application component in the integration scenario (see Section 3.3.1).

2. **B2B functions in the Integration Directory**
SAP XI 3.0 enables you to use not only *business systems*, but *parties* and *services* as logical senders and receivers for XI messages. In general, when a business message is sent to a partner, no information is available about its system landscape. The interfaces provided by the partner are bundled into logical units, that is, the services. The services are published and can be addressed during B2B communication. You make the corresponding entries for maintaining these services in the Integration Directory.

Conversely, the sender party (in our case, the SAP XI customer) may not want to reveal internal system information to its business partners. Here, too, it is possible to replace the information about the sender party's *own* business system with the neutral parameters *party* and *service* (see Section 6.4).

3. **Integration scenario configurator**
Once the integration scenarios have been created in the Integration Repository, you can use them to derive configuration rules in the Integration Directory. To do this, you assign the services in the Integration Directory to the integration scenarios created in the Integration Repository. The integration scenario configurator tool is available to guide you through the necessary configuration settings (see Section 6.3.1).

4. **UCCnet adapter from iWay**
The UCCnet adapter from iWay has two tasks during the connection of the UCCnet Data Pool to SAP XI. First, it establishes the technical connection between the two systems. Secondly, it converts the enhanced SOAP protocol of SAP XI to the proprietary data format of UCCnet Data Pool Services. The UCCnet adapter is bi-directional; it can send XI messages to the UCCnet Data Pool and receive UCCnet messages and forward them to the XI Runtime.

From a technical point of view, the UCCnet adapter is a resource adapter in the Java Connector Architecture (JCA)[1] sense, and can therefore be inserted in the Adapter Engine. For this purpose, iWay provides adapter metadata, which is saved in the Integration Repository. The actual adapter instance is implemented in the Integration Direc-

---

1 The Java Connector Architecture is part of the J2EE specification.

tory using the adapter metadata (see Section 10.3.4). Figure 10.1 contains an extract from the metadata of the UCCnet adapter showing the specifications for the possible transport and message protocols of the UCCnet adapter.

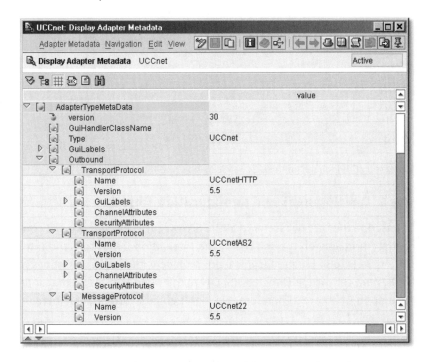

Figure 10.1 Extract from the Adapter Metadata of the UCCnet Adapter from iWay

10.3 Implementing the Scenario

This section gives a detailed description of the steps required to define the UCCnet scenario at the SAP XI customer site.

10.3.1 Components of the UCCnet Scenario

Figure 10.2 shows an overview of the components involved in the UCCnet scenario. Note that the catalog messages are not sent directly from the CRM application to the Integration Server, but via an IBM WebSphere message queue and the SAP XI Java Message Service (JMS) adapter before reaching the Integration Engine. The UCCnet adapter from iWay sends the data to the UCCnet catalog service. Messages with errors are not sent to UCCnet, but to the internal file system of the SAP XI customer (the *Garbage Collector*). The response messages from UCCnet reach the CRM system via the RFC adapter.

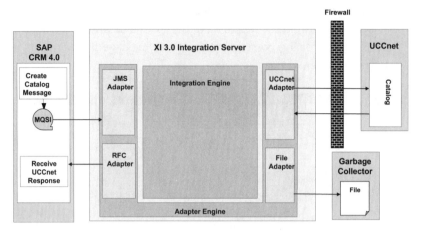

Figure 10.2 Components of the UCCnet Scenario

10.3.2 Development and Configuration Objects

To describe the UCCnet scenario at the SAP XI customer site, we will concentrate primarily on the settings in the Integration Repository and Integration Directory. From a technical point of view, the required settings in the System Landscape Directory (SLD) are the same as those of the Linde scenario in Chapter 9. Therefore, we won't go into further detail here.

Top-Down Approach

Unlike the Linde scenario, however, this implementation uses a *top-down approach* to create the Integration Repository objects. This means that the integration scenario is the starting point for developing the objects, and the first step is to define the message flow with the help of a graphical tool, the *integration scenario editor*. The next step is to create the required Integration Repository objects.

The description of the settings in the Integration Directory at the SAP XI customer site focuses on the B2B functions, the configuration of the iWay UCCnet adapter, and the use of the integration scenario configurator.

10.3.3 Using the Top-Down Approach to Create Integration Repository Objects

Integration Repository objects must be assigned to software component versions and namespaces. Therefore, the first step is to define the software component versions in the SLD and import them to the Integration Repository. Two software components are created for the UCCnet scenario.

Software Component Versions GL_CPE and NA_UCCNET

The software component GL_CPE contains all the Integration Repository objects related to XI messages sent or received by the SAP XI customer's CRM system. It is based on the software component SAP BBPCRM 4.0 shipped by SAP. Figure 10.3 shows how Version 1.0 of the software component GL_CPE is displayed in the Integration Repository. The **Details** tab page displays the namespaces that are inherited from the SAP software component SAP BBPCRM 4.0.

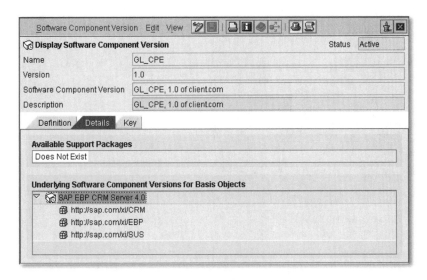

Figure 10.3 Version 1.0 of Software Component GL_CPE

NA_UCCNET contains all the objects related to the UCCnet Data Pool Service. According to convention as defined by the customer, all objects that relate to both sides of the communication (integration scenarios and mappings) belong to the software component NA_UCCNET. Once the current versions of the software components have been imported to the Integration Repository and the namespaces defined, development of the objects can begin.

Integration Scenario NA_CPE_UCCNET

Figure 10.4 shows the integration scenario NA_CPE_UCCNET. It is a graphical representation of all actions and message flows that are involved in the SAP XI customer's UCCnet scenario. It is a theoretical blueprint for the actual configuration settings to be made later (see Section 3.3). This blueprint is defined using logical application components instead of existing services and systems.

Application Component CPE

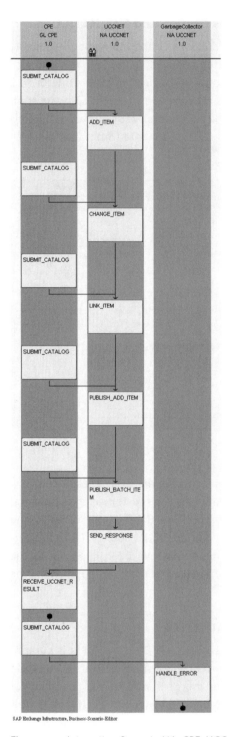

SAP Exchange Infrastructure, Business-Scenario-Editor

Figure 10.4 Integration Scenario NA_CPE_UCCNET

The application component CPE represents the SAP CRM application. Therefore, it is assigned the product GL_CPE 1.0, which contains the software component version of the same name.

UCCNET represents the UCCnet Data Pool Service. Since this is an application provided by a business partner, the **External Party with B2B Communication** checkbox is selected under **Communication Type**. The 🏬 icon appears in the header data for the application component. UCCNET references the product version NA_UCCNET 1.0 with the software component version of the same name.

Application Component UCCNET

The application component GarbageCollector represents a generic receiver for messages with errors.[2] Like the application component UCCNET, GarbageCollector uses Version 1.0 of the product NA_UCCNET.

Application Component GarbageCollector

Once the individual application components have been created, the development of the *actions* can begin. Actions represent elementary function units of an application and pertain to the sending and receiving of XI messages. They are displayed as white rectangles in the integration scenario (see Figure 10.4).

Actions

Since the top-down approach has been chosen for the design of Integration Repository objects, the actions are initially created just as shells. They're assigned message interfaces corresponding to their function later on in the design process.

The SUBMIT_CATALOG and RECEIVE_UCCNET_RESULT actions are created for the application component CPE, which represents the SAP CRM function at the SAP XI customer site. Note that the SUBMIT_CATALOG action represents a generic send step. It encompasses all functions that send messages to UCCnet.

CPE Actions

The SUBMIT_CATALOG action corresponds to the actions ADD_ITEM, CHANGE_ITEM, LINK_ITEM, PUBLISH_ADD_ITEM, and PUBLISH_BATCH_ITEM of the application component UCCNET. The SEND_RESPONSE action sends the response messages from UCCnet to the RECEIVE_UCCNET_RESULT action of the application component CPE.

UCCNET Actions

The application component GarbageCollector contains only the HANDLE_ERROR action.

---

2 Messages with errors are not sent to UCCnet; instead, they are collected in a file and processed manually.

Figure 10.5 shows the specific settings for the `ADD_ITEM` action as an example. The Create New Object function in the action editor has been used to define the asynchronous inbound interface `UCCNetItemAddIn` for the action.[3]

The following table gives an overview of the actions created in the UCCnet scenario, and the corresponding message interfaces.

Action	Message Interface	Direction
SUBMIT_CATALOG	UCCNetCatalogMessageOut	Outbound
ADD_ITEM	UCCNetItemAddIn	Inbound
CHANGE_ITEM	UCCNetItemChangeIn	Inbound
LINK_ITEM	UCCNetItemLinkIn	Inbound
PUBLISH_ADD_ITEM	UCCNetItemPublishAddIn	Inbound
PUBLISH_BATCH_ITEM	UCCNetItemPublishBatchIn	Inbound
SEND_RESPONSE	UCCNetResponseOut	Outbound
RECEIVE_UCCNET_RESULT	CPE_GET_XI_RESULT	Inbound
HANDLE_ERROR	UCCNetUnprocessedItemsIn	Inbound

Table 10.1 List of All Actions and Message Interfaces Used in the UCCnet Scenario

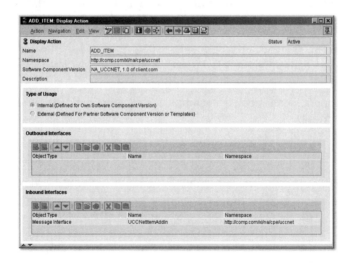

Figure 10.5 ADD_ITEM Action

---

3 Because the XI customer uses only XSLT mapping technology, it is not imperative that you save the exact structure of the XI message as a message type in the Integration Repository. However, you must specify a message type in the definition of a message interface. Therefore, dummy message types are used here.

Once the actions and the message interfaces used have been created, they can be added to the respective application component of the integration scenario. Then you can define the connections *between* the actions. Refer back to Figure 10.4 to see how the actions and their connections are arranged. Note that catalog messages do not have to pass through the entire process flow shown in the figure when they are sent. In the real integration process, it is more likely that in each case only *one* message is sent to the UCCnet Data Pool Service, which then sends a response message to the SAP XI customer's CRM system. The various connections of the SUBMIT_CATALOG action represent alternative communication paths. Creating all actions and their connections in one integration scenario does have certain advantages, as we will see in the section on configuring the scenario.

Adding Actions and Generating Connections

Figure 10.6 Connection of Type "Asynchronous Communication" Between the SUBMIT_CATALOG and ADD_ITEM Actions

Figure 10.6 shows an example of a connection. The SUBMIT_CATALOG action communicates with the ADD_ITEM action. The entries under **Connection Type** tell you that this is an asynchronous connection to a partner outside the SAP XI customer's own system landscape (**B2B Connection**). The steps required to define the assigned mappings are described in detail in the next section.

Imported Archives and Interface Mappings

The SAP XI customer has decided to use XSLT (Extensible Stylesheet Language Transformation) technology for the mappings in the UCCnet scenario. To be able to use this technology, the corresponding XSLT files are first defined outside SAP XI. Once the XSLT files have been bundled into a Java archive (JAR), they can be added to the Integration Repository as an imported archive. Figure 10.7 shows the imported archive UCCNET_ XSLT_Mappings containing the XSLT files.

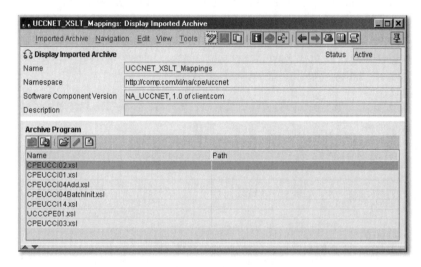

Figure 10.7 Imported Archive UCCNET_XSLT_Mappings

Interface Mapping The individual mapping programs of the imported archive can now be used to define the interface mappings in SAP XI. As we saw in the previous section, the message structures of the two applications CPE and UCCnet are different. Furthermore, each individual action on the side of the application UCCnet expects its own message structure. Therefore, a separate interface mapping must be defined for each connection between two actions in the integration scenario. The interface mapping itself references the respective XSLT program that connects the source message and the target message. Figure 10.8 shows how the mapping program CPEUCCi01 of type XSL (that is, XSLT) relates the messages of the outbound interface UCCNetCatalogMessageOut to the messages of the inbound interface UCCNetItemAddIn.

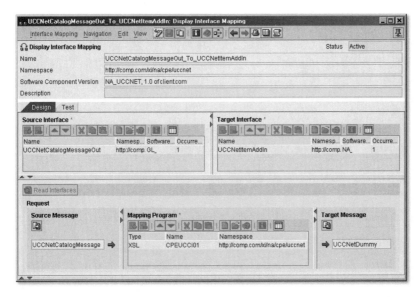

Figure 10.8 Interface Mapping UCCNetCatalogMessageOut_To_UCCNetItemAddIn

This defines all the required Integration Repository objects for the UCCnet scenario. The integration scenario configurator can now be used to derive the corresponding configuration objects.

10.3.4 Generating Integration Directory Objects Automatically

The previous section looked at the integration scenario NA_CPE_UCCNET, which is required for the XI connection between the SAP XI customer's CRM system and UCCnet. The next step is to use this blueprint for the integration process to derive the necessary logical routings. To do this, the *communication parties*, *services*, and *communication channels* that are involved in the scenario must be defined. These are then used to replace the theoretical application components in the integration scenario, and thus define the configuration.

Communication Party

Communicating beyond the boundaries of an SAP XI customer's system landscape requires not only services, but also the **Communication Party** parameter to identify the sender and receiver addresses. In this example, the two communication parties GL_COMP_T1 and NA_USA_UCCNET_T1 have been created. They represent the SAP XI customer and the UCCnet organization in B2B communication.

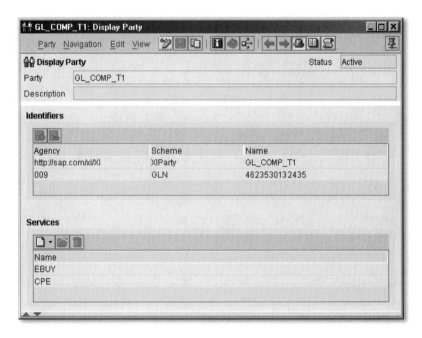

Figure 10.9 Communication Party GL_COMP_T1

Figure 10.9 illustrates the communication party object GL_COMP_T1, which represents the SAP XI customer in B2B communication. Under **Identifiers**, the first line shows the name automatically assigned for the party by SAP XI (Agency: http://sap.com/xi/XI, Scheme: XIParty), which is the same as the object name. In addition, the alternative identifier 4623530132435 (Agency: 009, Scheme: GLN) has been created. This is a Global Location Number (GLN), which identifies the SAP XI customer uniquely in the European Article Numbering (EAN) International or the UCC (Uniform Code Council) in the U.S.

Besides the identifiers, you can also see the services EBUY and CPE that are assigned to the communication party. The service CPE is discussed in the next section.

Services

In SAP XI, services can be created as a *business service*, a *business system*, or a *business process*. Note that when you define communication scenarios that go beyond the boundaries of your company's system landscape, you must create the services twice. You define them first as a *business service*, which is assigned to the communication party that represents your own company. Under this name, the service represents a specific internal function to the system environment outside the company's boundaries. You also define the service as a *business system*, which represents the service within the system landscape. In our scenario, the business service CPE and the business system CG1002LS represent two sides of the same coin.

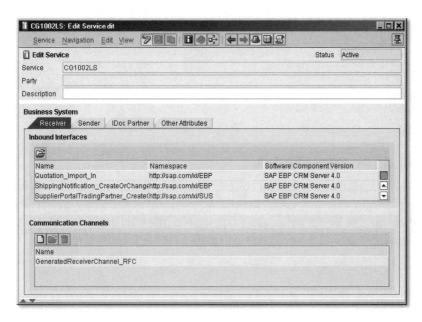

Figure 10.10 Service CG1002LS of Type Business System

Figure 10.10 shows the service represented by the business system CG1002LS. The interfaces used in the service (in this case, the inbound interfaces) are displayed automatically once the corresponding configuration settings have been made.

If messages with errors occur in the UCCnet scenario, they are not sent to UCCnet, but are collected in a file system within the SAP XI customer's system landscape. The business service NA_UCCNETGARBAGECOLLECTOR_S has been created for this purpose.

Messages with Errors

Besides the internal company services, another service must be created to receive and process the catalog messages on the side of the communication party NA_USA_UCCNET_T1. The business service CATALOG_PUBLISH performs this function.

The table below summarizes all the services involved in the UCCnet catalog scenario.

Service	Type	Description
CG1002LS	Business system	Represents the CRM system CG1 within the SAP XI customer's system landscape
CPE	Business service	Address of the CRM system CG1002LS in B2B communication
CATALOG_PUBLISH	Business service	UCCnet service for publishing catalog information
NA_UCCNETGARBAGECOLLECTOR_S	Business service	Generic service for processing error messages

Table 10.2 Services of the UCCnet Scenario

Communication Channels

The technical parameters for connecting application systems to SAP XI are defined in the *communication channel* Integration Directory object. As you can see in the component overview of the scenario in Figure 10.2, communication channels must be created for the following adapters:

▶ Sender adapters: JMS, UCCnet

▶ Receiver adapters: UCCnet, RFC, file

Let us look at the configuration of the JMS and UCCnet adapters as an example.

Configuring the Sender JMS Adapter

Figure 10.11 shows the technical parameters for establishing a connection to an IBM WebSphere message queue. Section 6.5 contains an overview of the general adapter parameters. Note that you must install the corresponding JMS driver before you can use the JMS adapter. The driver software is available from the respective vendor (in this case, IBM).

Configuring the UCCnet Adapter

Section 10.2 explained how the potential parameters for an adapter are made available in the Integration Repository in the form of adapter metadata. Let us now examine how these potential parameters are used for an actual adapter instance. Figure 10.12 shows some of the parameters used for the adapter in this particular scenario. For example, the transport and message protocols from the adapter metadata are shown in input help. Below this you can see the general parameters that are required to connect the adapter to the UCCnet Data Pool Service.

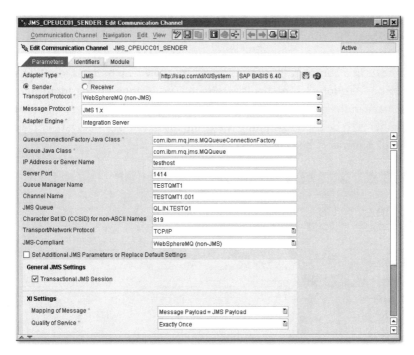

Figure 10.11 Communication Channel JMS_CPEUCC01_SENDER

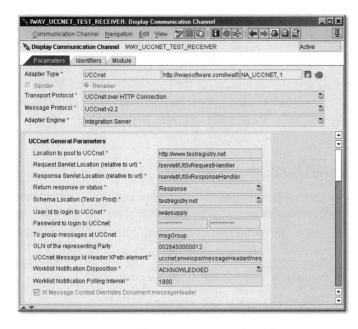

Figure 10.12 Parameters of the Communication Channel IWAY_UCCNET_TEST_
RECEIVER

The company-specific GLN number was defined as an additional identifier when the communication party GL_COMP_T1 was created (Figure 10.9). Since various identifiers can be created for the different business contexts at a company, it is necessary to specify which of these identifiers is to be used for each particular scenario. This is done on the **Identifiers** tab page in the communication channel. It is specified here that this GLN number is to be used to identify the company in the UCCnet Data Pool in this B2B scenario (see Figure 10.13).

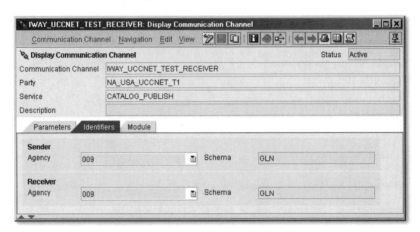

Figure 10.13 Identifiers of the Communication Channel IWAY_UCCNET_TEST_RECEIVER

Both the sender and receiver services and their communication channels are defined in this way. The template for the integration process (the integration scenario) is available in the Integration Repository. The integration scenario configurator uses both parts to create the logical routing automatically.

Integration Scenario Configurator

The SAP XI customer uses the integration scenario configurator to create the Integration Directory objects. The benefit of the integration scenario is twofold: It simplifies the definition of logical routings and it provides a graphical documentation for these logical routings.

Let's look at the individual steps of the automated process:

1. **Select Integration Scenario NA_CPE_UCCNET**
   Once you've started the integration scenario configurator (⊕ icon), you must first select the integration scenario that you want to configure

(in the UCCnet scenario of the SAP XI customer, this is NA_CPE_UCCNET). The task is to create a configuration scenario with the same name in the Integration Directory.

2. **Select Component View**

   Since there can be several component views for one integration scenario, you must select the relevant one. In the UCCnet scenario, only one component view exists at the time of generation. This is shown in Figure 10.14.

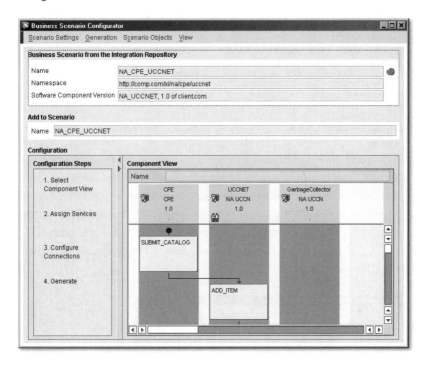

Figure 10.14 Component View of the Integration Scenario NA_CPE_UCCNET

3. **Assign Services**

   The next step is to assign the services maintained in the Integration Directory to the application components of the integration scenario NA_CPE_UCCNET.

   In Figure 10.15, you can see that the real business system CG1002LS performs the function of the theoretical role CPE when messages are exchanged within the SAP XI customer's system landscape.

Figure 10.15 Assigning the Business System CG1002LS to the Application Component CPE

In Section 10.3.3, it was explained that information about the business system should not be communicated outside the boundaries of the SAP XI customer's system landscape. Therefore, once the message leaves the XI pipeline, the technical name of the business system (CG1002LS) must be replaced by a neutral name for the party (GL_ COMP_T1) and service (CPE). This function is configured on the **Business Services for B2B** tab page.

Figure 10.16 Assigning the Business System CG1002LS with Party GL_COMP_T1 and Service CPE to the Application Component CPE

Figure 10.16 shows the settings required to define this assignment.

4. **Configure Connections**

Once a service has been assigned to all application components, the individual connections can be configured. To understand the required settings, let's look at the connection between the SUBMIT_CATALOG and ADD_ITEM actions (see also Figure 10.14).

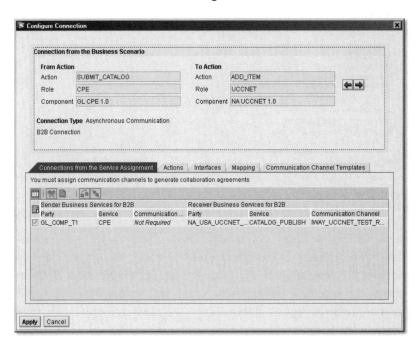

Figure 10.17 Configuration of Connection Between the SUBMIT_CATALOG and ADD_ITEM Actions

Once the services are assigned to the application components, the party-service combinations GL_COMP_T1-CPE (sender) and NA_USA_UCCNET_T1-CATALOG_PUBLISH (receiver) are displayed as the default values on the **Connections from the Service Assignment** tab page (see Figure 10.17). You assign the predefined communication channels that are to be used for this connection for the respective services.

Assigning Connections and Communication Channels

The actions, interfaces, and mappings that are involved in the connection are listed again on the **Actions**, **Interfaces**, and **Mapping** tab pages. These are for information purposes. You use these tab pages to view and check the settings made in the Integration Repository.

Assigning Actions, Interfaces, and Mappings

5. **Generate**

   Once all the connections are configured, you can start automatic generation of the logical routing. To do this, make the settings as shown in Figure 10.18.

Figure 10.18 Settings in the Integration Scenario Configurator for Automatic Generation of Logical Routing

Under **General Settings**, you specify whether you want to generate the objects immediately or execute a simulation run. You then define the scope of the generation. In the UCCnet scenario, the **Receiver Determination**, the **Interface Determination**, and the **Sender/Receiver Agreement** are to be generated automatically. The generated objects are to be added to the **Standard Change List**.

Created Objects

When you press **Start**, all receiver determinations, interface determinations, and sender/receiver agreements are generated automatically.

Figure 10.19 illustrates the receiver and interface determinations for the catalog messages sent from the CRM system. The XPath expressions were added to the receiver and interface determinations manually at a later time.

Once all the change lists are activated, the configuration objects are available in the SAP XI Runtime environment. The SAP XI customer can now automatically create, change, assign, and publish the catalog information defined in its CRM system in the UCCnet Data Pool Service.

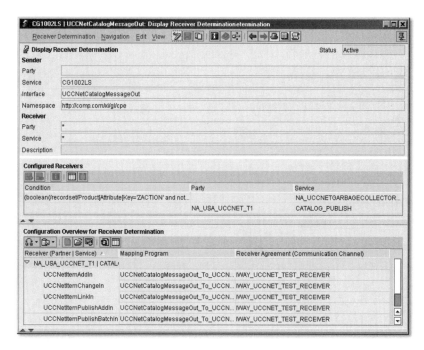

Figure 10.19 Automatically Generated Receiver and Interface Determinations for the Interface UCCNetCatalogMessageOut of the Service CG1002LS

10.4 Summary

SAP XI 3.0 enables the global foodstuffs manufacturer to publish its product data on the Internet, thus making it available to its partners at a central location. The integrated B2B functions conceal the SAP XI customer's internal system information from partners, thus reducing the risk of attacks from the Internet. The certified UCCnet adapter from iWay enables SAP XI to connect directly to the UCCnet Data Pool Service.

The integration scenario configurator makes creating configuration objects in the Integration Repository a fast and easy process. Integration scenarios from the Integration Repository are used as templates that provide detailed graphical documentation for the configuration.

A   Glossary

This is a short glossary containing definitions of some of the most important terms in SAP XI. It is not, however, a comprehensive list.

Abstract message interface   Interface without implementation in an application system. You cannot generate a proxy for this interface type. You use abstract message interfaces in integration processes, for example, to receive or send messages from application systems. Since abstract message interfaces are directionless, you can use the same abstract interface to receive or to send a message.

Acknowledgment message   A message sent to the sender to confirm that an asynchronous message has been processed successfully or that an error has occurred during message processing.

Action. An integration scenario object representing a function within an application component. It is not subdivided further. Actions focus on the exchange of messages between application components.

Adapter Engine. Runtime component for resource adapters for integrating applications and systems using SAP XI. The Adapter Engine contains the Adapter Framework and has functions for messaging and queuing, security, and for connectivity with the Integration Server. You can use this framework to add your own resource adapters, or those of your partners.

Application component. A component that represents a logical participant in an integration scenario and describes the business tasks and responsibilities of this participant in the scenario.

Business system   Logical sender or receiver that exchanges messages using

SAP XI and that is entered in the System Landscape Directory (SLD). Business systems pertain to a system landscape.

Change list   User-specific list of objects in the Integration Builder that are currently being edited.

Client proxy   Runtime representative used by an application to send a message to the Integration Server or via the Web service runtime.

Collaboration agreement   An agreement that defines which details in the collaboration profile apply to the message exchange for a particular sender/receiver pair.

Collaboration knowledge   All content of the Integration Repository and the Integration Directory.

Collaboration profile   A profile that describes the technical options of the communication parties for exchanging messages. It consists of an identifier, services, interfaces, and communication channels.

Collaborative process   An existing or new process from the real business world that will be implemented using a message exchange in SAP XI.

Communication channel   An object that defines the rules for handling messages in inbound and outbound processing. In particular, you use the communication channel to specify the type and the configuration of the adapter used for inbound or outbound processing.

Communication party   Configuration object for logically addressing a company in the collaborative process independently from the representation specified in the message header.

Configuration object   Object in the Integration Directory. The following object types exist: communication parties, services of various types, communication channels, receiver determinations, interface determinations, and sender and receiver agreements.

Configuration scenario   Object for grouping configuration objects in the Integration Directory. If you created a configuration scenario, you can select an integration scenario from the Integration Repository and use it as a template for configuration.

Configuration time   At configuration time, you use the Integration Builder to configure a collaborative process for a particular system landscape in the Integration Directory, so that it can be evaluated by the Integration Server at runtime.

Connection   Part of an integration scenario that connects two actions in a process flow to one another.

Design object   Object in the Integration Repository. The following object types exist: integration scenario objects, integration process objects, interface objects, mapping objects, and adapter objects.

Design time   Stage of development at which you define objects in the Integration Repository. You can ship these design objects and configure them for a particular scenario of a particular system landscape.

End-to-end monitoring   Function in the Runtime Workbench for monitoring the processing of individual messages within a preconfigured component set.

Identification scheme   An identification process that provides a context within which an object can be uniquely identified. Identification schemes are issued and managed by issuing agencies.

Identifier   A means of identification that comprises an agency, identification scheme, and a code for identifying a company.

Inbound interface   Superordinate term for interfaces that process messages at the receiver (for example RFCs, IDocs) and inbound message interfaces for which you generate server proxies in the application system.

Inbound processing   Processing step on the Integration Server for converting received messages in such a way that the Integration Engine of the Integration Server can process them. Inbound processing varies according to the adapter type used.

Integration Builder   Central tool for the design and configuration of collaborative processes with SAP XI.

Integration Directory   The directory where the Integration Builder stores the configuration for the collaborative process.

Integration process   Design object in the Integration Repository for describing the stateful processing of messages on the Integration Server. You address integration processes as services in the Integration Directory.

Integration Repository   The repository where the Integration Builder stores all information to be shipped regarding the collaborative process, for example, integration scenarios, integration processes, interfaces, and mappings.

Integration scenario   A scenario that describes the collaborative process in the Integration Repository as an exchange of messages between application components.

Integration Server   Central runtime distribution engine, for processing and forwarding messages.

Interface determination   Configuration object that describes the assignment of an outbound interface to an inbound interface and to an interface mapping.

Interface mapping   Design object in the Integration Repository for defining the mapping programs for request, response, and fault messages that are to be executed for a source and target interface. For transformation steps in integration processes, you can also specify several asynchronous source and target message interfaces to merge or split messages using a multi-mapping.

Issuing agency   Organization for managing and issuing one or more identification schemes to uniquely identify objects. The company Dun & Bradstreet, for example, manages the identification schema D&B D-U-N-S-Number for uniquely identifying company units.

Mapping program   Program for transforming a message. Mapping programs in the Integration Builder are the message mappings created there, mapping templates, or imported XSLT or Java mappings.

Mapping   Generic term for the transformation of a message regarding its structure and contained values.

Message interface   Language-independent interface object in the Integration Repository for describing the signature of a caller or a receiver in WSDL.

Message mapping   Mapping program that you define using the graphical mapping editor in the Integration Builder.

Message type   Language-independent interface object in the Integration Repository that defines the root element of a message.

Message   An instance for exchanging data between senders or receivers and the Integration Server. A message consists of a message header, the payload, and optionally any number of attachments (depending on the adapter type). The message header and payload are in XML format.

Multi-mapping   Mapping program for mapping m messages to n messages. Multi-mappings can be executed only in integration processes.

Namespace   Qualifier for XML names to identify objects uniquely.

Outbound interface   Superordinate term for interfaces used by senders to send messages to the Integration Server (for example RFCs, IDocs) and inbound message interfaces for which you generate client proxies in the application system.

Outbound processing   Processing step on the Integration Server for converting a message in such a way that it can be processed by an external receiver, depending on the receiver adapter used.

Payload   The body of a message with the business data in XML.

Pipeline   Defined sequence of Integration Engine services that a message passes through. The pipeline consists of individual pipeline elements, which call pipeline services.

Process integration content   All content of the Integration Repository.

Proxy generation   Tool that uses message interfaces in the Integration Repository to generate proxy objects in an application system to exchange messages.

Proxy object   Generated object in the application system, for example, a class, an interface, or a data type.

Proxy   Generic term for client and server proxies.

Quality of service   Attribute of a message that determines how the sender delivers the message.

Receiver adapter   Adapter called by the Integration Engine of the Integration Server to forward a message to a receiver.

Receiver agreement   An agreement that defines technical details for the communication between the Integration Server and a receiver.

Receiver determination   Configuration object in the Integration Directory that describes the assignment of a sender and an outbound interface to one or more receivers.

Release transfer   Transfer of objects of a software component version to another software component version of the same Integration Repository.

Request message   Message from a sender to a receiver to make a request or transfer data to the receiver.

Response message   Message from a receiver as a direct response to a request from the sender.

Runtime Workbench   Central tool in SAP XI for monitoring message processing, runtime components, and performance.

Sender adapter   Adapter for forwarding messages of a sender to the Integration Engine of the Integration Server.

Sender agreement   An agreement that defines technical details for the communication between a sender and the Integration Server.

Serialization context   A string enabling a sender to group asynchronous messages. All asynchronous messages with the same serialization context arrive at the receiver in the same sequence that they were sent from the sender.

Server proxy   Runtime representative used by an application to receive a message using the Integration Server or via the Web service runtime.

Service   Configuration object in the Integration Directory for addressing a sender or receiver. Services are usually provided by a communication party, but can also be used without parties. Possible service types are business systems, business services, and integration processes.

Software component version   Shipment unit for design objects in the Integration Repository. You import software component versions from the System Landscape Directory by using the Integration Builder.

XML   EXtensible Markup Language. Although there are parallels to HTML, XML was developed to describe data, unlike HTML. The structure and type of data in an XML document are defined using XML schema or a DTD (Document Type Definition). For a good introduction to different XML standards such as XML schema, XSLT, XPath, DTD, SOAP, and WSDL, see *http://www.w3schools.com*.

B   The Authors

Jens Stumpe joined SAP in 1998 with a degree in computer science. Since then, he has been responsible for documentation in several different technical areas. Currently, he is part of the SAP NetWeaver Product Management team. He spent the last three years documenting SAP Exchange Infrastructure (SAP XI), which enabled him to put to good use his many experiences with various SAP XI workshops.

Dr. Joachim Orb completed his doctorate in meteorology at the Swiss Federal Institute of Technology, Zurich. In 1998, he started working at SAP Labs France, where his main focus was the development of SAP standard interfaces. In 2002, he joined SAP AG's SAP NetWeaver Regional Implementation Group (RIG). Since then, he has been involved in the rollout of SAP XI in Europe, where he develops workshops, holds training courses, and advises customers on SAP XI implementation.

Index

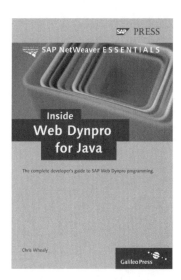

**Discover the full
potential of SAP's
new basis technology**

350 pp., approx. US$ 69.95
ISBN 1-59229-041-8, feb 2005

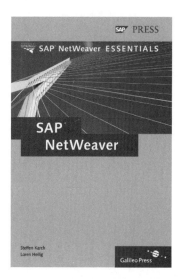

SAP NetWeaver

www.sap-press.de

S. Karch, L. Heilig, C. Bernhardt, A. Hardt, F.
Heidfeld, R. Pfennig

SAP NetWeaver

This book helps you understand each of SAP
NetWeaver's components and illustrates, using
practical examples, how SAP NetWeaver, and its
levels of integration, can be leveraged by a wide
range of organizations.
Readers benefit from in-depth analysis featuring four
actual case studies from various industries, which
describe in detail how integration with SAP
NetWeaver can contribute to the optimization of a
variety of essential business processes and how the
implementation works. Finally, detailed coverage of
SAP NetWeaver technology gives you the complete
picture in terms of architecture and functionality of
each component.

Web AS and Java: The guaranteed future for your Web business

360 pp., approx. US$ 59.95
ISBN 1-59229-020-5, Mar 2005

Java Programming with the SAP Web Application Server

www.sap-press.com

K. Kessler, P. Tillert, G. Frey, P. Dobrikov

Java Programming with the SAP Web Application Server

The 6.30 version of the Web Application Server represents the conclusion of Java Engine implementation by SAP.

This book covers all the areas in which Java can be applied on the WebAS in future, starting from the architecture of the Web AS and the installation of IDE. You get in-depth information on database and R/3-access and on surface-design using the new SAP technology Web Dynpro, plus development of Web services and basic information regarding Java messaging in SAP systems.

This book is aimed at Java-developers who want to branch out into the SAP-world and equally at ABAP programmers, who want to know in which direction Web AS is going in future.

Learn Java the easy way: from the ABAP point of view!

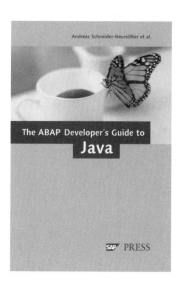

500 pp., 2005, US$ 69.95
ISBN 1-59229-027-2

The ABAP Developer's Guide to Java
www.sap-press.de

A. Schneider-Neureither (Ed.)

The ABAP Developer's Guide to Java

Leverage your ABAP skills to climb up the Java learning curve

This all-new reference book is an indispensable guide for ABAP developers who need a smooth transition to Java. The authors highlight each fundamental aspect pertaining to the development of business applications in both languages, and the differences as well as similarities are analyzed in detail. This book helps any developer learn techniques to master development tools and objects, application design, application layers and much more. Learn about Beans, OpenSQL for Java, JDBC, Security, and more.

Learn about the dos and don'ts in SAP EP 5.0 and SAP EP 6.0

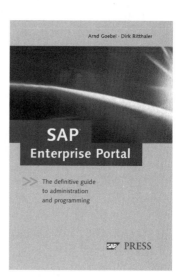

310 pp., US$ 59.95
ISBN 1-59229-018-3

SAP Enterprise Portal

www.sap-press.com

A. Goebel, D. Ritthaler

SAP Enterprise Portal

The definite guide to administration and programming

This book is a complete overview for the installation, operation and administration of a SAP-company portal (EP 6.0). Learn all there is to know about system requirements and the establishment of the portal in the system landscape. Get a step-by-step guide to the installation of a test system and discover how to adapt the portal to the requirements of the user and how to define roles.

The book focuses very much on content and application integration. You learn how to program Web-services and Portal-iViews, plus all there is to know about Unifer, and by use of the SAP Business Information Warehouse you get in-depth knowledge on content-integration.

Unlock the full potential of your SAP systems!

220 pp., 2004, US$
ISBN 1-59229-026-4

SAP System Landscape Optimization

www.sap-press.com

A. Schneider-Neureither (Ed.)

SAP System Landscape Optimization

This reference book serves as an essential collection of insights, procedures, processes and tools that help you unlock the full potential of your SAP systems. First, hit the ground running with a detailed introduction to SAP NetWeaver and the mySAP Business Suite. Then, elevate your mastery of key concepts such as system architecture, security, Change and Transport Mana- gement, to name just a few. All of the practical advice and detailed information provided is with a clear focus on helping you guide your team to achieve a faster return on investment.

Keep flexible while ptimizing cost structures

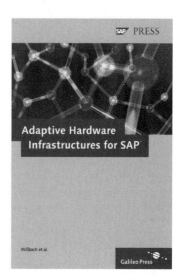

270 pp., approx. US$
ISBN 1-59229-035-3, may 2005

Adaptive Hardware
Infrastructures for SAP

www.sap-press.com

M. Missbach

Adaptive Hardware Infrastructures for SAP

Constantly changing business processes pose a critical challenge for today's hardware. In order to conquer this challenge, companies must respond quickly and in a cost-effective manner, without risking the future safety of their infrastructure. This unique new book helps you to understand the most important factors for determining what hardware you 'll need to support flexible software systems in the months and years ahead. Plus, discover the ins and outs of exactly how SAP systems support your business processes. In addition, you'll benefit from highly-detailed insights, essential for helping you calculate your true Total Cost of Ownership (TCO).